Maritime Mobilities

The central concerns of mobilities research – exploring the broader context and human aspects of movement – are fundamental to an understanding of the maritime freight transport sector.

Challenges to the environment, attempts at more sustainable practices, changes in the geoeconomic system, political power, labour, economic development and governance issues are all among the topics covered in this book. The aim of this volume is to address issues of maritime transport not only in the simple context of movement but also within the mobilities paradigm. The goal is to examine negative system effects caused by blockages and inefficiencies, examine delays and wastage of resources, identify negative externalities, explore power relations and identify the winners and losers in the globalised trade system with a particular focus on the maritime network. *Maritime Mobilities*, therefore, aims to build a bridge between "traditional" maritime academic approaches and the mobilities paradigm.

This volume is of great interest to those who study industrial economics, the shipping industry and transport geography.

Jason Monios is Associate Professor in Maritime Logistics at Kedge Business School, Marseille, France. His research areas include intermodal transport and logistics, port system evolution, collaboration and integration in port hinterlands, port governance and policy, institutional and regulatory settings and port sustainability.

Gordon Wilmsmeier holds the Kühne Professorial Chair in Logistics at the Universidad de los Andes in Bogotá, Colombia. From 2011 to 2017, he worked as Economic Affairs Officer in the Infrastructure Services Unit at the United Nations Economic Commission for Latin America and the Caribbean (UN-ECLAC).

Routledge Studies in Transport Analysis

Maritime Mobilities

**Edited by
Jason Monios and
Gordon Wilmsmeier**

LONDON AND NEW YORK

First published 2018
by Routledge

2 Park Square, Milton Park, Abingdon, Oxfordshire OX14 4RN
52 Vanderbilt Avenue, New York, NY 10017

Routledge is an imprint of the Taylor & Francis Group, an informa business

First issued in paperback 2020

British Library Cataloguing-in-Publication Data
A catalogue record for this book is available from the British Library

Library of Congress Cataloging-in-Publication Data
A catalog record for this book has been requested

ISBN: 978-1-138-23280-8 (hbk)
ISBN: 978-0-367-59368-1 (pbk)

Typeset in Times New Roman
by Apex CoVantage, LLC

Contents

Illustrations

Figures

Tables

Contributors

Lars Bomhauer-Beins is a geography PhD student at the University of Hamburg. He is studying small islands in the wider Caribbean region from a social geographical perspective. His current research project is dealing with the concepts of adaptability and resilience on social-ecological island systems from a complexity theory perspective.

Gang Chen is an associate professor of maritime law at Wuhan University of Technology. He graduated from World Maritime University, Malmo, Sweden, with master of science in maritime affairs. His recent articles include "Seafarers' Access to Jurisdictions over Labour Matters", Marine Policy (March 2017) and "Labour Rights of Merchant Seafarers Held Hostage by Pirates" (the Fifth International Research Seminar in Maritime, Port and Transport Law, held at the University of Bologna, Italy 2016). He focuses his research on maritime labour sectors.

Matej David completed undergraduate navigation studies (maritime transport engineer) and transport technologies (BSc). He sailed on merchant vessels and he is ship's officer. He got his doctoral degree (2007) in the field of maritime transport with a focus on ballast water management decision support based on risk assessment. He was professor at the University of Ljubljana (Slovenia), Faculty of Maritime Studies and Transport, and now he is visiting professor at the University of Rijeka (Croatia), Faculty of Maritime Studies. From 2009 onwards, he has run his private consultancy. He conducts researches and consultancy predominately predominantly at international level in the field of ballast water management (ballast water sampling, risk assessment and management, decision support systems, ballast water management systems) and oil and HNS pollution from vessels and in ports (contingency planning, illicit spills monitoring, port sustainable development). From 2002 to 2009, he was head or a member of the Slovenian Delegation in the International Maritime Organisation (IMO) Marine Environment Protection Committee, Bulk Liquids and Gasses (BLG) Sub-Committee and the Ballast Water Working Group (BWWG), and he was head of the Slovenian delegation at the Diplomatic Conference in 2004 in London when the BWM Convention was adopted. He is contributing to the development of ballast water management approaches mainly in the

Mediterranean, North, Baltic and Caspian Seas. He is an invited high-level expert and trainer for ballast water management issues for the European Maritime Safety Agency (EMSA) and IMO and GESAMP (The Joint Group of Experts on the Scientific Aspects of Marine Environmental Protection) BWWG expert.

Patrick DeDauw is a doctoral student in geography at the Graduate Center of the City University of New York. He holds a master's degree in political science and sociology from the John F. Kennedy Institute for North American Studies, Freie Universität Berlin. His research focuses on transport and prison infrastructure, land-market transformation and Canadian racial capitalism.

Mario Genco is partner of CSIL – Centre for Industrial Studies (Milan) and senior expert at the Evaluation and Development Unit. He holds a degree in nuclear engineering. He has been working for 15 years in the field of safety and licensing of nuclear facilities. Since 1982, he has covered several management roles in energy projects, water and integrated water service industry and in environmental sustainability programmes (for energy, air quality, natural and industrial risk, site pollution, water bodies' reclamation). During his professional career of more than 40 years, Mario has specialized in appraisal, cost-benefits analysis, planning and management of projects co-financed by European Funds. He has been appointed high professional profile advisor for several major infrastructure projects by national and international bodies.

Basil Germond is senior lecturer at Lancaster University. An expert in naval and maritime affairs as well as ocean governance, he has published two monographs and in excess of 25 peer-reviewed articles and book chapters on these topics. His latest book is titled *The Maritime Dimension of European Security* (Palgrave Macmillan, 2015). He also co-edited the *Routledge Handbook on Transatlantic Security* (Routledge, 2010). Basil is a fellow of the Royal Geographical Society (FRGS).

Celine Germond-Duret is senior lecturer in geography at Liverpool John Moores University. She is a critical geographer with an interdisciplinary background in international relations. Her research and publications discuss sustainability issues, discourse analysis, human geography of the marine environment, blue growth narrative and indigenous peoples. Celine is a FRGS.

Stephan Gollasch was involved in the first European ship sampling programme on ballast water, tank sediments and ship hull fouling (1992–1996). His PhD in marine biology, completed in 1996, is worldwide the first thesis based on ship sampling. He prepared the first risk assessment study for species invasions in the Baltic Sea, carried out for the Nordic Council of Ministers, Copenhagen (Denmark) in 1999. Dr. Gollasch became a member of several international working groups – e.g., International Council for the Exploration of the Sea and IMO. In addition to laboratory and desk studies he spent more than 300 days at sea and sampled ballast water of more than 250 vessels during several ship sampling programmes. As an independent scientific advisor, he runs his own consultancy company since 1999 and is today involved in projects related to biological invasions (e.g. ballast water management, ship sampling, risk assessment, biofouling). Other contracts included the German Ministry of Transport, German Federal Maritime and Hydrographic Agency, IMO and the Helsinki and European Commissions. He was involved in the EU-Projects DAISIE, MARTOB, IMPASSE, BaWaPla, BWO, VECTORS, e-CME and BALMAS. Further, he was involved in the development of risk assessments and ballast water management scenarios for the European Atlantic coast, North, Baltic, Caspian and Mediterranean Seas. Since 2005, he has undertaken more than 100 voyages to tests 20 ballast water management systems on different merchant vessels and was from February 2009 to December 2012 joining the evaluation team of active substances used to treat ballast water as a member of the GESAMP BWWG. Since 2008, he is an invited high level expert and trainer for ballast water management issues for the EMSA and IMO.

Marta Gonzalez-Aregall holds a PhD in economics (University of Barcelona). She is a postdoc researcher at the University of Gothenburg. She has conducted research stays at the Universities of British Columbia (Vancouver), Las Palmas de Gran Canaria (Spain) and UN-ECLAC (Chile). She has focused her research on evaluation of maritime transportation, competition and efficiency of port infrastructure, privatization and regulation of transport infrastructures and the spatial effects of transportation. She has presented her work in many international conferences, and she has published her papers in journals such as *Transport Policy* and the *International Journal of Shipping* and *Transport Logistics*.

Peter Hall is professor of urban studies at Simon Fraser University in Vancouver, Canada. His research examines the connections between port cities, seaports and logistics, as well as community, local economic and employment development. His publications include the co-edited *Integrating Seaports and Trade Corridors* (Ashgate, 2011) and *Cities, Regions and Flow* (Routledge, 2013). He is an associate editor of the *Journal of Transport Geography*.

Kristianne Hendricks recently completed her master's degree in the Department of Geography at Simon Fraser University. Her work explores the connections between labour and sustainability in the Canadian Port Authorities. Her work has been presented in Canada, Spain and the Netherlands, and her publications include "How Dockworkers Green the Port: Sustainability Measures in Vitória's Waterfront" (in Fronteras de Agua: La cuidades portuarias y su universe cultural, 2016).

Markus Hesse is a professor of urban studies at the University of Luxembourg, Faculty of Humanities and Social Sciences. He has an academic background in geography and spatial planning, which are also his teaching domains. His research focuses on urban and regional development; mobilities, logistics and global flows; metropolitan policy and governance; and spatial discourses and identities. He is an elected member of the Academy for Spatial Research and

Planning in Germany and sits on various advisory boards and scientific councils. Among recent publications are *"Cities, Regions and Flows"* (Routledge 2013, co-edited with Peter Hall) and "Selling the Region as Hub: the Promises, Beliefs and Contradictions of Economic Development Strategies Attracting Logistics and Flows" (book chapter in Cidell/Prytherch, eds.: *"Transport, Mobility, and the Production of Urban Space"*, Routledge 2015). Since 1975/76, he is addicted to the sort of music that is part of his chapter in this volume.

Jason Monios is associate professor in maritime logistics at Kedge Business School, Marseille, France. His research areas include intermodal transport and logistics; port system evolution, collaboration and integration in port hinterlands; port governance and policy; institutional and regulatory settings; and port sustainability. Jason has over 70 peer-reviewed academic publications in addition to numerous research and consultancy reports, covering Europe, North and South America, Asia, the Middle East and Africa. He has co-authored technical reports with UNCTAD and UN-ECLAC, and been advisor to the Scottish government. Previous book publications include two research monographs *Institutional Challenges to Intermodal Transport and Logistics* (2014) and *Intermodal Freight Terminals: A Life Cycle Governance Framework* (2016), and a textbook *Intermodal Freight Transport and Logistics* (2017).

Ricardo J. Sánchez is an economist graduated from the University of Salvador, Argentina, in 1983. His postgraduate studies include a PhD in economics (candidate) from the Pontificia Universidad Católica Argentina and MSc in economics and administration of public utilities from the University of Paris X and University Carlos III in Madrid, Spain. Ricardo is an internationally recognised expert in shipping and port economics, as well as in transport and infrastructure, with special focus on the region of Latin America and the Caribbean. He has worked either professionally or academically in 30 countries throughout the Americas for 33 years, as well as in Europe and Asia. His main research interests are shipping and port economics, including the maritime cycle, port devolution, national maritime policies and industrial organization applied to shipping markets. He holds more than 160 publications among books, chapters in books, peer-reviewed articles, working papers, etc. He is a United Nations senior economic affairs officer at UN-ECLAC. Currently he is the regional expert on ports, maritime transport and infrastructure. His main fields of work are infrastructure, maritime, ports and logistics affairs and physical regional integration.

Emanuela Sirtori earned a degree in economics from the University of Milan. She started her research activities at CSIL (Milan) in 2009, and she is currently a partner and project manager. She is an expert in the field of regional development, industrial policy and innovation and small business economics. Over the years, she has been involved in different evaluation studies on behalf of the European Commission, the European Investment Bank, the European Parliament and the European Organisation for Nuclear Research. Emanuela has command of a variety of research methodologies, both quantitative and qualitative, with in-depth knowledge of cost-benefit analysis both in its theoretical foundations and empirical application.

Anke Strüver is a professor for social geography at the University of Hamburg and studies mutual constructions of socio-economic, cultural and spatial processes at various scales. Her research profile is characterized by a continued and extensive critical study of spatial issues and their adjoining methodological perspectives at the interface between political, social and economic problems.

Lijun Tang is lecturer in international shipping and port management at the University of Plymouth. He obtained his PhD from Cardiff University. His research interests and publications are in the areas of employment relations in shipping, occupational health and safety, training and technology in shipping and Internet culture and politics in China.

Silvia Vignetti is an economist and currently director of the evaluation and development unit at CSIL – Centre for Industrial Studies (Milan). She is specialised in the evaluation of regional development and cohesion policy with a long-standing track records of study and evaluation assignments. As cost-benefit analysis expert, she has experience in training to civil servants and practitioners in Italy and abroad (e.g. Lithuania, Romania, Croatia, Slovenia, FYROM, Ghana), practice on project evaluation and advisory to the European Commission by reviewing the application forms of Italian major projects in the transport and environment sector asking for co-financing. She has also had teaching appointments at the University of Milan in macroeconomics, economics of European integration and cost-benefit analysis.

Boris Vormann is professor of politics at Bard College Berlin. Vormann's most recent books are *Global Port Cities in North America: Urbanization Processes and Global Production Networks* from Routledge (2015) and a handbook on politics and policy in the United States for a German-speaking audience (Springer VS, 2016). His current research project examines the role of states in building the urban infrastructures of expanding global trade networks across the globe.

Yuhong Wang is professor in maritime transport at the Faculty of Maritime and Transportation, Ningbo University, China. He obtained his doctoral degree from the University of Newcastle, and won the second-best prize of the Fourth Palgrave Macmillan PhD Competition in Maritime Economics and Logistics (2008–2011). Prior to joining Ningbo University, he worked for six years at the Transport Research Institute, Edinburgh Napier University, United Kingdom, with particular research interests in liner shipping transportation and container supply chains.

Gordon Wilmsmeier holds the Kühne professorial chair in logistics at the Universidad de los Andes in Bogotá, Colombia. From 2011 to 2017, he worked as economic affairs officer in the Infrastructure Services Unit at the United Nations

Economic Commission for Latin America and the Caribbean (UN-ECLAC). Previously he worked at Edinburgh Napier University's Transport Research Institute and as consultant for UN-ECLAC, UNCTAD, UN-OHRLLS, the World Bank, Adelphi Research, JICA, IDB, CAF, OAS. He is an internationally recognized expert in maritime transport geography and economics; port economics and inland shipping issues with particular interests in shipping networks, governance, competition, transport costs, sustainability; and energy efficiency. Gordon is honorary professor for maritime geography at the University of Applied Sciences in Bremen and visiting lecturer at Göteborg University, Sweden and Universidad Nacional de San Martín, Argentina. He has published over 100 book chapters, journal papers, institutional publications and working papers. He is leader of the global port performance research network (https://pprn.network). Gordon is member of the International Association of Maritime Economists (council member 2010–2016), the Sustainability Working Group of the European Freight and Logistics Leaders Forum and associate member of PortEconomics.

1 Introduction

Applying the mobilities paradigm to the maritime sector

Jason Monios and Gordon Wilmsmeier

In the name of the primacy of infrastructures, of structures or systems, subjectivity still gets a bad press, and those who deal with it, in practice or theory, will generally only approach it at arm's length, with infinite precautions, taking care never to move too far away from pseudo-scientific paradigms, preferably borrowed from the hard sciences: thermodynamics, topology, information theory, systems theory, linguistics, etc. It is as though a scientific superego demands that psychic entities are reified and insists that they are only understood by means of extrinsic coordinates. Under such conditions, it is no surprise that the human and social sciences have condemned themselves to missing the intrinsically progressive, creative and auto-positioning dimensions of processes of subjectification.

Félix Guattari (2000: 36)

Introduction

Understanding the social and political construction of movement is essential to any analysis of transport systems. This is perhaps even more true of maritime transport than other modes due to the large range of scales from the very local to the global, to the peopled space of ships and ports and the temporal nature of the changing industry and the transitoriality of placemaking as people and goods move through a space that is variously striated and smooth.

The aim of this volume is to address issues of maritime transport not only in the simple context of movement but also within the mobilities paradigm. The goal is to examine negative system effects caused by blockages and inefficiencies, examine delays and wastage of resources, identify negative externalities, explore power relations and identify the winners and losers in the globalised trade system with a particular focus on the maritime network. The book also aims to build a bridge between "traditional" maritime academic approaches and the mobilities paradigm.

The development of the maritime system

While people and goods have been transported in ships for millennia, a truly global shipping network evolved through the ages of sail and steam before maturing in the age of containerisation. The development of the container by Malcom McLean in 1956[1] revolutionised ports, as the stevedoring industry was transformed over a few decades from a labour-intensive operation to an increasingly automated activity. Vessels once spent weeks in port being unloaded manually by teams of workers; they can now be discharged of thousands of containers in a matter of hours by large cranes, with the boxes being repositioned in the stacks by automatic guided vehicles. This in turn means that ships can spend a much higher proportion of their time at sea, becoming far more profitable.

As shipping and port operations were transformed by the container revolution, a wave of consolidation and globalisation took place. Shipping lines grew and then merged to form massive companies that spanned the globe. Container ports expanded out of origins as general cargo ports, or were built entirely from scratch. Some existing major ports today show their legacy as river ports and require dredging to keep pace with larger vessels with deep drafts (e.g. Hamburg), whereas newer container ports are built in deep water, requiring not dredging but filling in to create the terminal land area (e.g. Maasvlakte 2, Rotterdam). The move to purpose-built facilities with deeper water severed the link between port and city, with job numbers reduced and those remaining moved far from the local community, altering the economic geography of port cities (Hesse, 2013; Martin, 2013).

Most of the new generation of container ports are operated by one of a handful of globalised port terminal operators such as Hutchison Port Holdings or APM. This is the result of the trend towards consolidation across the industry in the decade leading up to the onset of the global economic crisis in 2008, in which many mergers and acquisitions took place in both shipping liner services and port terminal operations. There has also been much vertical integration, with shipping lines investing in port terminals (e.g. Maersk/APM and others). The increasing integration between shipping lines and ports has created an almost entirely vertically-integrated system from port to shipping line to port within the same company.

As a result of these changing industry dynamics, ports changed from city-based centres of local trade to major hubs for cargo to pass through, with distant origins and destinations. This development was driven to a large degree by the container revolution, as distribution centres (DCs) located in key inland locations became key traffic generators. Port hinterlands began to overlap as any port could service the same hinterland. Shipping services were rationalised, with large vessels traversing major routes between a limited number of hub ports.

Despite such consolidation in shipping and port terminals, the business of maritime transport remains highly volatile, not only cyclical but also dramatically so, exhibiting widely divergent peaks and troughs. According to a senior executive from Maersk: '2009 for Maersk Line was the worst year we have ever had and 2010 was the best – that is not very healthy' (Port Strategy, 2011). Therefore, port actors seek stability where possible, needing to anchor or capture traffic to make themselves less susceptible to revenue loss when the market is low.

While the shipping market remains very much a scale-driven industry, emerging developments are changing the source of port competitiveness from economies of scale based on basic production factors (capital, land, labour), to economies of scope based on advanced production (service) factors (Sánchez and Wilmsmeier, 2011).

The nature of the required services is changing from standard services with long life cycles to differentiated service requirements which tend to have short life cycles.

Government responses to the development of the maritime system must also be considered. How have planners responded to this emerging system? Governments have encouraged it through supporting globalisation and "free trade" (or forcing poorer countries to open their economies to FDI and resource extraction) and encouraged private participation through privatisation of port infrastructure and devolution of port governance. Many of the negative aspects of globalisation, particularly as they apply to geographical studies, have been clearly identified for some time (e.g. Janelle and Beuthe, 1997) but have not been taken up by transport geographers. Have countries given up too much control in the obsession with supposed efficiency gains? Is it just rent extraction? Has it solved long-term infrastructure deficits or just postponed the next crisis while simultaneously ensuring that it will be more severe? How should the maritime system be governed in the interests of the nation, the global community and the planet? And what about the individuals caught up in this system, from local residents living near a port to port workers, seafarers, exporters, consumers and everyone who relies on this system for their livelihood, directly or indirectly?

The intrinsic instability of capitalism as a mode of production (cf. the analysis of Harvey and Marx in Wilmsmeier and Monios, 2015 and Chapter 3) has far-reaching effects for our understanding of the port sector, because in order to avoid the inevitable devaluation as a result of over-accumulation, capital will shift geographically or be deferred, meaning that it is only ever fixed in space for a temporary period. According to Harvey (1985: 150):

> Capitalism perpetually strives . . . to create a social and physical landscape in its own image and requisite to its own needs at a particular point in time, only just as certainly to undermine, disrupt or even destroy that landscape at a later point in time. The inner contradictions of capitalism are expressed through the restless formation and reformation of geographical landscapes.

This is particularly relevant for the port sector, because "the fixed capital required in the transport industry is extensive and a lot of it is embedded in the built environment as roads, rails, terminals, etc." (Harvey, 2006 [1982]: 378). Thus the "restless formation and reformation" of the port industry should be read critically by port scholars, alert to what it reveals about underlying processes of power and control. A paucity of research on the aforementioned questions must be laid at the door of academic researchers. Have geographers paid sufficient attention to these issues? Can the application of the mobilities paradigm help?

Maritime transport geography

Geographers working in the port sector contributed some of the early works of transport geography. Such early approaches to the geography of port system evolution were predominately taken from a spatial perspective (Bird, 1963; Taaffe et al., 1963; Rimmer, 1967; Hoyle, 1968; Hayuth, 1981; Barke, 1986; Van Klink, 1998). As the industry developed, analysis has turned to address port competition through hinterland accessibility (Notteboom and Rodrigue, 2005; Monios and Wilmsmeier, 2013), the structure of maritime services (Sánchez and Wilmsmeier, 2006; Rodrigue and Notteboom, 2010) and the influence of liner service concentration (e.g. Frémont and Soppé, 2007; Lee et al., 2008; Sánchez and Wilmsmeier, 2011; Wang and Ducruet, 2012).

A key spatial principle established by port geographers is that port system concentration eventually reaches its limits (Barke, 1986; Hayuth, 1981), leading to a process of deconcentration (Slack and Wang, 2002; Notteboom, 2005; Frémont and Soppé, 2007; Ducruet et al., 2009; Wilmsmeier and Monios, 2013). Spatial approaches tend not to differentiate between spatial deconcentration that emerges upon failure of a system in a reactive manner, deconcentration that materializes from proactive port development strategies and deconcentration that emerges from new economic and industrial development. Thus there tends to be an implicit assumption that port systems will follow a dependent path, with the result that potentially contingent elements are less visible.

The emergence and location of secondary ports (e.g. Slack and Wang, 2002; Wang and Ng, 2011, in China; Wilmsmeier and Monios, 2013, in the United Kingdom; Wilmsmeier et al., 2014, in Latin America) has not been explained satisfactorily by the natural location advantages that have in most cases driven the location of dominant ports. If such developments are instead driven by other factors, such as the planning and regulatory regimes in each country, then research is needed to uncover and classify them, particularly if they differ between regions rather than following a generic path. In order to address these issues, geographers should seek interdisciplinary methodologies incorporating institutional and economic approaches (Hall et al., 2006). More recognition is needed of the port's place in the market, meaning that transport geography must learn more from economic and political geographies, sub-disciplines that perhaps devote more attention to contingent processes.

While some key early papers on transport geography were based on ports, in later years, the sub-discipline moved more towards passenger transport (Rodrigue, 2006), as have other disciplines studying transport issues. This could partly be a result of the increasingly private sector dominated world of freight, leaving policy actors interested mostly in passenger transport, meaning that much of the work on governance has been in that field, with the notable exception being the wave of port governance research over the last decade, particularly the landmark publication by Brooks and Cullinane (2007). Rodrigue's (2006: 386) view that "transport geography should follow the freight" lamented the bias towards passengers in transport geography, especially considering that "the intensity of freight movements has a much more significant variety of geographical conditions." In the decade since that paper, freight transport (and particularly the study of ports) has been the site of some of the more interesting discussions within transport geography. Nevertheless, unlike geographical approaches to passenger transport, which have increasingly considered cultural and social factors and taken more from other branches of study such as sociology and political science, freight transport geography has tended to be less questioning about these forces underpinning freight flows and focused more on cartographic approaches. It has tended to accept the private globalised system as a fait accompli and chosen to rearrange deckchairs rather than looking out for the iceberg that threatened to sink the maritime transport system post-2008 when all the forecasts were proved wrong.

Doel's "pointillist" (1999, 2000) critique suggests that geography as a discipline is overly focused on cartographic representations, leading to a superficial account that tends to the descriptive and misses key underlying processes that constitute space. Sheller (2015: 16) asks, "How, indeed, can the quantitative description of the trends be mobilised into qualitative narratives that contest business as usual in the field of transportation planning by framing issues in new ways informed by a mobilities perspective?" Peters (2010: 1266) points out that,

> Unlike approaches in transport geography, mobilities research seeks to uncover the social, cultural and human intricacies of movement rather than quantitative patterns and trends. Contemporary "maritime geographies" could be strengthened through the lens of the "new mobilities paradigm", following work within tourism studies by asking questions such as: What politics are involved in contemporary movements across the oceans? Do these politics vary with different vessels, their owners, and the flags ships fly under? What meanings are embodied in journeys? How are identities forged and contested across the seas? How does experience differ depending upon the capacity in which those onboard travel (as crew or passenger?).

Much work on the social, cultural and political aspects of transport itself and on the other fields influencing and influenced by transport (e.g. urban planning, regional development, market structure) has taken place in other disciplines than geography. While sociologists have explored power differentials and social exclusion and economists have examined unequal regional development and political scientists have looked at the role of scale and state restructuring, geographers have tended to over-rely on positivist approaches (Goetz, 2006; Hall et al., 2006). Particularly transport geographers have evinced less interest in these themes. Could this be a reason for the suggested lack of prominence of the sub-discipline within human geography as a whole, noted by Shaw and Hesse (2010: 305): "Despite its vintage, frequently absent from major human geography texts." Shaw and Sidaway (2010: 504) consider that this could be because transport geography has been "only marginally associated with key social, political and cultural imperatives," while others are critical that geographers have tended to neglect questions arising from the role of neoliberalism in transport (Wilmsmeier and Monios, 2015; Pyrtherch and Cidell, 2015). This is even more evident in port geography, which may be characterised as suffering from what Smith (2005) sees as the co-opting of geographers by the dominant neoliberal narrative. Hanson's (2003) criticism of transport geography as overly reliant on outdated frameworks, though refuted by some other scholars (e.g. Goetz, 2006), still resonates.

This lacuna has begun to be filled in recent years (Lin, 2016) and evidence can be seen of bridges between transport geography and other disciplines as well as other sub-disciplines within geography (e.g. economic geography), but these remain in the minority. Taking a self-conscious mobilities perspective is one way to work actively towards bridging this gap and bringing such work together under one umbrella, from both a subject point of view as well as methodological, bridging the gap between quantitative and qualitative research (Goetz et al., 2009). While large-scale, data-rich quantitative models are essential, more attention needs to be paid to the underlying assumptions and the outliers ironed out of focus to produce unrealistically smooth outcomes. It is important to draw only relevant conclusions from such studies (e.g. total demand for transport) and not necessarily a total conclusion (e.g. invest in infrastructure at a specific location) without examining the many other forces and influences at play in making up the transport system. So it is not to criticise geography for the use of necessarily abstract macro models, but to remain alive to their simplifications of reality and aware of the non-neutrality of interpretation of such models (Schwanen, 2016; Kwan and Schwanen, 2016). The fact that this space-time compression is a selective process that benefits some at the expense of others (Thrift, 1996; Knowles, 2006; Schwanen and Kwan, 2012) has been insufficiently addressed by port scholars.

The general trend of port geography research in recent decades has been away from traditional geographical approaches and towards more applied and operational perspectives (Ng et al., 2014). Perhaps as a consequence of this trend, analysis of the significant concentration of ownership and operations of ports and shipping lines has, besides a few exceptions (e.g. Olivier and Slack, 2006; Sánchez and Wilmsmeier, 2011; Debrie et al., 2013), tended to address only the operational impacts. Thus questions relating to the new conceptions and configurations of space, networks and power created through geoeconomic and political imperatives, as well as the corporatisation of the sector remain unanswered (Wilmsmeier and Monios, 2015).

Keeling (2007: 219) defines the needs of transport geography as follows: "Theories about transportation geography must move beyond the strictly utilitarian or orthodox and challenge the very essence of the social processes that take place in myriad spatial milieus." Turning to the maritime system, Steinberg (2013: 157) reminds us that the ocean is "continually being reconstituted by a variety of elements: the non-human and the human, the biological and the geophysical, the historic and the contemporary." That is why the current volume is turning to the mobilities paradigm for insight.

The mobilities paradigm

The establishment of the mobilities paradigm in the seminal papers by Sheller and Urry (2006) and Hannam et al. (2006) led to a rapidly developing field of enquiry, with its own journal *Mobilities*. Sheller and Urry recognise mobilities as an inherently multidisciplinary field, identifying the growth of mobilities approaches through disciplines as diverse as anthropology and sociology to geography and tourism studies. They identify the "mobility turn" as an opportunity for "transcending the dichotomy between transport research and social research." (208). Pyrtherch and Cidell (2015: 26) suggest that the rapid growth of this field is due to "a latent desire to understand the social and cultural aspects of transportation [and] dissatisfaction with existing and largely quantitative approaches."

The common thread linking this stream of work is that the central concern of mobilities research is "of too little movement or too much, or of the wrong sort or at the wrong time" (Sheller and Urry, 2006: 208). They want to explore "the concomitant patterns of concentration that create zones of connectivity, centrality and empowerment in some cases, and of disconnection, social exclusion and inaudibility in other cases" (210). They object to the prioritisation of fixed spaces over mobile connections, while at the same time recognising "how all mobilities entail specific often highly embedded and immobile infrastructures" (210). They object to transport demand being accepted as given rather than seeking to understand the forces behind it. This chimes with the notion of transport solely as a derived demand being challenged and reformulated as an integrated demand (Hesse and Rodrigue, 2004).

Cidell and Lechtenberg (2016) identify three key developments: debates over the neutrality of scale, the spatial turn of many social sciences and the impact of relational spaces. There is certainly a need to recognise the extent to which mobilities are politically constructed (Cresswell, 2010b). Hannam et al. (2006: 3) note that "mobilities cannot be described without attention to the necessary spatial, infrastructural and institutional moorings that configure and enable mobilities" and go on to describe these underpinnings as sites "through which mobilisations of locality are performed and re-arrangements of place and scale materialised," sites that "enable the fluidities of liquid modernity, and especially of capital." They recognise the performativity of mobility (what Cresswell [2010a: 550] calls "the universal but always particularly constructed fact of moving") and its spatially unequal instantiations through differently accessed and constructed moorings: "mobility is a resource to which not everyone has an equal relationship." In the current volume, such relations are enacted through the institutional and regulatory makeups of the global shipping system and port governance. Hannam et al. (2006) specifically note the role of unequal power relations and the need to be alert to a "flexible and dynamic scalar shifting, polymorphism of spatial forms and overlapping regulatory regimes." Thus these immobilities are contested and constantly in flux.

Over a decade ago, Hall et al. (2006) noted that transport geographers had not yet engaged with the emerging mobilities paradigm, and little has changed since then. Only a handful of key papers have developed the nexus between transport and mobilities, while at the same time exploring the sub-discipline of transport geography, seeking to delineate on one hand the role of geography in transport studies and on the other the contribution of transport geography to wider debates and concerns within geography. Transport geography has proved fertile ground for aspects of economic geography, dealing as it does with issues of economic development, growth, jobs, commuting and, for the purposes of this book, movements of freight and major freight transport infrastructure. But at the same time, transport "is not just about modes and movement but also about politics, money, people and power, and there is a need for transport geography to be a more human geography" (Shaw and Sidaway, 2010: 515). Shaw and Sidaway see an opportunity for transport geography to improve its relevance to social and cultural issues by engaging more closely with mobilities. Similarly, Shaw and Hesse (2010) call for a greater interaction between transport geography and mobilities. Pyrtherch and Cidell (2015) note that mobilities scholars seldom cite the work of transport specialists, while Shaw and Hesse (2010: 306) note that transport geographers are "conspicuously under-represented" in the flagship *Mobilities* journal. Shaw and Hesse (2010: 307) suggest that transport geography and mobilities "might be thought of as distributed along a continuum." More recently, Schwanen (2015) identified increasing dialogues between transport geographers and mobilities scholars as one part of geographers other than traditional transport geographers reengaging with transport through research on topics such as the economy, energy and health. Elsewhere, it is suggested that mobility has itself already become a core geographical concept, alongside such traditional concepts as space, place, scale and network (Kwan and Schwanen, 2016)

Schwanen (2016: 355) recognised the value of big data and network approaches to transport geography, while cautioning that in some instances, they may have "made acceptable and even normalized a focus on supposedly universal laws that explain the functioning of mobility systems and on space and time independent of explanations of hierarchies, inequalities and vulnerabilities in transport systems and patterns." The goal of uniting transport and mobilities in the present volume stems from a similar concern, neatly described by Schwanen (2016: 356): "Balancing and somehow integrating generality and particularity benefits transport geography in light of the deep divisions over the ontological status of mobility within the broader discipline."

There has been a limited amount of work on freight transport and logistics considered from the mobilities perspective and recently Cresswell (2014) identified logistics and off-shoring as two key activities that could benefit from a mobilities perspective. These will both be examined in the present collection, exploring the many activities and forces that conspire to keep the logistics flow in circulation as well as the off-shoring of some undesirable elements of the mobile system (e.g. ship breaking in Pakistan discussed in Chapter 9). Such subjects have begun to receive attention in recent years. Cidell (2012) explored the movement of containers (see this volume Chapter 13) inland and particularly what local authorities can do when unhappy about the immobility of stored empty containers far inland. Other authors (Steinberg, 2001; Martin, 2013) have considered the role of standardisation in attempting to annihilate local difference and produce a frictionless surface of logistics mobility, which in reality is underpinned by much work in the industry and political manoeuvring to regulate, control and access this system. As summarised neatly by Creswell and Martin (2012: 521):

> As mobilities of all kinds multiply and collide, becoming more complex and more central to the world we inhabit, so, by implication, do the entanglements

of order and disorder, manifested by the complexity of interactions between various actors in the mobilities assemblage.

Cowen (2014) uncovers and explores the dangers, challenges, risks and rewards derived from the military and political underpinnings lying beneath the logistics surface.

Other authors have explored other negative aspects of the freight mobilities system. Creswell and Martin (2012) examined what happens when the system breaks down and containers are damaged and spill their contents. They classify this situation as indicative of turbulence, which they define as "disordered and unpredictable mobilities." Similar unpredictable mobilities can be observed in the bankruptcy of Hanjin, the world's seventh-largest shipping line, resulting in several aporias, from terminals and depots full of containers, ships impounded with crew and cargo aboard and unpaid, creditors seeking payment, ports demanding fees and shippers across the globe unable to access their goods. Gregson and Crang (2015) examined flows of waste and Gregson (2017) recently applied a mobilities perspective to the precarious mobilities of truck drivers, highlighting the often neglected role of labour changes in the logistics system, analogous to the discussion of seafarers in Chapter 6 of the present volume.

Building on this notion of disordered mobilities, Peters's (2015) work on drifting explores how the concept is often considered as transgressive, to stray from a designated path, deviate from the ordinary, often without any aim but not necessarily entirely devoid of agency. Yet the designation of ordinary and accepted or outside and rejected is subjective and changes over time due to shifts in power. Seafarers stranded onboard for months without pay or papers (not as uncommon as might be expected, but receiving a higher profile in recent times in the Hanjin case) can be considered a form of drift. The seafarers are not drifting physically as their ship is berthed in a port, but neither the ship nor the workers are able to leave and thus drifting institutionally outside the norms of the system. Throughout history, certain forms of movement have been deemed acceptable, especially those that are seen to contribute to the economic well-being of a privileged group, such as "urban migrations [and] imperialising sea voyages" (Peters, 2015: 264). Regarding the latter, one could argue that the drift of institutional power from Western ports to Asian ports was initially considered transgressive and had to be reined in by international pressure to adopt Western port governance norms. Peters's work is also useful as a link between some of the land-focused concerns of mobilities research and their more recent application to the maritime mode.

Looking specifically at the maritime mode, Hasty and Peters (2012) explored the mobilities of ships themselves and raised several issues for further research, such as shipowning and governance of flags and port docking, the mobility of seafarers, tourism, physical and institutional governance of the sea itself and immobilities such as ports and anchored vessels. Following Cresswell's (2010a: 555) suggestion that "it would be nice to see an edited collection on watery mobilities to sit alongside the collection on car and air travel," some of these topics were explored in an edited collection by Anim-Addo et al. (2015), *The Mobilities of Ships*, which covered subjects such as piracy, mutiny, tourism, surveillance and the efficiency of packaging in the shipping container. Similarly, another edited collection by Anderson and Peters (2014) *Water Worlds: Human Geographies of the Ocean* explored a diverse range of maritime topics such as ocean knowledge and imaginaries, conservation, leisure, fishing and governance. While these chapters searched towards "more-than-human geographies," there has thus far not been sustained attention to maritime freight transport. The vast literature on maritime freight transport, particularly container ports and shipping, whether treated explicitly through a geographical lens or through other disciplines, has almost never interacted with the mobilities literature, not even the literature on maritime mobilities just discussed.

An edited volume on *Cargomobilities* (Birtchnell et al., 2015) contained chapters addressing topics as diverse as distribution centres, oil transport and petrochemicals, smuggling, representation, security and 3D printing. Our chapter on maritime mobilities identified material, geographical and intuitional mobilities in the maritime transport sector, producing a research agenda signalling the need for a new volume dedicated to freight and logistics aspects of maritime mobilities. Thus as the two maritime collections mentioned primarily addressed peopled mobilities and the *Cargomobilities* volume addressed all modes with only some focus on maritime, there remains significant scope to address more freight-focused maritime issues in the present volume. There is certainly the need in maritime transport geography for "critical mobilities," defined by Söderström et al. (2013) and described by Cresswell (2014: 712) as "mobilities which interrupt the taken-for-granted world of flows and force us to question how things move and the meanings given to those movements."

Maritime mobilities

It is important to emphasise that Sheller and Urry (2006: 210) "do not insist on a new 'grand narrative' of mobility, fluidity or liquidity." Nor do Pyrtherch and Cidell (2015). Nor are we aiming to downplay the role of infrastructure and material movements. What we want to do is unite traditional transport approaches with the more social and cultural aspects of mobilities, not reduce the role of infrastructure planning and analysis, nor to downplay the built environment or the traditional spatial analysis via nodes, corridors and networks.

A differentiation between productive, unproductive and induced mobilities is essential to an understanding of material mobility. Furthermore, the relation and interaction between immobile and mobile infrastructures necessitated by mobility (see Sheller and Urry, 2006: 219) requires further exploration. Just as the immobility of ports and airports underpins the mobility of people and goods, the unproductive mobility in container shipping manufactures new relations and influences decisions relating to productive mobility, as industry actors strive to minimise unproductive mobility.

Immobility has also emerged as a key theme in mobilities research (Cresswell, 2012), which applies strongly to the maritime sector. Ships spend much of their time still, being loaded and unloaded, while goods spend much of their time waiting on the quay or in the stack or at various interchange points in the network, and, indeed, the very provision and operation of interchange points such as ports are essential parts of the provision of mobility but are themselves subject to ongoing pressures, influences and challenges from political and institutional viewpoints. Their physical immobility indeed masks an institutional mobility as ports are privatised or concessioned or reformed (Monios and Wilmsmeier, 2015).

A mobilities approach teases out some of the questions that tend to be neglected in traditional geographical approaches. Schwanen (2016: 360) asks, "Why are apparently critical or vulnerable nodes or links located in particular sites and corridors . . . why have transport networks been configured as they are in the first place?" Monios and Wilmsmeier (2015) identified many practical maritime issues that are relevant to mobilities, such as ballast water (see Chapter 8), which is water held in storage tanks to stabilise empty or minimally loaded vessels. This transport of water across water could be viewed as unproductive or indeed induced mobility. It is a necessary part of maritime trade in order to cope with imbalances, but what is traded is not goods between distant countries but an almost invisible mobility of marine life forms that are part of visible mobilities. Like undocumented and unaccounted human immigrants using containers to cross national borders, marine life forms are now being scrutinised to determine if they will be allowed to enter new territorial waters, and regulations are being developed to manage this process. Similar operational and governance challenges include how to transition away from fossil fuels in an effective and equitable manner and how to deal with climate change impacts.

(Im)mobilities are also reflected in the stasis of international crew traversing the world on vessels but not leaving the vessel for months, and in many cases spending up to a year with the only trips off the ship to a narrowly circumscribed area of the port where they can undertake basic necessities and purchases before needing to be back on board. Seafarers are more mobile than most people in the world (see Chapter 6), but simultaneously immobile, as they rarely leave the ship, have few rights and can even be stranded through piracy or bankruptcy or even sometimes the simple negligence of the shipping line employing them. Cases exist of such employees being left with no money and food, but unable to enter the country where they happen to be stranded, with no rights, papers or prospects of returning home. Such essential workers in the maritime industry have no control over their mobility (either simple physical mobility or mobility in the sense of legal entry to a country or ability to secure employment), even as it is necessary to permit the mobility of maritime trade.

The differential in access between developed and developing countries in access to flights, travel, trade and other essential mobilities of modern life is also seen in maritime trade in which peripheral ports and regions with poorer and more expensive access are disadvantaged. This is exemplified by the existence of pure transhipment hubs where freight congregates then moves on but never actually leaves the port to enter the country. Thus a poor region may have huge amounts of trade massing on its doorstep while obtaining little benefit for its own economy. For example, 99.0 percent of the 1.1m TEU handled at Freeport in the Caribbean and 95.6 percent of the 2.3m TEU handled at Marsaxlokk in Malta are transhipped. So there is little access to the economic benefits of mobility that these ports facilitate for the distant regions utilising these transhipment ports. The port of Gioia Tauro in Italy has received large public subsidies in order to develop economic activity in the poor south of Italy, but the port has remained almost exclusively a transhipment port (94.0 percent) due to a variety of industrial and institutional factors (see Chapter 12).

Introducing the chapters

The authors for this volume are drawn from a range of backgrounds, mostly transport rather than mobility specialists. This is because, as noted earlier, most of these concerns are not being addressed in the mobilities literature, hence the requirement for this book. Thus each author engages to their own preferred depth with the mobilities literature. What is brought by each author, however, is an approach that goes beyond traditional descriptive analysis to consider imbalances, inefficiencies and unproductive aspects of the maritime system. Challenges to the environment, attempts at more sustainable practices, changes in the geoeconomic system, political power, labour, security and governance issues are all among the topics covered in this book.

The volume begins with geographic and institutional mobilities. Germond and Germond-Duret explore ocean governance and the placefulness of oceans. Building on the previous work of mobilities scholars Philip Steinberg and Kim Peters, they identify that in fact mobilities has been an object of enquiry before the seminal Sheller and Urry (2006) paper defined the mobilities paradigm. The central questions of their chapter are what/who is mobile at/across/from the sea and what types of social and political interactions result from these maritime mobilities. To answer these questions, they consider the role of sea power in strengthening the liberal world order and the power of capitalist entities, and highlight differences in representations of the sea between Western and non-Western countries. Their analysis of the relational nature of the construction of the ocean continues as they proceed to draw on Deleuze and Guattari in their discussion of the territorialisation of the sea. They find that

> the process of re-territorialisation of the seas that is currently taking place can certainly be conceived as a neo-modern element within the post-modern world order. As such, the deterritorialisation that characterises post-modern world politics bears the seeds of a re-territorialisation of the seas in the form of ocean governance.

There are clear parallels with the chapter by Monios and Wilmsmeier, which draws on similar theoretical underpinnings to consider ports as capitalist spaces. In that chapter, we recap a recent paper in which we applied the concept of smooth space of Deleuze and Guattari to the global port system. We apply a mobilities perspective to that work, finding that many private players have extracted rents in many cases and avoided competition wherever possible, thus the role of national and international regulators has been required to place limits on market power. Thus the apparently mobile world of global trade is predicated on several constructed and contested mobilities and on many similarly constructed and contested immobilities, revealing these immobilities themselves to be (perhaps counterintuitively) mobile, in the way their geographies, particularly institutionally, are constructed, leading back into the dialectic of smooth and striated space. There is thus a clear recursive relationship between the smooth space discussion and the mobilities paradigm.

Hendricks and Hall look at the human element in their examination of the role of people in green port strategies, seeking to understand how dockworkers mediate the acceptance or rejection of particular cargo regimes. Their analysis of labour geographies provides a welcome contribution to the freight transport literature which often overlooks this crucial aspect in its assumptions of speed, flow and frictionless supply chains (leading us towards the next section on economic mobilities). The authors demonstrate how an actor-centric approach questions these assumptions that attempt to distance the port from its cargo. At the heart of this question is the role of scale, a disjunction and even conflict between global scales of cargo flows and local scales of cities and actors handling this cargo, the points of immobility underpinning the mobility of global trade. Much of the public relations undertaken by ports these days does not always bear close relation to the reality as experienced by dockworkers, questioning the degree to which corporate social responsibility is simply greenwash.

The volume then proceeds to economic mobilities. Vormann and DeDauw examine globalised supply chains and logistics cities. They contrast the "powerful narrative of smart and green growth" with "gentrification processes and the dissolution and relocation of long-standing communities." Moreover, the importance of scale to mobilities is once more revealed in that it is not only a local issue but also the dependence of these urban renewal schemes on global production networks. The authors discuss waterfront developments from New York and Dublin to Lagos and Shanghai. Drawing on the work of David Harvey, they consider the systemic changes that produced the conditions for the emergence of the postindustrial waterfront, such as outsourcing negative externalities and the costs of overcapacity to individual residents and workers who do not benefit from the redevelopments. Once again, the governance issue is raised by the lack of regulation that has driven such developments.

Tang and Chen look at the role of Chinese seafarers, who are geographically mobile due to their working conditions but also institutionally mobile by working for various different companies in many cases flying different flags thus subject to different labour regulations. The authors point out that the mobility of shipping capital drives cost cutting and profit maximisation, hence the number of seafarers from OECD countries has fallen markedly, replaced by employees from developing countries. They note both national attempts at regulation in China and international regulation, such as the 2013 commencement of the Maritime Labour Convention. What is interesting is their identification of the growth of freelance seafarers in China who choose higher salaries and lower insurance benefits, which is what the employers also prefer, but which undermines attempts to protect seafarers from weak labour regulations.

Hesse considers the economic geography of cruise touring through the case study of rock bands hosting mobile concerts as part of an integrated cruise package for music fans. This commodification of the music fan experience links into tourism studies, which the author notes has also experienced its own mobilities turn. The author also makes the connection with previous mobilities work on cruising and drifting, unpacking the relation between the mobility of the ship and the immobility of the passengers within the cruise ship, wherein the actual port destinations are secondary to life on board. This is potentially the case with the regular cruise experience but even more so in this case with the focus being on the music performances and meeting the band members and other fans. The importance of the topic of cruise shipping within maritime transport studies has expanded in recent years as it becomes an increasingly important revenue stream for ports, and the decisions of which ports to call are big business decisions, while at the same time there are some questions as to whether the port cities actually benefit economically from such calls.

The third section of the volume turns to sustainable mobilities. David and Gollasch explore ballast water mobilities, which is a topic rarely considered outside of the technical literature, but one of great importance for the environmental sustainability of maritime transport. While much focus of environmental analysis is on emissions, the authors point out that "the transfer of non-indigenous species across biogeographic barriers is among the greatest threats to the world's oceans and seas," and they discuss the case of a cholera epidemic in Peruvian port cities directly linked to ballast water discharge. It has taken decades of work by various organisations to produce the IMO ballast water management convention, coming into force in September 2017, reflecting both the challenges of global environmental governance and the timeliness of this contribution to the volume.

Bomhauer-Beins and Strüver research ship breaking and recycling through a case study in Pakistan. Their work raises a familiar topic throughout this volume of flagging out, not only during the life of the vessel but also particularly at the end of its life, impacting the regulations regarding its disposal. The authors explore waste mobilities that underpin global commodity flows, in which the ship itself becomes a commodity for recycling. Overcapacity since 2008 has resulted in low freight rates which make scrapping vessels, even at low prices, a necessity for many ship owners, and they interrogate the legally unclear area of vessel sales on the demolition market. The case study reveals the highly manual task of ship breaking, the unofficial role of child labour and the local tax laws. Moreover, the authors demonstrate that waste mobilities are complex, not a simple linear argument that developing countries break the ships of developed countries, but that it is actually a profitable business segment. Nevertheless, the spatial relocation of this environmentally damaging activity suggests the weakness of global regulation identified in many chapter contributions.

The final section covers induced and unproductive mobilities. Wilmsmeier and Monios explore overcapacity and undercapacity as emblematic of unproductive mobilities. These exist in several forms in maritime transport, from transporting empty containers or fuel wastage to service and ship overcapacity. Two specific and related forms are analysed in this chapter: overcapacity of vessels due to the rush to order ultra-large container ships, which leads to a cascading down of vessels to medium routes that do not need them, and infrastructure undercapacity of ports facing the prospect of vessels cascading all the way down to the lowest tier, which may not possess the physical infrastructure to handle them. The empirical application of these concepts in the chapter indicates that these strategies derive in part from an oligopolistic market structure that regulators have done little to address. Governance and regulation are essential aspects of an understanding of mobility, particularly at the international level, and it seems certain that shipping regulation is one of the big questions to be addressed by scholars in the next decade.

Wilmsmeier, Gonzalez-Aregall and Sánchez examine how concentration and cyclical effects in the liner shipping market, in tandem with the seeking of economies of scale, are prolonging the "party" of low freight rates which acts to mask the growing dangers that may likely lead to the "hangover." The underlying issue is the potential abuse of a dominant position in the liner shipping industry which might reach far beyond creating barriers for new entrants and privileges for setting prices. The behaviour of shipping lines in continuing to expand capacity is not reacting to the state of the market, but it is rather a potential sign of anti-competitive practices. From a mobilities perspective, these actions indicate the role of power of individual players under the guise of a supposedly smoothly functioning market sending signals to players to match supply and demand. The authors demonstrate the gap between supply and demand and actions that appear not to be in line with the shipping market cycle.

Genco, Sirtori and Vignetti consider the economic development effect of transhipment port development. This contribution thus also contributes to the discussion on economic mobilities, but, as with cruise shipping, transhipment port development incorporates both the operational decisions of the shipping market (i.e. which ports to call) and the economic imperatives of land development and labour markets. Again, as with cruise calls, the link between transhipment calls and economic multipliers for the region is disputed. Many transhipment port developments try to attract more revenue through hinterland transport of containers and logistics operations but these opportunities are limited given that most of the cargo is simply containers being transhipped without being moved or opened. One important finding is that if the port had been developed specially for this market then it would not have been economically beneficial, but taking the pre-existing port infrastructure (it had previously been used for the steel market) produced a positive long-term economic rate of return. The other key outcome from this analysis was the institutional challenges, as the authors reveal that many actions required to improve the port's performance were understood but the governance structure was too complex to facilitate clear and timely decision making.

Monios and Wang look at empty container repositioning through a case study of Scotland, a country that is a net exporter within the context of the United Kingdom, which is a net importer (like most Western countries). Containers emptied of their imported goods in inland distribution centres in England are not shipped north overland for the use of Scottish exporters but rather returned to south-eastern ports and then moved north by sea. Scottish imports arrive mostly overland in trucks as picked loads from centralised DCs. This system is driven by the centralising logic of UK import logistics but causes additional costs in certain locations such as Scotland. Local stakeholders attempt to resolve this issue, but they have difficulties interacting with the global scale, where decisions are made by global shipping lines.

Conclusion

Transport geographers should identify the "location of power that needs to be talked back to, challenged, or transformed" (Smith, 2005: 894). This endeavour can be aided by using the theoretical tools of critical, radical and relational geographies, and from the wider post-structuralist enterprise to analyse ports as socially constructed, contingent and, in many cases, contested spaces (Wilmsmeier and Monios, 2015). Peters (2010: 1264) notes that,

> Given the sea has been often regarded as a different or marginal space, it is perhaps unsurprising that one route by which contemporary social and cultural geographies have begun to recognise the sea as a site of study is through "critical geographies," an approach that seeks to redress "unequal power relations," achieve "social justice" and "transform politics" (Johnston et al., 2000: 127). Critical geographies seeking to give voice to the marginalised (usually underrepresented groups or forgotten places) have begun to recognise the sea and people who live and work in these marginal spaces, who too are often outside of mainstream society.

Yet very little of this work has filtered through to the large literature on maritime freight transport and logistics, hence the need for this current volume. We want to expand the conversation with our colleagues working in the field of ocean shipping and container ports to engage with the topics raised in this volume.

There is clearly a high degree of interaction between the different kinds of mobility used to segment the chapter contributions to this volume. Governance and (lack of) regulation, particularly as they are complicated by scale, emerge as the key themes running throughout the volume. Several chapters consider whether globalisation has developed equitably within the current form of increasingly unregulated neoliberalism, drawing on a shared pool of theoretical concepts such as smooth space, the spatial fix and the continued importance of the work of David Harvey. The role of the state has been transformed in recent decades, and state intervention is more likely to take the form of enforced privatisation of transport infrastructure management than regulation of transport provision. According to Enright (2013: 804),

> The state maintains a high level of involvement in leading capital accumulation, but does so not to correct the failures of the naturally functioning market,

but to intervene and marketize those social and political forms that would not otherwise conform to a market logic.

Each of the different kinds of mobilities discussed in this book, but represented most directly by the category of induced and unproductive mobilities, demonstrate the sometimes artificial and counter-intuitive decisions underpinning what appears to be a smooth surface of frictionless mobility. The global system of maritime transport can be explored in all its richness by drawing on the mobilities literature discussed earlier, utilising concepts such as drifting, mooring and turbulence. Peters (2015: 263) suggests that, "The sea offers an important spatiality for unlocking knowledge beyond the confines of the nation state and the grounded materiality of land." The work in this book demonstrates that mobilities are politically, culturally and socially constructed. Moreover, they are frequently contested, albeit usually within unequal power relations.

It is possible to criticise the mobilities paradigm along the lines of whether it contributes a clearly distinct approach to other ways of understanding transport, notably through transport geography but increasingly in economics through discussions of regulation. While that must remain an open question, our view is that if consciously using a mobilities approach has enabled the development of a stream of work that has sought the inconsistencies, the aporias, the gaps, the conflicts, the lives and the experiences of those left behind and other critics of the neoliberal consensus, then it will have served its purpose.

Note

1   See *The Box* (Levinson, 2006) for a historical account of the advent of containerisation.

References

Anderson, J., Peters, K. (eds.) (2014). *Water Worlds: Human Geographies of the Ocean.* Abingdon: Routledge.

Anim-Addo, A., Hasty, W., Peters, K. (eds.) (2015). *The Mobilities of Ships.* Abingdon: Routledge.

Barke, M. (1986). *Transport and Trade: Conceptual Frameworks in Geography.* Edinburgh: Oliver & Boyd.

Bird, J. (1963). *The Major Seaports of the United Kingdom.* London: Hutchinson & Co.

Birtchnell, T., Savitzky, S., Urry, J. (eds.) (2015). *Cargomobilities: Moving Materials in a Global Age.* Abingdon: Routledge.

Brooks, M. R., Cullinane, K. (eds.) (2007). Devolution, port governance and port performance. *Research in Transport Economics*, special issue. 17. Elsevier, London.

Cidell, J. (2012). Flows and pauses in the urban logistics landscape: The municipal regulation of shipping container mobilities. *Mobilities.* 7 (2): 233–246.

Cidell, J., Lechtenberg, D. (2016). Developing a framework for the spaces and spatialities of transportation and mobilities. *Annals of the American Association of Geographers.* 106 (2): 257–265.

Cowen, D. (2014). *The Deadly Life of Logistics.* Minneapolis, MN: University of Minnesota Press.

Cresswell, T. (2010a). Mobilities I: Catching up. *Progress in Human Geography*. 35 (4): 550–558.

Cresswell, T. (2010b). Towards a politics of mobility. *Environment & Planning D*. 28: 17–31.

Cresswell, T. (2012). Mobilities II: Still. *Progress in Human Geography*. 36 (5): 645–653.

Cresswell, T. (2014). Mobilities III: Moving on. *Progress in Human Geography*. 38 (5): 712–721.

Creswell, T., Martin, C. (2012). On turbulence: Entanglements of disorder and order on a Devon beach. *Tijdschrift voor Sociale en Economische Geografie*. 103 (5): 516–529.

Debrie, J., Lavaud-Letilleul, V., Parola, F. (2013). Shaping port governance: The territorial trajectories of reform. *Journal of Transport Geography*. 27: 56–65.

Doel, M. (1999). *Poststructuralist Geographies: The Diabolical Art of Spatial Science*. Edinburgh: Edinburgh University Press.

Doel, M. (2000). Un-Glunking Geography: Spatial Science after Dr Seuss and Gilles Deleuze. In: M. Crang and N. Thrift (eds.), *Thinking Space*. London: Routledge. pp. 117–135.

Ducruet, C., Roussin, S., Jo, J.-C. (2009). Going west? Spatial polarization of the North Korean port system. *Journal of Transport Geography*. 17 (5): 357–368.

Enright, T. E. (2013). Mass transit in the neoliberal city: The mobilizing myths of the Grand Paris Express. *Environment and Planning A*. 45: 797–813.

Frémont, A., Soppé, M. (2007). Northern European Range: Shipping Line Concentration and Port Hierarchy. In: D. Olivier, T. Notteboom and B. Slack (eds.), *Ports, Cities and Global Supply Chains*. Aldershot: Ashgate. pp. 105–120.

Goetz, A. R. (2006). Transport geography: Reflecting on a subdiscipline and identifying future research trajectories: The insularity issue in transport geography. *Journal of Transport Geography*. 14: 230–231.

Goetz, A. R., Vowles, T. M., Tierney, S. (2009). Bridging the qualitative-quantitative divide in transport geography. *The Professional Geographer*. 61 (3): 323–335.

Gregson, N. (2017). Logistics at work: Trucks, containers and the friction of circulation in the UK. *Mobilities*. 12 (3): 343–364.

Gregson, N., Crang, M. A. (2015). From waste to resource: The trade in wastes and global recycling economies. *Annual Review of Environment and Resources*. 40: 151–176.

Guattari, F. (2000 [1989]). *The Three Ecologies*. Trans. I. Pindar, P. Sutton. London: The Athlone Press.

Hall, P., Hesse, M., Rodrigue, J.-P. (2006). Reexploring the interface between economic and transport geography. *Environment and Planning A*. 38: 1401–1408.

Hannam, K., Sheller, M., Urry, J. (2006). Editorial: Mobilities, immobilities and moorings. *Mobilities*. 1 (1): 1–22.

Hanson, S. (2003). Transportation: Hooked on Speed, Eyeing Sustainability. In: E. Sheppard and T. Barnes (eds.), *A Companion to Economic Geography*. Oxford: Blackwell. pp. 468–483.

Harvey, D. (1985). The Geopolitics of Capitalism. In: D. Gregory and J. Urry (eds.), *Social Relations and Spatial Structures*. MacMillian: London. pp. 128–163.

Harvey, D. (2006 [1982]). *The Limits to Capital*. New and fully updated ed. London: Verso.

Hasty, W., Peters, K. (2012). The ship in geography and the geographies of ships. *Geography Compass*. 6 (11): 660–676.

Hayuth, Y. (1981). Containerization and the load center concept. *Economic Geography*. 57: 160–176.

Hesse, M. (2013). Cities and flows: Re-asserting a relationship as fundamental as it is delicate. *Journal of Transport Geography*. 29: 33–42.

Hesse, M., Rodrigue, J.-P. (2004). The transport geography of logistics and freight distribution. *Journal of Transport Geography*. 12 (3): 171–184.

Hoyle, B. S. (1968). East African seaports: An application of the concept of 'anyport'. *Transactions & Papers of the Institute of British Geographers*. 44: 163–183.

Janelle, D. G., Beuthe, M. (1997). Globalization and research issues in transportation. *Journal of Transport Geography*. 5 (3): 199–206.

Johnston, R. J., Gregory, D., Pratt, G., Watts, M. (eds.) (2000). *The Dictionary of Human Geography*. 4th ed. Oxford: Blackwell.

Keeling, D. J. (2007). Transportation geography: New directions on well-worn trails. *Progress in Human Geography*. 31 (2): 217–225.

Knowles, R. D. (2006). Transport shaping space: Differential collapse in time-space. *Journal of Transport Geography*. 14 (6): 407–425.

Kwan, M.-P., Schwanen, T. (2016). Geographies of mobility. *Annals of the American Association of Geographers*. 106 (2): 243–256.

Lee, S. W., Song, D. W., Ducruet, C. (2008). A tale of Asia's world ports: The spatial evolution in global hub port cities. *Geoforum*. 39 (1): 372–395.

Levinson, M. (2006). *The Box: How the Shipping Container Made the World Smaller and the World Economy Bigger*. Princeton: Princeton University Press.

Lin, W. (2016). Transport provision and the practice of mobilities production. *Progress in Human Geography*. In press.

Martin, C. (2013). Shipping container mobilities, seamless compatibility and the global surface of logistical integration. *Environment & Planning A*. 45 (5): 1021–1036.

Monios, J., Wilmsmeier, G. (2013). The role of intermodal transport in port regionalisation. *Transport Policy*. 30: 161–172.

Monios, J., Wilmsmeier, G. (2015). Identifying Material, Geographical and Institutional Mobilities in the Global Maritime Trade System. In: T. Birtchnell, S. Savitzky and J. Urry (eds.), *Cargomobilities: Moving Materials in a Global Age*. Abingdon: Routledge. pp. 125–148.

Ng, A.K.Y., Ducruet, C., Jacobs, W., Monios, J., Notteboom, T., Rodrigue, J., Slack, B., Tam, K., Wilmsmeier, G. (2014). Port geography at the crossroads with human geography: Between flows and spaces. *Journal of Transport Geography*. 41: 84–96.

Notteboom, T. E. (2005). The Peripheral Port Challenge in Container Port Systems. In: H. Leggate, J. McConville and A. Morvillo (eds.), *International Maritime Transport: Perspectives*. London: Routledge. pp. 173–188.

Notteboom, T. E., Rodrigue, J.-P. (2005). Port regionalization: Towards a new phase in port development. *Maritime Policy & Management*. 32 (3): 297–313.

Olivier, D., Slack, B. (2006). Rethinking the port. *Environment & Planning A*. 38 (8): 1409–1427.

Peters, K. (2010). Future promises for contemporary social and cultural geographies of the seas. *Geography Compass*. 2 (6): 1260–1272.

Peters, K. (2015). Drifting: Towards mobilities at sea. *Transactions of the Institute of British Geographers*. 40: 262–272.

Port Strategy (2011). Maersk calls ports to the table. Port Strategy. 17 October 2011. Available at: www.portstrategy.com/news101/products-and-services/maersk-calls-ports-to-the-table Accessed 2 September 2013.

Pyrtherch, D., Cidell, J. (2015). Transportation, Mobilities and Rethinking Urban Geogrpahies of Flow. In: J. Cidell and D. Prytherch (eds.), *Transport, Mobility and the Production of Urban Space*. New York: Routledge. pp. 19–44.

Rimmer, P. J. (1967). The search for spatial regularities in the development of Australian seaports 1861–1961/2. *Geograkiska Annaler*. 49: 42–54.

Rodrigue, J-P. (2006). Transport geography should follow the freight. *Journal of Transport Geography*. 14 (5): 386–388.

Rodrigue, J.-P., Notteboom, T. E. (2010). Foreland-based regionalization: Integrating intermediate hubs with port hinterlands. *Research in Transportation Economics*. 27: 19–29.

Sánchez, R. J., Wilmsmeier, G. (2006). The river plate basin: A comparison of port devolution processes on the east coast of South America. *Research in Transportation Economics*. 17: 185–205.

Sánchez, R. J., Wilmsmeier, G. (2011). Liner Shipping Networks and Market Concentration. In: K. Cullinane (ed.), *International Handbook of Maritime Economics*. Cheltenham: Edward Elgar. pp. 162–206.

Schwanen, T. (2015). Geographies of transport I: Reinventing a field? *Progress in Human Geography*. 40 (1): 126–137.

Schwanen, T. (2016). Geographies of transport II: Reconciling the general and the particular. *Progress in Human Geography*. 41 (3): 355–364.

Schwanen, T., Kwan, M.-P. (2012). Critical space – time geographies. *Environment and Planning A*. 44 (9): 2043–2048.

Shaw, J., Hesse, M. (2010). Transport, geography and the 'new' mobilities. *Transactions of the Institute of British Geographers*. 35 (3): 305–312.

Shaw, J., Sidaway, J. D. (2010). Making links: On (re)engaging with transport and transport geography. *Progress in Human Geography*. 35 (4): 502–520.

Sheller, M. (2015). Mobilizing Transportation, Transporting Mobilities. In: J. Cidell and D. Prytherch (eds.), *Tranöport, Mobility and the Production of Urban Space*. New York: Routledge. pp. 12–18.

Sheller, M., Urry, J. (2006). The new mobilities paradigm. *Environment & Planning A*. 38 (2): 207–226.

Slack, B., Wang, J. J. (2002). The challenge of peripheral ports: An Asian perspective. *Geojournal*. 56: 159–166.

Smith, N. (2005). Neo-critical geography, or, the flat pluralist world of business class. *Antipode*. 37 (5): 887–889.

Söderström, O., Randeria, S., Ruedin, D., D'Amato, G., Panese, F. (2013). *Critical Mobilities*. Lausanne: EPFL.

Steinberg, P. E. (2001). *The Social Construction of the Ocean*. Cambridge: Cambridge University Press.

Steinberg, P. E. (2013). Of other seas: Metaphors and materialities in maritime regions. *Atlantic Studies*. 10 (2): 156–169.

Taaffe, E. J., Morrill, R. L., Gould, P. R. (1963). Transport expansion in underdeveloped countries: A comparative analysis. *Geographical Review*. 53: 503–529.

Thrift, N. (1996). *Spatial Formations*. London: Sage.

Van Klink, H. A. (1998). The port network as a new stage in port development: The case of Rotterdam. *Environment and Planning A*. 30 (1): 143–160.

Wang, C., Ducruet, C. (2012). New port development and global city making: Emergence of the Shanghai-Yangshan multi-layered gateway hub. *Journal of Transport Geography*. 25: 58–69.

Wang, J. J., Ng, A.K.Y. (2011). The geographical connectedness of Chinese seaports with foreland markets: A new trend? *Tijdschrift voor Economische en Sociale Geografie*. 102 (2): 188–204.

Wilmsmeier, G., Monios, J. (2013). Counterbalancing peripherality and concentration: An analysis of the UK container port system. *Maritime Policy & Management.* 40 (2): 116–132.

Wilmsmeier, G., Monios, J. (2015). The production of capitalist 'smooth' space in global port operations. *Journal of Transport Geography.* 47: 59–69.

Wilmsmeier, G., Monios, J., Pérez-Salas, G. (2014). Port system evolution: The case of Latin America and the Caribbean. *Journal of Transport Geography.* 39: 208–221.

Part 1

Geographic and institutional mobilities

2 Critical geographies of the ocean

Mobilities, placefulness and maritime relationalism

Basil Germond and Celine Germond-Duret

Introduction

In collective imaginaries, the sea has traditionally been represented as an unknown, hazardous, unpredictable, inhospitable, infinite, unregulated, lawless and, ultimately, uninhabitable space. Therefore, the sea has been constructed as the land's other, or in other words it is where 'we are not' or where 'we', as human beings, are not supposed to be, or at least to stay and to settle. This has resulted in recurring binary oppositions, such as the fluid/liquid nature of water opposed to the solid/static nature of the land. Indeed, as stated by Anderson and Peters (2014: 5), "The sea's physical constitution renders it as intrinsically 'other'; it is a fluid world rather than a solid one. Our normative experiences of the world centre on engagements on solid ground; rather than in liquid sea."

Since the sea has traditionally been considered and represented as a "placeless void" (Steinberg, 2001) – i.e. an 'empty' space outside of human and social experience, human geography as an academic discipline has not been much interested in the sea, to the point that it has been defined as a "landlocked field" (Lambert et al., 2006: 480). The ocean was "best left to the natural sciences" (Gillis, 2011: 17), including physical geography. However, as Smith explains, "Historically, geography has always played a central role in bringing together the natural and social sciences through the study of inter-relationships between people and environments on both land and sea." (2002: 577). In other words, human geography could further develop a maritime ontology, which goes along with the realisation that the sea is placeful (Germond and Germond-Duret, 2016) and that the 'maritime object' can be studied within a mobilities framework (Steinberg and Peters, 2015; Peters, 2015) that further allows taking into account social interactions within the maritime domain as well as the relationalist nature of the interactions between the sea and human agents.

The "scholarly turn to the ocean", already noticed by Connery in 2006 (496) is perhaps still limited or even "premature" (Bear, 2012: 22), but it has nevertheless materialised in a variety of academic disciplines, such as economy, anthropology, law and even in those disciplines that had previously neglected the sea such as international relations (e.g. Germond, 2015b). In this chapter, we contribute to the human geography's turn to the sea with a particular focus on critical geographies and the concepts of placefulness and mobilities. The chapter discusses the way forward in terms of ontology and analytical framework.

Critical geographies of the ocean

It is not surprising to find that the geographers who have developed a strong interest in the oceans are mainly critical geographers (as also noticed by Peters, 2010: 1264), since the source of this ontology and related epistemology can be traced back to continental philosophy, in particular Foucault's description of the ship as "heterotopia" on a placeless sea; "a floating piece of space, a place without a place" (Foucault and Miskowiec, 1986: 27), as well as Deleuze and Guattari's discussion of the maritime space as space of mobility, which is both striated and smooth (Deleuze and Guattari, 1988: 387, 479; see also Steinberg, 1999a, 1999b). In fact, beyond the conceptualisation of the sea as "the realm of the unbound" (Connery, 2006: 497), continental philosophy acknowledges the 'colonisation' of the sea by the land, not only in the form of power projection (such as the Foucauldian knowledge-power matrix that acknowledges the practical consequences of a certain representation of the ocean in terms of power projection) but also in terms of the interactions between what is a place and what is a space, and the mutually constituting relationship between place and space at sea as well as the deterritorialisation-reterritorialisation dialectic within the modernity-postmodernity debate. Indeed, in recurring representations, the sea "epitomizes wilderness" (a "wild place"), whereas the land is more "civilized" (Casey, 1993: 204), which demonstrates the cultural colonization of the sea by the land.

The two most prominent (critical-cultural) geographers of the 21st century who have largely contributed to the debate on maritime geographies are Philip Steinberg and Kimberley Peters. They have been at the forefront of the current academic debates in geography on the specificities, nature and dynamics of the maritime space, and have clearly pushed for a disciplinary turn towards the oceans.

Philip Steinberg is well known for his application of critical approaches to the understanding of what he calls "ocean-space"[1] as well as his role in promoting a human, cultural, social, economic and political geography of the seas. The origin of his ocean research has to be found in critical political economy, following a realisation that critical economic geography in the age of globalisation actually ignores a crucial global space – i.e., the ocean. Continental philosophy can be considered as a "maturation" of his ocean research beyond political economy (e.g. Steinberg, 2001: 38; personal correspondence with Steinberg). His ideas have originally been exposed in two articles published in 1999 as well as in a seminal book titled *The Social Construction of the Ocean* published in 2001. Three main claims are particularly relevant to this discussion on critical maritime geographies:

1) Geographers have misunderstood and understated the importance of the sea from a social perspective: they have indeed traditionally considered the sea "as a space that shares little with the land-space studied by the bulk of the discipline", which Steinberg claims "is inadequate as the sea emerges

as a central arena for many of the key social and physical problems of concern to policymakers, scholars, and citizens [since] it is a space that, like land, shapes and is shaped by a host of physical and social processes" (1999a: 367). In other words, "the world-ocean is a significant space continually transformed amidst an array of social and physical processes, some of which operate on land, some of which operate at sea, and some of which span the coastal divide" (1999a: 372). Steinberg explains that this lack of interest by human geographers is due to the uninhabitable nature of the sea, which puts its "location beyond any of the sovereign states that frequently bound the scope of inquiry for students of 'national' polities, economies, cultures, etc." – a "location outside of [the] 'world region'" (1999a: 369). Another explanation is that geographers have rather "focussed on issues of direct policy relevance, particularly in the coastal areas, where human interaction and impacts are most intense" (1999a: 367).

2) Ocean-space is constructed as 'empty' (and thus disposable) but is nonetheless 'regulated' (and thus controlled). Steinberg builds on continental philosophers' work from the 1980s, notably Deleuze and Guattari, who "highlight the ocean as a unique 'smooth' space of movement that resists regulation" while still prone to "striation" and thus control (1999a: 369). He also contrasts Virilio's claim that "the incorporation of the marine domain within the controlled perpetual motion of capitalism and statist militarism represents a victory for modernity" with Foucault's interest for the ocean as a domain resisting states' control (369). Steinberg discusses the way representing the ocean as an 'empty' space[2] has engendered a practice consisting in managing the ocean. He mainly applied this framework to resource management by deconstructing the so-called stewardship discourse – i.e. a "resource-rich but fragile ocean in need of comprehensive management and planning" (1999b: 419). Steinberg claims that this "managerial environmentalist perspective is supportive of general guidelines for governing the uses of the sea without actually mandating its governance as territory. [. . .] The ocean is recognized as a crucial space for essential social processes but care is taken to protect it from the ravages of competitive territorial states. [The sea is] a special space of commerce [. . .], immune to territorial appropriation but susceptible to exertions of social power" (1999b: 419). In other words, this discourse tends to justify the non-territorial exercise of power at sea. In his *Social Construction of the Ocean* (2001), Steinberg expands on the hegemonic nature of the discourse consisting in representing ocean-space as an empty space, a void or an 'other', and analyses the contradiction between a discourse constructing the ocean as an empty space and the practice consisting in a certain territorialisation of ocean-space, not least to assure the stewardship of the ocean (see also Steinberg, 1999c).

3) Mobility characterises ocean-space: Steinberg explains, "Many scholars have noted the important role that speed and the conquest of distance play in contemporary capitalism" (1999b: 416), and he emphasises that "within this system of hypermobile capitalism, the ocean has taken on special

importance as a seemingly friction-free surface across which capital can move without hindrance" (1999b: 416). Steinberg also builds on continental philosophy to draw links between this notion of mobility and the idea of the ocean as an empty space/void conquered and put at the service of both capitalism and militarism (1999b: 417): a "spatial ideology" at the service of the Capital (2001: 165) or in other words what Connery calls the "bourgeois idealisation of sea power" (1994: 40). It is interesting to note that Steinberg's reference to the notion of mobility appeared several years before it became 'academically trendy' following Sheller and Urry's (2006) seminal article. However, mobility in geography was already discussed in the 1990s (e.g. by Tim Cresswell). This influenced Steinberg's idea to integrate mobility and its spaces into social theory, but his original aim was first and foremost to bring political economy to the sea (personal correspondence with Steinberg).

Since 2010, Kimberley Peters has greatly contributed to the debate on maritime geographies and mobilities, building on Steinberg as well as Lambert et al. (2006) to stress the importance of developing a geography of the sea, as well as the relevance of the "mobilities paradigm" (Sheller and Urry, 2006) to tackle sea-related processes. Peters's starting point is the recognition of cultural and social geographers' lack of interest in the sea: "There's no 'sea' in current geographies" (Peters, 2010: 1262). Like Steinberg, she incriminates the uninhabitable nature of the sea, which has, she regrets, resulted in the sea being "typically understood as inferior to and marginal from the land and invisible in modern consciousness" (1260). She also points the finger at scholars' and practitioners' current "[obsession] with speed" (1263). In other words, the importance given to speed in social constructions and the lack of maritime mobilities research (compared to positivist maritime transport studies and transportation geography) has resulted in a lack of interest for the ship in particular and the sea in general within the discipline of geography (1265). In sum, Peters proposes, "Contemporary 'maritime geographies' could be strengthened through the lens of the 'new mobilities paradigm'", by asking questions such as "what politics are involved in contemporary movements across the oceans? [. . .] How are identities forged and contested across the seas?" (1266). Peters claims that maritime mobilities are central to our lives and life experiences as well as social interactions, which demonstrates the relevance of maritime geographies (also see Anim-Addo et al., 2014).

In 2015, Steinberg and Peters proposed to develop a "wet ontology" that accounts for the importance of the mobilities paradigm. Therefore, their idea is

> not merely to endorse the perspective of a world of flows, connections, liquidities, and becomings, but also to propose a means by which the sea's material and phenomenological distinctiveness can facilitate the reimagining and reenlivening of a world ever on the move.
>
> (Steinberg and Peters, 2015: 248)

Talking about the mapping and delimitation of zones at sea, they notice, "Attempts at mapping vertically fail. The drawing of lines through water in an attempt to constitute levels of legal authority fails to account for the dynamic fluidity of the various elements that constitute the marine assemblage" (2015: 253). However, they acknowledge the fact that "legal institutions will always attempt to delimit volumes into strata just as they will always attempt to delimit horizontal spaces into areas" (258). Referring to Lagrangian fluid dynamics, they propose that the ocean shall be conceptualised not "as a space of discrete points between which objects move but rather as a dynamic environment of flows and continual recomposition where, because there is no static background, 'place' can be understood only in the context of mobility" (257). In other words, the fluid nature of the maritime milieu contributes to the relationalist nature of the sea as a place.

In sum, Steinberg and Peters have started to develop a stream of research that tries to bring the sea into human geography's ontology: "To shift the sea to the centre of human geographical studies" (Anderson and Peters, 2016: 4). According to them, two central elements shall steer this scholarly move: first, "the sea is not a material or metaphorical void, but alive with embodies human experiences" (ibid) and secondly, "the ocean is an actual experienced place of mobilities" (Steinberg, 2011: 274). In other words, they propose a framework that brings together critical maritime geographies and (maritime) mobilities.

Steinberg's works engaged with the critical geopolitical tradition, such as critically discussing the links between space and politics or deconstructing policy documents or popular geopolitics. However, in general, critical geographers of the sea have not so much engaged into the discussion of the practical implications of geopolitical discourses in terms of the justification and normalisation of policies and practices. So critical geopolitics can further be integrated into a critical maritime geography framework. Drawing from international relations, Germond (2013, 2015a) and Germond and Germond-Duret (2016) have used critical geopolitics, notably drawing on Agnew and Ó Thuatail, to demonstrate the link between the construction of threats at sea and the normalisation of policies that consist in controlling or governing the maritime domain. They have shown how certain geographical representations contribute to the normalisation of certain practices via the construction of certain 'truths', including on the (geographical) origin of threats and the characteristics of the maritime milieu. Discourse and practice mutually reinforce each other: "Geography is not a natural given but a power-knowledge relationship" (Ó Tuathail, 1996: 10).

> Applied to the maritime domain, critical geopolitics, as an approach, reveals useful in exposing the way maritime spaces are constructed in relation to one's own identity and to perceived (or constructed) external threats, and how this contributes to normalizing a practice that consists in projecting power onto, and controlling, the maritime domain beyond one's territorial and jurisdictional waters.
>
> (Germond and Germond-Duret, 2016)

This fits with Glück's point about the "production of security space" at sea that contributes to secure the free flow of goods (capital) (2015). Indeed, beyond the management of marine resources, ocean governance and maritime security practices are increasingly aimed at controlling the flows of goods and people across the maritime domain, which is related to Steinberg's point about the growing territorialisation of the sea (2001). This practice does not lead to an 'occupation' of the sea (which beyond political and legal considerations would certainly not be possible from a practical, material perspective), but to the control of sea lanes of communication as well as of people and goods moving along those lanes. This results in hybrid territorialisation practices in a deterritorialized world and space, which are hardly taken into account by traditional maritime historians, lawyers and spatial planners. Whereas "the mobility of either the water or the fish" (Steinberg and Peters, 2015: 253) must be taken into account, "fish cross borders" (Germond, 2015b) and do not respect the immaterial (constructed) lines drawn by politicians and spatial planners, but so do fishermen, migrants and other actors who interact at sea, with the sea and from the sea. This again calls for the mobilities paradigm to be incorporated into critical maritime geography.

In sum, human geography is still very much a 'landlocked' discipline, and there is a need to expand the study of maritime geographies. The earlier discussion highlighted the relevance of adopting a framework for analysis that brings together the mobilities paradigm, critical geopolitics and the Foucauldian knowledge-power matrix so as to study maritime geographies in a way that accounts for the placefulness of the ocean – i.e., a place of social and political interactions that is both deterritorialized and territorialized, and whose nature is relationalist. We propose to apply this framework to the following questions: What/who is mobile at/across/from the sea? What type of social or political interactions result from these maritime mobilities? By doing so, we aim at highlighting the relevance of adopting a maritime relationalist ontology that accounts for the placefulness of the sea.

Maritime mobilities in a placeful environment

Hannam et al. (2006: 1) explain that,

> The concept of mobilities encompasses both the large-scale movements of people, objects, capital and information across the world, as well as the more local processes of daily transportation, movement through public space and the travel of material things within everyday life.

It appears clearly that the mobilities paradigm implies that something or someone is mobile or in motion (at least potentially) and that the act of moving (or not moving in the case of mobilities exclusion) is constitutive of that someone's identity and of the nature of social/political interactions in a given place and at a given time beyond (and not always in relations to) the place of departure and arrival. So the crucial questions to explore are what/who is mobile/in motion at/across/from the sea? And then what type of social or political interactions result from these various maritime mobilities?

The most obvious subject of maritime mobilities is the ship. Foucault's description of the ship as heterotopia (Foucault and Miskowiec, 1986: 27) has contributed to foster research, including by social and cultural geographers, on ships as places of/for contestation, located outside the realm of sovereign states and regulated space (see also Hasty and Peters, 2012: 664–5). Sailors, fishermen or else tourists experience the sea through the ship, which is the place of human experience, 'floating' on the blue void, which itself "is a space of circulation because it is constituted through its very geophysical mobility" (Steinberg, 2013:165; see also Steinberg and Peters, 2015). Interestingly, whereas the ship is conceived as a likely place (e.g. Gilroy, 1993), it is a place that is in motion on the seas. This has certainly contributed to render the sea placeless, since in collective imaginaries the ship is the place of social interactions (after all it represents materiality versus the liquidity of the sea), not the sea, which is 'just' the (natural – physical) environment in/on/through which the ship and its passengers/cargo move. Drawing from Mack (2011) and Steinberg (2013: 159) explains that in literature and historical studies what is presented (at least in a Western context) as "life at sea" is actually a discussion of "life on ship". This narrative is in line with what Steinberg (2001: 163) calls the annihilation of ocean-space – i.e., the construction of ocean-space as "a mere surface" or "an empty void to be annihilated by hypermobile capital" (1999b: 403). According to him, the cruise ship industry contributes to this representation, since the ship and not the sea is presented as the "primary destination". That said, as noticed by Hasty and Peters (2012: 661), the ship is often acknowledged but seldom considered in the academic literature. In sum, ships are not given the attention they deserve; in collective imaginaries, the ship is the 'place' where people 'are' when they travel through the sea, which has contributed to the representation of the sea as placeless. More attention shall be paid to the ship not only as a place of social interactions but also as a vector for not only people and goods but also ideas, norms, values and identities. In sum, the ship can be studied in relation to the sea as a place. The ship's agency as well as the agency of those who are (and the cargo which is) on the ship contribute to perform the sea as a place. Also, a relational framework fits well with the mobilities paradigm, since it puts an emphasis on the relational nature of the sea as a place rather than the interactions at sea between 'existing' entities such as ships and sailors.

Beyond the ship itself, goods and people can move across the oceans thanks to the ship, which is the vector. In fact, before the existence of ships capable of traveling beyond the horizon, the human experience of the sea was evidently more limited. Scholars working on the movement of goods have essentially conducted statistical and economic studies (Peters, 2010: 1266) and discussed issues such as risk and safety management (e.g. Kristiansen, 2013), which fits with a traditional positivist framework. But it is interesting to note that such transport studies contribute to the perception of the sea as placeless, since goods are understood to be at sea only to be transported as efficiently as possible from port to port (land to land) across the blue void. Steinberg (e.g. 2001) and Connery (1994, 2006) discussed the movement of capital across the sea. They propose that the sea has been conceived as a great common that states and commercial actors should be free to use for travel and transportation. As mentioned earlier, this is what Steinberg calls a "spatial ideology" at the service of the Capital (2001: 165) and Connery the "bourgeois idealization of sea power" (1994: 40). Maritime transportation in particular and sea power in general has seemingly resulted in the strengthening of the liberal world order (Germond, 2015b: 8–10) via obvious advantages for capitalist entities as well as states via commerce and naval power projection: "Naval scholars have also contributed to representing the sea as a mere lane of communication, which allows commerce to flourish and navies to protect the commerce and to reach any (land) place in the world" (Germond and Germond-Duret, 2016: 125). Corbett, for example states that "the only positive value which the high seas have for national life" (1911: 93) is to serve as a means of communication. Sea power (understood as both naval and civilian) has also contributed to the consolidation of nation-states (Glete, 2000) and to the spread of Western/European values in general (Herder, 1803: 119). Whereas this demonstrates the importance of the sea to explain societal and political developments on land (such as modernity, nation-states and liberalism), this may also contribute to the representation of the sea as placeless, since the movement of goods and ideas does not seems to be impacted by the sea itself, but only by the degree of command or control some actors have of the sea.

If one now turns to people (human beings) who (directly) experience the sea, the identity argument is central to most reflections on the concept of place. However, the lack of consideration for the importance of the sea as a place of identity building has contributed to the underlying idea that the sea is placeless: the sea is an "anonymous" space (Relph, 1976: 143) devoid of social interactions and does not contribute to shaping identity beyond being a mere context for human, social and political interactions. Against that limited (and, as mentioned earlier, Western) understanding of the sea, several studies have pointed at the link between the sea and people's identity. In a general manner, the identity of fishing communities (i.e. those who work at sea and live by the sea) can probably be said to strongly relate to the sea. Daily encounter with the marine element (either at sea fishing or at home facing the waterfront and waiting for the return of loved ones) and the dependence on the sea for living (either as a source of revenue or as a direct source of food for the community) have impacts on those communities' identities (see the following). The sea is also linked to the identity of several other communities, who can feel a 'sense of place'.

Brstilo (2013) discusses the case of Filipino sailors and shows that they constitute a "sea-based diaspora", with the sea being a place of "human experience" for them (31). Sampson (2003) also uses the case of Filipino sailors to discuss the extent to which their experience of the sea does impact on their identity. Hannam, Sheller and Urry mention "fears of illicit mobilities and their attendant security risks increasingly determine logics of governance and liability protection within both the public and private sectors" (2006: 1). Whereas drug or arms trafficking directly relate to illegal maritime mobilities, the case of illegal migrant is particular, since the criminals are the human smugglers. Scholars in the field of international relations, geography, law and sociology have discussed the case of migrants at sea. The current refugee/boat people crisis in the Mediterranean has only highlighted a phenomenon that had already become apparent in Europe since the 1990s. It is interesting to discuss the relevance of the sea in understanding the underlying social and political interactions that characterise sea migrants as well as the nature of their relation with the sea itself and how this may impact on their own identity construction. How do they conceive the sea? As a barrier that prevent them from accessing the European 'Eldorado'? Or, on the contrary, as a medium for hope; hope to reach a 'better destination' and access a 'better life'? Following their journey, when they are again settled on land (whether in Europe or back in their country of origin), to what extent has those migrants' identity been, if at all, influenced or even transformed by their experience at and of the sea? Migrants who cross the Mediterranean at high risk may perceive the sea as

> both a place of hope (leading to a 'better' life) and despair (facing dangers); a place of life and death, which becomes forcibly linked to their (evolving) identity, or at least to their identity as constructed by others. [For example], migrants are associated with boats and their attempts at crossing the sea; their identity is often reduced to the act of crossing the sea (and dying at sea).
>
> (Germond and Germond-Duret, 2016: 125)

In sum, fishermen, sailors and to a certain extent migrants are examples of people whose identity is linked to their experience of, at and from the sea. Many studies (mainly in cultural history, anthropology or geography) have shown that non-Western communities tend to develop a different representation of the sea, which grants the sea with more placeful characteristics. Jackson's discussion of the conception of the sea in Aboriginal culture and the implication in terms of sea rights highlights the fact that "there are other world-views that are not as terrestrially bound (*terra-centric*) as are western world-views" (1995: 94). Anderson and Peters take the example of gift-giving rituals at sea in the Western Pacific and explain, "Despite Western culture's willingness to reduce the water world to an empty space, many 'indigenous' cultures refute this essentialism" (2016: 8). Gillis acknowledges the existence of a Pacific and Asiatic vision which differs from the Western one:

> For Pacific islanders, the ocean is not a placeless place, but a sea of islands with its own unique geography. For them, history does not begin and end with land, but it is inextricably bound up with the sea itself.
>
> (2011: 17)

In her study of the Sri Lanka's east coast, Lehman (2013) shows that while the sea is often depicted as being unpredictable (adding to the inhospitable argument playing in favour of its placelessness), the fisherfolks she interviewed seemed on the contrary to find the ocean very reliable. Similarly, in her ethnographic work on the people of Hudson Bay, Tyrrell (2006) shows the extent to which

> the sea is important, not only as an economic resource and as a means to travel and movement, but as a place where identity is formed, where memories are

created, and where the history of the community lives amongst the rocks, the seaweed and the ever-changing water.

(222)

These examples (also discussed in Germond and Germond-Duret, 2016: 125) illustrate the need to account for the sea as a "social space" (Cusack, 2014) or even a place.

Some 'alternative' communities have also favoured 'maritime' settlements so as to live the lifestyle they have chosen at the edge of 'normal' society, such as the marginal community living on houseboats in Shoreham-on-sea in Sussex (Smith, 2007) or even at the edge of sovereignty, as envisaged by some libertarian seasteading projects (Steinberg et al., 2012). In these cases, the sea is experienced as a 'safe haven' as it offers some sort of protection or physical separation from the dominant society. This shows an inversion of the dominant narrative on the sea represented as a dangerous, inhabitable 'other', since for those 'alternative' communities, the sea is rather considered as a safer or 'nicer' habitable place, where it may be easier to live the life they have chosen (e.g. anti-consumerism, sustainable) at the margin of society. In this case, the sea becomes a place following the meaning that those community members wish to grant the sea with. In other words, the relation between the sea and the community performs the place.

Studying fish stock within the mobilities framework allows pointing out the irrelevance of the process consisting in (over)territorializing the sea. Indeed, the movement of fish illustrates the fact that the sea remains mainly alien to the Westphalian striation practice (on liquidity, see also Steinberg and Peters, 2015). Bush and Mol's study on fishing and sustainability (2015) makes the postulate that oceans are placeless. They refer to oceans' relative inaccessibility and the abstracted ways in which one experiences them. They consider the United Nations Convention on the Law of the Sea's (UNCLOS) attempts to create territories in the marine environment as abstract and placeless (resulting in "highly stylised, homogenising and placeless geography of the marine environment", 2–3). This is debatable, as UNCLOS could on the contrary illustrate a move towards placefulness, since it extends to the sea the political interactions and political/social realities found on land (such as borders, jurisdictions, etc.). This raises questions about the link between the placefulness of the sea, the advancement of modernity and the impact of human beings on the conception of a natural environment. Indeed, the growing territorialisation of the sea seems to contribute to render it placeful and human encroachment into the sea seems to be a necessary condition for the sea to be a place rather than a natural space. Thus environmental protection studies (see Steinberg, 1999a: 370–1) may allow understanding the ocean as an ecosystem, but not really as a place. By contrast, the concept of hybrid geography (Whatmore, 2002) allows grasping the relationality of the interactions between the human and the non-human. Thus a 'more-than-human geography' can examine the intersubjective relationships between ecosystems and places of human and political interactions. For example, in his discussion of the 'surfed wave as a relational place', Anderson makes it clear that "places are no longer solely considered as static and sedentary but also seen as formed through the meeting of movements and the pausing of practices" (2012: 575); the surfed wave is a place as a result of an ongoing relational process involving the surfer, the board, the water: "places enjoy a relational agency" (574). In his study of Cardigan Bay scallop fishery, Bear (2012) draws on assemblage theory to include in the analysis of resource management narrative and practice "actants such as fish and other marine wildlife, and encourages critical focus on the relationships between the stability and/or mobility of these" (3). This highlights different relationalities beyond the expected ones such as "fishermen, fishing boats and scallops" (16).

The importance of the sea for tourism and recreational activities also contributes to its representation as a commodity (Trist, 1999, quoted in Peters, 2010: 1266), which also fits with the utilitarian concept of marine ecosystem services. In their study of the strategic role of ports for cruise business Gui and Russo (2011) postulates that "most part of [tourists'] experience happens in a placeless environment" (129). Their argument is based on the growing marginalisation of destination ports compared to the ships themselves, which are becoming the true destination place for tourists embarking on a cruise (as already mentioned by Steinberg, 2001: 163). The sea itself is not even considered as a likely place. This, again, points to the ship, which is represented as the place of human experience at sea. But if we adopt a relationalist approach to places, then the ship is a place through the activities that are performed on it, from it and via it.

Finally, places themselves are in motion, since they are continuously reconstructing and reinventing themselves, whether through agency or relationality. Maritime places are constantly reconstructing and reimagining themselves via representations and practices and the interactions between various representations and various practices that evolve intersubjectively in time and space. This represents a form of ideational mobility. Whereas the relations between the sea and human agents perform the sea as a place, the placeful nature of the sea is in perpetual motion. From space to place and from place to space, the sea perpetually evolves and reinvents itself depending on time and location as well as on the nature and orientation of the relations under scrutiny.

As Sheller and Urry state, "Social science has largely ignored or trivialised the importance of the systematic movements of people for work and family life, for leisure and pleasure, and for politics and protest" (2006: 208). At sea, maritime mobilities are crucial to understand the placefulness of the sea. Maritime mobilities induce social and political interactions at sea, with the sea and from the sea. Within the mobilities framework, the sea can definitely be studied as a place, although, as Steinberg and Peters remind us, the materiality of oceanspace "can never be separated from either the experience of the ocean or the meanings that we attach to oceanic experiences" (2015: 256). In other words, the ocean as a place of social and political interactions (with all that entails in terms of identity) cannot be separated from the ocean as a space (with all its material and physical characteristics such as liquidity, fluidity, depth, unboundness, etc.). The mobilities framework allows grasping the relationalist nature of the sea as a place.

Maritime mobilities in a territorialized ocean

The earlier discussion highlighted the narrative that tends to represent the sea as placeless and thus both vulnerable to illegal activities and free to use for states and commercial actors, which calls for a practice that consists in governing and controlling the sea. Paradoxically, from placeless in the narrative the sea becomes placeful in practice, via the practice of ocean governance (Germond and Germond-Duret, 2016). Bringing mobilities and placeless/fullness together has also highlighted the importance of de/re/territorialisation of the sea, which has implications for maritime geography.

Ocean governance as a set of policies and a practice is driven by post-modern considerations such as environmental protection and management, as well as modern considerations such as states' control of entire sections of the maritime domain in peacetime. In practice, ocean governance in the form of public policies in territorial waters, EEZs and even beyond has initiated a certain territorialisation of the sea, which has been facilitated by the UNCLOS, which is an example of modern/post-modern mix of interests and conceptions of the freedom of the sea:

> When the rights of sovereignty are projected over seas and oceans, States and their various political and territorial structures [. . .] have begun to introduce new patterns of territorial organisation with which to formalise the political and economic control, which to differing degrees are defined in the various regulatory, strategic, legal, and spatial planning documents.
>
> (Suárez de Vivero et al., 2009: 628)

In other words, states "incorporate new maritime spaces into their national jurisdictions", which creates "a new sea-based territoriality" (Suárez de Vivero and Rodríguez Mateos, 2014: 62). The dialectic of smoothness (deterritorialisation) and striation (territorialisation) expressed by Deleuze and Guattari (1988) appears to resolve in the transformation of the sea into a hybrid space that combines elements of unboundness and territoriality both from a legal/jurisdictional and a social interactions perspective.

While interventions in other states' domestic affairs, as well as traditional naval power and forces projection, can be conceived as post-modern in that it challenges the tenets of the Wesphalian system/order, this process of territorialisation of the seas under the umbrella of ocean governance bears neo-modern characteristics, since it aims at affirming states' or regional organisations' control over space/territory, albeit maritime. Steinberg proposes, "During the industrial era, this territorialisation of the sea was restricted to discrete coastal zones. Recently, however, there have been movements to extend this territorialisation to ever larger areas of ocean-space" (2001: 169). Interestingly, he situates this process within post-modern capitalism (as opposed to post-fordism or post-industrialism), which creates the conditions for a limited territorialisation of the seas. Now, if nascent neo-modern characteristics have to be found in the post-modern world just like post-modern characteristics find their roots within the modern world (Bauman,

1987; Lyotard, 1988; Osborne, 1992), the process of territorialisation of the seas that is currently taking place can certainly be conceived as a neo-modern element within the post-modern world order. As such, the deterritorialisation that characterises post-modern world politics bears the seeds of a territorialisation of the seas in the form of ocean governance. Indeed, the increasing number and the growing power of non-state actors operating at sea (including criminals) as well as the transnational and global nature of threats (including environmental ones) have obliged states to find ways to secure and properly govern the 'global commons' rather than to 'leave it alone' as if a 'blank void', which would entail a policy consisting in washing one's hand of any responsibility of what is happening on the (high) seas. The process of deterritorialisation of security that consists in projecting one's security beyond one's boundary and territorial waters has thus led to a process of territorialisation of the maritime space, or, in other words, a neo-modern form of territorialisation that is particularly apparent at sea.

This discussion can be lined to the concept of ocean stewardship developed by Steinberg to account for the fact that oceans, due to their importance, notably in terms of resources, while remaining outside states' jurisdiction (at least on the high seas) must nevertheless be controlled: "The community of states, and/or non-state actors are permitted to exercise social power in the interest of stewarding marine resources" (2001: 177). Whereas the inclusion of environmental concerns in public policy is understandably post-modern, this translates into neo-modern practices of territorialisation. For example, the European Union has developed a marine strategy, with a focus on resources management that has geopolitical consequences (Germond and Germond-Duret, 2016). For instance, EU norms and rules can de facto apply to other stakeholders and states within the same marine basin due to an imbalance in political and economic power. This results in the development of maritime margins – i.e., "hybrid spaces, which legally are situated out of the Union but functionally inside its strategic zone of interest and competencies" (Germond, 2010: 41).

Steinberg is right to highlight the influence of post-modern capitalism in explaining the territorialisation of the seas, but today's practice is clearly neo-modern, in that the aim is to secure control, if not legal titles, over portions of the sea, or at least to be in a position to manage human activities taking place in the maritime domain. This shows that in practice the sea is placeful – i.e., a place of social (and political) interactions, hence the need, responsibility, right and legitimacy to govern it. Ocean governance and maritime security are concerned with the management and control of human activities at sea as well as of the movements associated with human activities, which constitutes a response to the challenge of maritime mobilities. States' willingness to govern the oceans and control the maritime domain has created various layers of human, social and political interactions related to, and within, the oceans. States represent the embodiment of public power; they are granted with, or claim, the right and responsibility to guide, constrain, monitor, control and repress human activities at sea. This represents social interactions, which tend to play in favour of the argument that the sea is placeful. The mobilities framework goes beyond substantialist approaches "that treat place, stability and dwelling as a natural steady-state" so as to embrace the importance of "mobility, fluidity or liquidity as a pervasive condition of postmodernity or globalization" (Hannam et al., 2006: 5). As such, this approach applies relationalism to the understanding of deterritorialisation and territorialisation practices at sea.

Conclusion: towards maritime relationalism

Human geography is still clearly a "landlocked" discipline. Apart from the extensive works of Steinberg and Peters, very few scholars in the field have paid attention to the sea as a place of social and political interactions. In this chapter, we have shown that bringing frameworks together – i.e., mobilities, critical geopolitics, knowledge-power matrix – allows for grasping the placeful nature of the oceans. The mobilities framework in particular has revealed crucial in pointing out the way forward in research.

So far, transport and strategic studies have been interested in the free movement of capital, goods and military forces in a void without constraints. This could be called 'Mahan's world'; the glorification of free movement which goes along with a narrative that "attempt to annihilate the ocean" (Steinberg, 2001: 166). To this we could oppose 'Urry's world', which is better analysed by using a mobilities framework. A place is in motion and understood through the movements from, to and within it. The seas are places of social and political interactions and the relations between the sea and human agents perform the place.

Ocean governance and the current deterritorialisation and territorialisation of the sea follow the evolution that is taking place from modernity to postmodernity to neo-modernity. Geographers shall pay more attention to the link between maritime mobilities and the debate on post/neo-modernity. Future research shall further discuss the extent to which the sea is placeful, and how to account for its placefulness. To what extent is the sea a deterritorialized or a territorialized space/place? What is in motion at/from the sea? How do entities such as ships, people, goods, capital, resources and water interact with each other? How are those interactions constitutive of the sea as a place? What are the implications in terms of actors' identity building? To what extent are dominant Western narratives different from non-Western narratives and practices?

This chapter showed that since a mobilities framework highlights the social interactions that are taking place between the point of departure and the point of arrival, then acknowledging the placefulness of the sea allows applying this framework to maritime geographies. Considering the sea as placeful allows going beyond substantialism in the analysis of mobilities. Indeed, rather than a product of the interactions between existing fixed entities (such as ship, sailors, goods), the placeful sea is itself an entity produced or performed by the continuous interactions of actors, nature and ideas and is therefore continuously defined and redefined (relationalism). Maritime mobilities as a framework allows grasping the impact of continuous interactions and processes at sea on the creation and evolution of entities such as ships, maritime communities, and eventually the sea itself. It is therefore crucial to further develop the concept of maritime relationalism so as to account for the fact that those relations perform the sea as a place of social and political interactions.

Acknowledgements

The authors would like to thank Phil Steinberg and Kim Peters for their valuable comments on a draft of this chapter. Some sentences and references to the literature come from Germond and Germond-Duret (2016).

Notes

1 Steinberg notably proposed this term in 1999 stressing the need for geography to account for the socially and physically constructed dimensions of the ocean (1999a), although he already developed the concept before.
2 Representing the ocean as 'empty' or as a 'void' is Western-bound (Jackson, 1995, cited in Steinberg, 1999a: 369; see also Gillis, 2011: 17).

References

Anderson, J. (2012). Relational places: The surfed wave as assemblage and convergence. *Environment & Planning D.* 30 (4): 570–587.
Anderson, J., Peters, K. (2014). 'A Perfect and Absolute Blank': Human Geographies of Water Worlds. In: J. Anderson and K. Peters (eds.), *Water Worlds: Human Geographies of the Ocean.* Abingdon: Routledge, first published by Ashgate, 2014. pp. 3–22.
Anim-Addo, A., Hasty, W., Peters, K. (2014). The mobilities of ships and shipped mobilities. *Mobilities.* 9 (3): 337–349.
Bauman, Z. (1987). *Legislators and Interpreters.* Oxford: Blackwell.
Bear, C. (2012). Assembling the sea: Materiality, movement and regulatory practices in the Cardigan Bay scallop fishery. *Cultural Geographies.* 20 (1): 21–41.
Brstilo, I. (2013). Filipino seafarers as seabased global diaspora: Contribution to maritime sociology. *Annuals of Marine Sociology* (Roczniki Socjologii Morskiej). 22: 27–37.
Bush, S. R., Mol, A.P.J. (2015). Governing in a placeless environment: Sustainability and fish aggregating devices. *Environmental Science & Policy.* 53 (A): 27–37.
Casey, E. (1993). *Getting Back into Place: Toward a Renewed Understanding of the Place-World.* Bloomington: Indian University Press.
Connery, C. L. (1994). Pacific rim discourse: The U. S. global imaginary in the late cold war years. *Boundary 2.* 21 (1): 30–56.
Connery, C. L. (2006). There was no more sea: The supersession of the ocean, from the bible to cyberspace. *Journal of Historical Geography.* 32 (3): 494–511.
Corbett, J. (1911). *Some Principles of Maritime Strategy.* Annapolis: United States Naval Institute, 1988. First published by Longmans, London, 1911.
Cusack, T. (2014). Introduction: Framing the Ocean, 1700 to the Present: Envisaging the Sea as Social Space. In: T. Cusack (ed.), *Framing the Ocean, 1700 to the Present, Envisaging the Sea as Social Space.* Farnham: Ashgate. pp. 1–22.
Deleuze, G., Guattari, F. (1988). *A Thousand Plateaus: Capitalism and Schizophrenia.* Trans. B. Massumi. Minneapolis, MN: University of Minnesota Press.
Foucault, M., Miskowiec, J. (1986). Of other spaces. *Diacritics.* 16 (1): 22–27.
Germond, B. (2010). From frontier to boundary and back again: The European Union's maritime margins. *European Foreign Affairs Review.* 15 (1): 39–55.
Germond, B. (2013). The European Union at the Horn of Africa: Contribution of critical geopolitics to piracy studies. *Global Policy.* 4 (1): 80–85.
Germond, B. (2015a). The geopolitical dimension of maritime security. *Marine Policy.* 54: 137–142.

Germond, B. (2015b). *The Maritime Dimension of European Security: Seapower and the European Union*. London and New York: Palgrave Macmillan.

Germond, B., Germond-Duret, C. (2016). Ocean governance and maritime security in a placeful environment: The case of the European Union. *Marine Policy*. 66: 124–131.

Gillis, J. R. (2011). Filling the Blue Hole in Environmental History. In: K. Coulter and C. Mauch (eds.), *The Future of Environmental History Needs and Opportunities*. Munich: Rachel Carson Center for Environment and Society. pp. 16–18.

Gilroy, P. (1993). *The Black Atlantic: Modernity and Double Consciousness*. Cambridge, MA: Harvard University Press.

Glete, J. (2000). *Warfare at Sea, 1500–1650: Maritime Conflicts and the Transformation of Europe*. Abingdon: Routledge.

Glück, Z. (2015). Piracy and the production of security space. *Environment and Planning D: Society and Space*. 33 (4): 642–659.

Gui, L., Russo, A. P. (2011). Cruise ports: A strategic nexus between regions and global lines – evidence from the Mediterranean. *Maritime Policy & Management*. 38 (2): 129–150.

Hannam, K., Sheller, M., Urry, J. (2006). Editorial: Mobilities, immobilities and moorings. *Mobilities*. 1 (1): 1–22.

Hasty, W., Peters, K. (2012). The ship in geography and the geographies of ships. *Geography Compass*. 6 (11): 660–676.

Herder, J. G. (1803). *Outlines of a Philosophy of the History of Man*. Trans. T. Churchill. New York: Bergman.

Jackson, S. E. (1995). The water is not empty: Cross-cultural issues in conceptualising sea space. *Australian Geographer*. 26 (1): 87–96.

Kristiansen, S. (2013). *Maritime Transportation: Safety Management and Risk Analysis*. Abingdon: Routledge, first published, 2005.

Lambert, D., Martins, L., Ogborn, M. (2006). Currents, visions and voyages: Historical geographies of the sea. *Journal of Historical Geography*. 32 (3): 479–493.

Lehman, J. S. (2013). Relating to the sea: Enlivening the ocean as an actor in Eastern Sri Lanka. *Environment and Planning D: Society and Space*. 31 (3): 485–501.

Lyotard, J.-F. (1988). Reecrire la modernité. *Cahiers de Philosophie*. 5: 193–203.

Mack, J. (2011). *The Sea: A Cultural History*. London: Reaktion.

Osborne, P. (1992). Modernity is a qualitative, not a chronological, category. *New Left Review*. 192 (1): 65–84.

Ó Tuathail, G. (1996). *Critical Geopolitics*. London: Routledge.

Peters, K. (2010). Future promises for contemporary social and cultural geographies of the sea. *Geography Compass*. 4 (9): 1260–1272.

Peters, K. (2015). Drifting: Towards mobilities at sea. *Transactions of the Institute of British Geographers*. 40 (2): 262–272.

Relph, E. (1976). *Place and Placelessness*. London: Pion Ltd.

Sampson, H. (2003). Transnational drifters or hyperspace dwellers: An exploration of the lives of Filipino seafarers aboard and ashore. *Ethnic and Racial Studies*. 26 (2): 253–277.

Sheller, M., Urry, J. (2006). The new mobilities paradigm. *Environment & Planning A*. 38 (2): 207–226.

Smith, D. P. (2007). The 'buoyancy' of 'other' geographies of gentrification: Going 'back-to-the water' and the commodification of marginality. *Tijdschrift voor economische en sociale geografie*. 98 (1): 53–67.

Smith, H. D. (2002). The role of the social sciences in capacity building in ocean and coastal management. *Ocean & Coastal Management*. 45 (9–10): 573–582.

Steinberg, P. E. (1999a). Navigating to multiple horizons: Toward a geography of ocean-space. *The Professional Geographer.* 51 (3): 366–375.

Steinberg, P. E. (1999b). The maritime mystique: Sustainable development, capital mobility, and nostalgia in the world ocean. *Environment & Planning D: Society and Space.* 17 (4): 403–426.

Steinberg, P. E. (1999c). Lines of division, lines of connection: Stewardship in the world ocean. *Geographical Review.* 89 (2): 254–264.

Steinberg, P. E. (2001). *The Social Construction of the Ocean.* Cambridge: Cambridge University Press.

Steinberg, P. E. (2011). Free Sea. In: S. Legg (ed.), *Spatiality, Sovereignty and Carl Schmitt: Geographies of the Nomos.* Abingdon: Routledge. pp. 268–275.

Steinberg, P. E. (2013). Of other seas: Metaphors and materialities in maritime regions. *Atlantic Studies.* 10 (2): 156–169.

Steinberg, P. E., Nyman, E., Caraccioli, M. J. (2012). Atlas swam: Freedom, capital, and floating sovereignties in the seasteading vision. *Antipode.* 44 (4): 1532–1550.

Steinberg, P. E., Peters, K. (2015). Wet ontologies, fluid spaces: Giving depth to volume through oceanic thinking. *Environment & Planning D: Society and Space.* 33 (2): 247–264.

Suárez-de Vivero, J. L., Rodríguez Mateos, J. C. (2014). Changing maritime scenarios: The geopolitical dimension of the EU Atlantic Strategy. *Marine Policy.* 48: 59–72.

Suárez de Vivero, J. L., Rodríguez Mateos, J. C., Florido del Corral, D. (2009). Geopolitical factors of maritime policies and marine spatial planning: State, regions, and geographical planning scope. *Marine Policy.* 33 (4): 624–634.

Tyrrell, M. (2006). From placelessness to place: An ethnographer's experience of growing to know places at sea. *Worldviews: Global Religions, Culture, and Ecology.* 10 (2): 220–238.

Whatmore, S. (2002). *Hybrid Geographies: Natures Cultures Spaces.* Thousand Oaks, CA: Sage Publications.

3   Ports as capitalist spaces

Jason Monios and Gordon Wilmsmeier

Introduction

One of the key themes of this book is to build a bridge between mobilities and (trans)port geography. In a recent paper (Wilmsmeier and Monios, 2015), we identified several drivers for the creation of smooth space in global port operations and characterised ports as capitalist spaces, working on a capitalist logic of value creation, migration and destruction. In this chapter, we want to apply a mobilities perspective to our previous work in order to determine what the mobilities perspective can add to the previous analysis, for three reasons. First, to see what can be learned about ports from the mobilities perspective. Second, as a proxy for discovering what a mobilities approach adds to a more traditional geography approach. Finally, and conversely, what insights can we derive from an analysis of the global port system to feed back into mobility studies?

Ports as capitalist spaces

The introduction to this volume provided a brief overview of the developments that took place in the global port sector throughout the second half of the 20th century. The changing economic nature of the system is evident, moving from dispersed, slow, individual vessels and ports served directly, to a much more homogenised system of large ships serving large hub ports with universal handling systems and management approaches. These economic factors are reflected in the trend towards port devolution that, first, moved port operations from the public into the private sector and second, transferred responsibilities from central government to more decentralised regional and local entities. This opened up new development opportunities for international terminal operators and favoured processes of merger and acquisition that resulted in a handful of multinational corporations operating large portfolios of port terminals across the globe. Since the 1980s, significant changes have occurred in the way ports are owned and operated. Commercialization, devolution, privatisation, internationalization and corporatization of port operations are now global phenomena (Notteboom and Rodrigue, 2005; Brooks and Cullinane, 2007; Ng and Pallis, 2010; Sánchez and Wilmsmeier, 2010; Jacobs and Notteboom, 2011; Notteboom et al., 2013; Wilmsmeier and Monios,

2015). A large literature addresses the devolution of political responsibility from the national to the state level as well as the public to private sector.

Despite a recent growth in the institutional analysis of ports (Ng and Pallis, 2010; Jacobs and Notteboom, 2011; Notteboom et al., 2013; Wilmsmeier and Monios, 2016), missing from previous analyses has been a critique of the role of the dominant neoliberal narrative. This criticism has been directed at geography more widely (Smith, 2005) and at transport studies (whether specifically approached through geography, economics or other disciplines). The role of neoliberalism in the transport sector has been defined as seeking "to maximise the role of market mechanisms in public policy and service provision" (Docherty et al., 2004: 257). In recent decades, the provision of transport services and to a lesser extent the development of infrastructure have been increasingly outsourced to the private sector, sometimes through regulated franchise monopolies (e.g. the right to operate a port terminal for a fixed time period) and in others through an open competitive market where the public sector operator competes directly with private operators or withdraws from the market, perhaps performing only those unprofitable services that are unattractive to private operators but deemed as necessary by the government or local community (e.g. a small locally administered port). The wide-ranging changes in the fundamental nature of the port sector due to the widespread privatisation of ports means that now if a disruptive policy is attempted, it must be enacted within a neoliberal paradigm that limits the range of acceptable actions (Monios, 2017).

Little attention has been given to these processes in the port sector or in freight transport more generally, but some authors have considered the issue in passenger transport. Aldred (2012: 95) demonstrates that "cycling became embedded in public policy only after policy-making had been variously outsourced to private, quasi-private, and voluntary organisations." Thus, rather than introducing strong policy instruments, the state relied on non-state organisations to deliver change, avoiding the need to introduce unpopular policies, devote resources or modify the wider policy setting. Henderson (2011) showed how cycling activists overcame a pro-car road space allocation system, although it was achieved counter-intuitively by building an alliance with property developers who see value in improving urban space for their intended client market. This need for any policy to align with property development priorities can certainly be seen in many port development projects and a similarity can be seen here with urban property developments by private investors linked to high public sector investment in public transport links. Enright (2013: 797) suggests, "The state-directed transportation plan of Grand Paris is not primarily aimed at facilitating capacities for public movement, so much as it is designed to channel investment flows throughout metropolitan Paris and to catalyse private development."

In an example perhaps more comparable to ports, Paget-Seekins (2015) showed how the introduction of private Bus Rapid Transit (BRT) schemes has been used in South America to overcome a fragmented and unregulated public transport sector that was providing low quality services and leading to congestion and emissions problems. By restructuring the bus market through the construction of route-based monopolies contracted to private operators, the government was able to regulate service levels and quality, and the new system also provides workers with collective action opportunities to protect their interests unavailable in the previous informal market. On the other hand, small local operators are forced out of the market and the state now pays subsidy to large private operators, so while neoliberalism can in some cases counterintuitively lead to progressive goals, these are still achieved within market-based assumptions and norms. This is the challenge currently facing port governance. While it is beyond doubt that the influx of private operators has brought productivity and efficiency benefits to port operation, it has come at the expense of a changed governance framework, which is later very difficult to adapt or challenge when needed. Monios (2017) identified a process of institutional isomorphism represented by the increasing similarity of state forms, the better to be co-opted into globalised neoliberal norms. From here, what is politically acceptable becomes narrower (Peck, 2001), and any real disjunctive policy intervention, such as one that is perceived to threaten economic growth, becomes less likely. Again, it is not to be mindlessly critical of an increased role for the private sector, but to recognise that the dominant neoliberal paradigm, according to which the role of the state is seen as less interventional, shapes institutional structure and the kind of policies selected.

A lack of analysis of the neoliberalisation of transport provision can be observed in transport geography and even more so in freight and port geography, its global nature reflecting the essence of globalisation and neoliberalism more than other transport modes. The institutional setting in which ports are now embedded requires methods of analysis that go beyond those traditionally applied in transport geography, but neither transport nor port geography has embraced critical, radical or relational geographies. In the absence of a theoretical underpinning, such approaches ignore the evidence of a capitalist trend towards oligopoly and the inevitable accumulation crisis that leads to value destruction in one space and recreation in another. (Quasi)oligopoly can be observed in the maritime sector in both ports (increasing concentration of port concessions held by global terminal operators) and shipping (merger and acquisition of carriers, conferences/alliances), as well as in many formerly national and now privatised utility sectors, from passenger transport to telecommunications to energy provision (Wilmsmeier and Hoffmann, 2008; Sánchez and Wilmsmeier, 2011).

As we argued in our paper on capitalist port spaces (Wilmsmeier and Monios, 2015), ports can be viewed as exemplars of the inherently unstable spatial fix of mobile capital (Monios and Wilmsmeier, 2012). We argued that ports, therefore, cannot be understood in the absence of a critique of their capitalist context. That paper was based on two streams of literature. The first part of the argument was centred on the work of David Harvey, whose development of the concept of the spatial fix (Harvey, 1981, 1982) provided the spatial dimension to Marx's theories of capitalist accumulation (Harvey, 1975). Harvey (2001: 25) defined the spatial fix as

one of the central contradictions of capital: that it has to build a fixed space (or 'landscape') necessary for its own functioning at a certain point in its history only to have to destroy that space (and devalue much of the capital invested therein) at a later point in order to make way for a new 'spatial fix' (openings for fresh accumulation in new spaces and territories) at a later point in its history.

The evolution of ports and port systems follows just such a trajectory as mobile capital identifies new port locations in which to create value, while value is destroyed in traditional port locations, either through obsolescent infrastructure or a location that is no longer suitable for new routes or even due to processes of horizontal and vertical integration that favour competing ports.

Our analysis took the spatial fix forward into the political dimension via Brenner's (1998) scalar fix. According to Brenner (1998: 470), drawing on Lefebvre (1991), each temporary scalar fix must be approached in terms of its formation, stabilisation and eventual rupture. However, the role of the state is to attempt to maintain these equilibria, and to this end, it "deploys a wide range of geographically specific policies oriented differentially towards cities, industrial districts, regions, growth poles, peripheries, 'underdeveloped' zones, rural areas, and so forth." The state's aim is to harness the power of capital to achieve its own aims through various combinations of privatisation, public-private partnerships, deregulation and subsidies; however, "the state is denied the power to control the flow of those resources which are nevertheless indispensable for the exercise of state power" (Offe, 1984: 120).

The second part of the analysis and the main theoretical construct of the paper was based on an exploration of the nuances at the heart of the social production of space via the smooth space conceptualisation of Deleuze and Guattari (1987). Viewing the capitalist context of global port operations as a deterritorialised smooth space allows an appreciation of the relational construction of power and place, thus providing the tools of analysis currently absent from port geography. Deleuze and Guattari's conception of smooth space fits within the broader arc of post-structuralist thought, with its key elements of difference, multiplicity and becoming, as opposed to identity, singularity and being.

Marx identified how the over-accumulation of capital leads to periodic crises, whereby a correction is produced through value destruction and migration. Harvey's theory of crisis was based on his notion of the temporary spatial fix of mobile capital. Adapting this with the work of Brenner raises the importance of the scalar fix, showing the essential role played by states in providing an appropriate planning and regulatory apparatus to underpin the capitalist spatial fix. The question then is how to understand this fix more deeply, to understand the relation between capital and the state in producing and maintaining the scalar fix. This is where the work of Deleuze and Guattari is useful, replacing the Marxian notion of an evolution in successive modes of production with an ongoing relation between smooth and striated space, between capital and the state, between deterritorialisation and reterritorialisation.

Deleuze and Guattari proposed a "smooth" space outside the state, contrasted with "striated" space, space that has been gridded, measured, demarcated and controlled by state powers. Smooth space is deterritorialised, without borders, uncontrolled and heterogeneous, whereas striated space is territorialised by the state and homogenised. With devolution and privatization, the "complementary and dominant level of integrated (or rather integrating) world capitalism," represented by global terminal operators, is creating a new smooth space in global port operations. This is produced when "capital reaches its 'absolute' speed," where "multinationals fabricate a kind of deterritorialized smooth space" (Deleuze and Guattari, 1987: 543).

In that paper, we concluded that the initial smoothing of space by capitalism can lead to a new type of striation due to the convergence and strategy replication of global terminal operators, producing a new homogeneous and striated space of port management. In an empirical paper on port devolution in Latin America (Wilmsmeier and Monios, 2016), we demonstrated that it is quite possible to move from an unresponsive and inflexible public path dependency to a similarly inflexible private path dependency. Governments may find that they have insufficient levers to address issues of national priority – e.g., labour strikes in the port, complaints by port users of poor service or environmental dangers. Such examples could be considered as potential disruptors of capitalist attempts to impose a smooth space on global port operations, but it could equally be argued that such conflicts are in fact predicated upon such smooth space because they are no longer embedded in local/regional planning and policy but take place in an artificial supranational space where actions and decisions transcend national borders, which indeed represents the essence of globalisation.

The current economic system tries to evade crisis through the spatial expansion of activity (in this case, shipping and port operations) through the destruction of value in one region and the opening of new spaces of capital accumulation in other regions (as witnessed in the migration of port dominance from West to East). The conclusion of the paper was that new challenges to the system cannot be identified in the absence of an understanding of ports as spatial fixes of mobile capital, recognised as part of an ongoing process of value destruction, migration and creation. Such processes work within and against an ongoing deterritorialisation and reterritorialization of smooth and striated space in which national interests are increasingly ceded to global corporations, producing a relational space in which public institutions often lack influence.

Applying a mobilities perspective to port geography

As discussed in the introduction chapter, many of the seminal works in transport geography have been based on the study of ports. The spatial concepts of nodes, corridors and networks have been explored through the evolution of the numerous regional port systems, observing the concentration of traffic at major hubs and mainline connections. Convergence of institutional approaches has also been identified through the devolution of port governance and the mergers and acquisitions in the ports and shipping industry. On the operational side, less geographical issues but nonetheless related to the discussion are the increasing competition in the sector leading to massive investments, producing overcapacity of vessel and port provision and a variety of strategies to resolve this problem such as slow steaming and vessel cascading. These actions impact on spatial development as some evidence is now appearing of deconcentration of flows due to diseconomies of scale and disbenefits of agglomeration. All of these issues contain political, social and cultural dimensions that have thus far been overlooked.

Many of these topics have been examined through more traditional geographical approaches – that is to say, large-scale descriptive studies that map flows but with insufficient attention to the local scale and the drivers behind the flows. A mobilities approach looks more at the social and cultural aspects, the winners and losers, the inequalities in this system. These aspects are not just worthy of study in their own right and for giving a voice to those less powerful that often lose out from such systems, but, as recent political events have shown, rising inequality is leading to increased political division and crisis.

Turning to the mobilities paradigm (discussed at greater length in the introductory chapter to this volume), one of the seminal papers (Hannam et al., 2006: 3) also drew briefly on Harvey and Brenner. They wrote, "Mobilities cannot be described without attention to the necessary spatial, infrastructural and institutional moorings that configure and enable mobilities – creating what Harvey (1989) called the 'spatial fix.'" They drew attention to the

> immobile platforms . . . through which mobilisations of locality are performed and re-arrangements of place and scale materialised . . . . multiple fixities or moorings often on a substantial physical scale that enable the fluidities of liquid modernity, and especially of capital.

As we noted in the introduction, immobility has emerged as a key theme in mobilities research (Sheller and Urry, 2006; Cresswell, 2012; Hasty and Peters, 2012), which applies strongly to the maritime sector. The very provision and operation of interchange points such as ports are essential parts of the provision of mobility but are themselves subject to ongoing pressures, influences and challenges from political and institutional viewpoints. Their physical immobility masks an institutional mobility as ports are privatised or concessioned or reformed (Monios and Wilmsmeier, 2015). The smooth space conceptualisation discussed earlier clearly has a strong overlap of ideas with the mobilities paradigm. Indeed, Hannam et al. (2006: 3) mention "rhizomatic attachments and reterritorialisations", terminology drawn from Deleuze and Guattari.

Building on these ideas, the next step is to discuss the issues outlined earlier to determine what can be learned from applying a mobilities perspective. The key theme running through this chapter is how the focus on, indeed obsession with, mobility in the presentation of the modern shipping and port sectors masks both the importance of providing the immobile infrastructure (and all the policy, planning, risk and investment entailed) and the institutional mobility underlying these developments, often taking place through unequal power relations and a changing neoliberal discourse through which the logic of globalisation drowns any local, regional or even national priorities. As Hannam et al. (2006: 3) remind us, "Mobility is a resource to which not everyone has an equal relationship."

Processes of concentration and deconcentration of port traffic

The processes of concentration, and particularly the deconcentration that has emerged as a result of diseconomies of scale, reflects the blind logic operating at the global scale. The "tragedy of the commons" is evident as shipping lines continue purchasing larger vessels that they cannot fill, and create more problems with cascading of vessels down to other trade lanes that cannot fill them, creating an ongoing system of unproductive and induced mobility. While the deconcentration away from hubs may produce some benefits for smaller regional ports which had lost out to major hubs from the earlier processes of concentration, the future remains uncertain and the process is unlikely to be free from disruption. Managing such processes for the benefits of local and regional stakeholders will create significant governance challenges for port managers. Particularly, modern governance models have weakened the levers of public actors to ensure the quality of port services and the readiness for transition.

At the macro scale often taken by geographers, such evolution in freight flows is just a conceptual matter, but the mobilities perspective reminds us of the inefficiencies and blockages inherent in each of these shifts. What appears as a thicker and thinner line on a chart represents the aggregation of many individual ports gaining and losing traffic, and the reordering of supply chains by thousands of individual shippers and freight forwarders. Of course, this is not always a problem and individual businesses will often be changing ports and transport providers to obtain savings and new deals, but it represents a smaller scale migration of value destruction and creation. We will return to this later when considering port and vessel investments, but even from the operational perspective, the making and breaking of local and regional networks due to decisions taken at the global level represents an inefficient and constrained mobility system. Policymakers at all scales, but particularly local and regional, need to devise policies for investment and employment, but a system that incentivises footloose traffic makes this difficult and often produces redundant investment (both public and private).

Devolution of port governance

The devolution of port governance from the public to the private sector has created governance challenges, exacerbated by the devolution of the public sector responsibility from the national to the regional and local level in many cases, although this depends on the country. This can be a good arrangement, allowing individual locally governed ports to compete against each other directly and react swiftly to signals from the market, sometimes a challenge for centrally governed national port systems. On the other hand, such institutions have less power than national organisations and struggle to influence global terminal operators. Moreover, the length of port concessions further reduces the influence of the port authority.

In addition to the common 20–30 year concessions for container terminals, we are now seeing ports being concessioned for around 100 years (e.g. Brisbane, Australia), effectively a full privatisation of the port asset. Until recently, such full privatisation of ports was unusual, the United Kingdom being the most well-known case of selling ports in their entirety (Baird, 2000), including handing regulatory responsibilities for harbour safety, pilotage, etc., to the private operators. But long concessions are being seen now in countries such as Australia. This brings short-term funds to the government but relinquishes influence on this nationally strategic sector. While it is not a simple handover of influence as the port will still be subject to various planning regulations regarding development as well as environmental protection and so on, the ongoing negotiations over the port space will be drastically changed and indeed lead to delays caused by misaligned development plans. In the last decade there were some cases in the United Kingdom of taking several years to consider port expansion plans, a particular issue in the case of Southampton, which was eventually rejected due to environmental concerns. While the slow progress was blamed on the national planning authority, it could be argued that better communication and coordinated planning (rather than the planning authority having only a reactive capability to approve or reject proposed plans) might have at least alleviated the situation.

From a mobilities perspective, handing over control and even influence of strategic infrastructure provides a constraint on future mobility. With an only limited and mechanistic kind of regulation on port performance, services offered, investment plans, etc., as a result of privatisation or long concessions, how can future challenges be dealt with in a way that benefits all port stakeholders? The private company purchasing the port or long concession will probably not be in business that long and the port may well change hands several times (as has happened in the United Kingdom).

Concentration of global terminal operators and shipping lines

While the global container port devolution trend has brought valuable private sector expertise into the management of ports around the globe, it has come at the price of a major handover of power and influence. This is particularly the case because of the trend towards merger and acquisition that has produced an oligopolistic market of massive operating companies with portfolios of ports across the globe. Coupled with the same process in shipping lines and the vertical integration of some of these companies to produce port and ship operating giants, such as Maersk (some also involved in inland transport), a significant power differential has been produced. While such companies do compete against each other, real concerns of collusion (tacit or otherwise) have been raised (Sánchez and Wilmsmeier, 2011), such as the 2016 EU investigation into collusion in general rate increases by shipping lines. Are the various economic influences on the system as currently operating producing an efficient resource allocation or is it rather market power leading to rent extraction?

The oligopoly trend has been observed in other transport markets as well. Some transport analysts suggest that the market provides flexibility and responsiveness unachievable by central planning, such as Rodrigue (2006: 387): "Central planning does not work effectively as a means to allocate scarce resources and often makes matters worse. It disconnects those involved from the clear signals a market often sends." While indeed there are many examples of central planning governments wasting resources, the current overcapacity strategies of shipping lines suggest private operators suffer from similar failings. Of course, it is better for a private operator to lose their investment than public money being wasted, but it will often be governments needing to pick up the pieces and support their shippers and economies when the crash comes, so they would rather do what they can to avoid such an outcome. More importantly, the oligopolistic and anti-competitive behaviour of large transport providers shows that, far from reacting to market signals, they might prefer to control and "milk" the market, suggesting that they are in favour of central planning and lack of competition as long as they are doing the planning. A free market does not exist when such vast power differentials are at play, thus attuning ourselves to such constructions of market space helps the identification of sites of contestation. Sheller (2015: 14) reminds us of the importance of the "politics of mobility", the "logics of justification" and the "power relations", adding that the actors shaping this space are sometimes "specific individuals or groups, but other times, they are agreed upon forms of 'objectivity' and rationality such as cost-benefit analyses, or 'level of service' measurements."

Countries privatise their national transport systems in order to introduce competition between several private transport providers, only for these providers to merge into a handful of large organisations, often with local, regional or international monopolies that do not provide any better service that the previous public monopoly, all the while extracting rents from their situation. In addition, nonprofitable services are usually still provided by the public sector, as they are not rolled into the concession or purchase agreement. This is similar with ports, although the way they are generally viewed is different. Freight transport is not usually considered as a socially necessary service in the same way as access to passenger transport. However, society tends to forget that their daily consumption of strawberries and wines might be as socially 'necessary' as a local bus service. When the latter is threatened then there will be an expectation that the public sector will step in to remedy the situation, whereas if a port is congested or does not invest in better facilities and trade is threatened, it is considered simply a private sector issue in an openly competitive market and not a reason for government intervention if traffic were to move to another port doing a better job. In some cases, such as a port range where several ports compete to serve an overlapping hinterland, this may not necessarily impact on the shipper or consumer, but in other cases, it will. So the question is whose responsibility should it be to ensure a smooth passage of freight through the port to service the local economy? A supplementary question is whether the institutional mobility acting all the time behind the actions of the port is constraining the ability of the various stakeholders to act where necessary to resolve these issues.

Is a global market logic suitable for managing this process on behalf of less well located shippers and consumers? Is the market too concentrated? We have recently seen the P3 vessel sharing agreement proposed in 2013 rejected. It was proposed by the three largest global shipping lines (Maersk, MSC and CMA CGM) to supposedly increase efficiency and cut costs by sharing space on each other's vessels, which would have comprised almost half of all container movements on Asia-Europe and transatlantic routes. The proposal was approved by European and American regulators but rejected by the Chinese government and was thus discontinued. A 'smaller' 2M initiative including only Maersk and MSC has since been established. The EU's exemption on liner shipping alliances from the anti-competitive regulations applied to mergers expires in 2020 and some shippers (e.g. the European Shippers' Council) are urging stronger action. Thus while it is easy to point to acts of deregulation that have been of great benefit to the freight industry (e.g. the Staggers Act in the US rail sector and the 1989 abolition of the National Dock Labour Scheme in the UK port sector), it does not follow that further deregulation is the answer, as without shipping regulation, there would be (even) less competition leading to a poorer result for the customer. A simplistic "big government versus free market" binary is unhelpful here; rather, the goal of scholars and industry analysts should be to determine the best blend of public and private interests.

From the mobilities perspective, how should such a global market be regulated? The IMO has shown sufficient power to institute some environmental regulations such as sulphur emissions control zones. Who regulates and constrains access to mobility for all? Is access to cheap ocean shipping equally available to all countries? There is currently no supranational regulatory body that could take such a decision on behalf of all jurisdictions for the shipping sector. But would such a body actually be a good idea? It would potentially concentrate too much power in one organisation and an objection from one part of the world (e.g. the Chinese rejection of the proposed P3 alliance) could potentially be overruled.

Operational challenges and responses

A number of operational challenges to the current system have been observed, along with some emerging responses. Port competition and strategy replication in ports across the globe have led to large investments in expanded port infrastructure and new vessels. Ports are forced to upgrade their infra- and superstructure to handle increasingly large vessels, but some will inevitably lose out and such investment might prove wasteful. Even if they win the business, such large (sea side) demand spikes means that their expensive cranes will be inefficiently used and sit idle large periods of time, a situation worsened by the current disconnect of supply and demand (Wilmsmeier and Sánchez, 2017). This is already a problem at major ports who compete for large business, but it can be considered more acute for smaller ports needing to upgrade to handle the increasing size of feeder vessels. Such ports are not necessarily competing directly with other ports, but they rely on these services to serve local demand, and it will be a blow to their economy if they lose these links.

Overcapacity in vessel supply is a familiar reality to observers of the shipping sector. Strategies of slow steaming, marketed as caring for the environment and a contribution to sustainability and 'cannibalising' freight rates to utilise overcapacity of vessels are common but have only made a small difference considering the scale of the challenge. When rates are so low that carriers are not even covering their costs on some routes and are struggling to implement general rate increases, should we feel concern over their plight or have they brought it upon themselves? Moreover, the inefficiencies in the port and inland transport systems as a result of such large lumpy container drops causes problems for the other actors in the transport and supply chains. While the sea is still a 'free' highway dominated by the private sector, the infrastructure of ports and their hinterlands remains in many cases the burden of the taxpayer.

The logic of the competitive market suggests that high competition produces low prices and good service for shippers and if some carriers cannot compete then they will exit the market. We are now seeing this with Hanjin and others, albeit on a fairly small scale that will not make much difference to the overall market capacity. Furthermore, it is happening much later than initially thought. How have they hung on for so long? State subsidy (e.g. Hanjin)? Cross-subsidy from other parts of their group portfolio (e.g. Maersk)? Such market distortion is impossible to eradicate fully and must be accepted as the downside against the positives of an overall competitive market, but considering the tacit collusion in alliances, the question to be asked is whether they are really competing. Liner shipping is a curious business from an economic perspective, seeming to include both oligopoly and strong competition. Yet it is more due to drops in demand and 'scale-race' strategies of buying large vessels that has lowered rates rather than competition per se. When demand was high pre-2008 then rates were high – even 'fierce' competition did not seem to lower rates then.

At first, the overcapacity was due to a drop in demand in combination with the arrival of new capacity that had been ordered before 2008, but many years later, even without recovery of demand, operators are still ordering more and larger ships. Is this following the siren song of economies of scale? How can the economic trade-off between a partially full 20,000 TEU vessel and a full 15,000 TEU vessel be explained? To paraphrase Baudrillard (2009), maybe it is when a thing is beginning to disappear that the concept appears. Take economies of scale: if there is so much talk of it, as obvious fact, as indisputable reality, that is perhaps because it is already no longer at its height and the shipping industry is already contending with something else. What if we consider the container industry as a multi-output industry and the main driver is economies of scope and not scale? Is the current level of freight rates the last 'party' of traditional beliefs? What can explain such strategies?

Other threats to the system

The dramatic change in the world shipping system brought about by containerisation could not have been predicted, nor could the influences of various external shocks such as from the oil market, and before the global economic crisis in 2008 all forecasts predicted continuous growth. Thus it seems reasonable to predict that future changes will be unpredictable. There are already some signs that stagnation is the new normal. At a system level, weak or stagnant growth remains likely in the near future at least, while individual trades (e.g. the dominant east-west trade) face several challenges, such as the debt crisis in China and the changing role (or lack) of a newly isolationist US foreign policy. Some reshoring of manufacturing is possible, particularly through the rise of automation and 3D printing as it reduces the labour cost differential between high and low labour cost countries if fewer employees are needed. Threats of terrorism, increasing political instability, breaking down of international politics such as the EU and NATO may lead to protectionist trade policies. All of these may change radically the global shipping system as we have come to know it in recent decades. How will the market react? What effect will this have on the trade of individual countries? Some countries, or regions within countries (e.g. ex-manufacturing regions that have lost jobs), feel that they have lost out to globalisation and a return to protectionism will benefit them. This remains to be seen. But there do seem some reasons to expect globalised cheap ocean shipping to be less ubiquitous than in the past.

Just as the banking system has never properly adjusted to the global economic crisis and the big crash has merely been deferred, this also seems to be the case in the global shipping sector (more so than with ports). They are living on borrowed time and some small causalities such as Hanjin are not the market correction that is needed. In the absence of economic growth, they cannot hold out forever, and eventually some large reduction in capacity is inevitable. In theory, that will produce a healthier shipping market with smaller operators and smaller, fewer vessels, more able to react to the market. But this process will not happen easily. Much political and economic power play will be entailed and shippers and the governments representing them will need to be careful to ensure they are not caught in the crossfire.

Conclusion

The first point to underscore before concluding is that we are not claiming that public actors are always the best managers of the port and shipping systems. Major gains have been made in recent decades through the influx of private operators and the growth in competition. But it is also beyond doubt that many private players have extracted rents in many cases and avoided competition wherever possible, thus the role of national and international regulators has been required to place limits on market power. So the question remains, as it does in any study of governance, what is the best mix of public and private interests? How does the public sector (representing the interests of their citizens) intervene to keep the market competitive and ensure good and fair service for shippers and thus keep trade healthy? How can they incentivise market players to compete and innovate without stifling such activities?

The aim of our smooth space paper was to explore how space is not given but constructed and, in particular, how it is contested and shaped by different power relations that are themselves based on shifting spatial and scalar constructions.

Expanding these ideas in this chapter via the mobilities paradigm has explored how likewise the apparently mobile world is not a given either. It is predicated on several constructed and contested mobilities and on many similarly constructed and contested immobilities, revealing these immobilities themselves to be (perhaps counter-intuitively) mobile, in the way their geographies, particularly institutionally, are constructed, leading back into the dialectic of smooth and striated space. There is thus a clear recursive relationship between the smooth space discussion and the mobilities paradigm. So where does that leave port geography?

The first aim of this chapter was to see what can be learned about ports from the mobilities perspective. The institutional mobility underpinning the immobile port infrastructure is evident in the changing governance systems that are not simply a change from public to private but an ongoing negotiation of power and regulation. The rather static cartographic approaches common in port geography mask major power plays and negotiation. This leads into the second aim, which was to explore what a mobilities approach adds to a more traditional geography approach. This can be seen in the dominant neoliberal discourse claiming that globalisation is good for all and that a competitive market will correct itself. The ongoing mergers and alliances in both the port and shipping industries are rarely challenged in transport geography but merely depicted and illustrated. There is strong evidence that shippers relying on this system have serious questions about this and seek greater protection from regulators to prevent ever more concentrated market power. A mobilities perspective reminds us that no specific system is a natural occurrence, but individual stakeholders in several agencies and organisations across the public and private sectors negotiated and agreed upon it.

Finally, what insights can we derive from an analysis of the global maritime and port system to feed back into mobility studies? The analysis in this chapter suggests that while beginning with a mobilities approach helps keep us alert to inequalities and contested power plays, it is not always clear what is precisely a mobilities issue rather than the traditional concerns of other disciplines. Certainly, many of the issues raised in this chapter overlooked in port and maritime transport research are indeed primarily economic issues such as market power and regulation. Taking a self-consciously mobilities perspective reminds us of the necessity of interdisciplinarity, perhaps suggesting that mobilities scholars need to make greater effort to delineate the roles of the traditional disciplines within the wider mobilities discussion.

References

Aldred, R. (2012). Governing transport from welfare state to hollow state: The case of cycling in the UK. *Transport Policy*. 23: 95–102.

Baird, A. J. (2000). Port privatisation: Objectives, extent, process and the UK experience. *International Journal of Maritime Economics*. 2 (2): 177–194.

Baudrillard, J. (2009). *Why Hasn't Everything Already Disappeared?* Seagull: Calcutta.

Brenner, N. (1998). Between fixity and motion: Accumulation, territorial organization and the historical geography of spatial scales. *Environment & Planning D*. 16 (5): 459–481.

Brooks, M. R., Cullinane, K. (eds.) (2007). Devolution, port governance and port performance. *Research in Transport Economics*. 17. Elsevier, London.

Cresswell, T. (2012). Mobilities II: Still. *Progress in Human Geography*. 36 (5): 645–653.

Deleuze, G., Guattari, F. (1987). *A Thousand Plateaus*. Minneapolis, MN: University of Minnesota Press.

Docherty, I., Shaw, J., Gather, M. (2004). State intervention in contemporary transport. *Journal of Transport Geography*. 12: 257–264.

Enright, T. E. (2013). Mass transit in the neoliberal city: The mobilizing myths of the Grand Paris Express. *Environment and Planning A*. 45: 797–813.

Hannam, K., Sheller, M., Urry, J. (2006). Editorial: Mobilities, immobilities and moorings. *Mobilities*. 1 (1): 1–22.

Harvey, D. (1975). The geography of capitalist accumulation: A reconstruction of the Marxian theory. *Antipode*. 7 (2): 9–21.

Harvey, D. (1981). The spatial fix – Hegel, Von Thunen and Marx. *Antipode*. 13 (3): 1–12.

Harvey, D. (1982). *The Limits to Capital*. Oxford: Blackwell.

Harvey, D. (1989). *The Condition of Postmodernity: An Enquiry into the Origins of Cultural Change*. Oxford England and Cambridge, MA: Blackwell.

Harvey, D. (2001). Globalization and the 'spatial fix'. *Geographische Revue*. 2: 23–30.

Hasty, W., Peters, K. (2012). The ship in geography and the geographies of ships. *Geography Compass*. 6: 660–676.

Henderson, J. (2011). Level of service: The politics of reconfiguring urban streets in San Francisco, CA. *Journal of Transport Geography*. 19: 1138–1144.

Jacobs, W., Notteboom, T. (2011). An evolutionary perspective on regional port systems: The role of windows of opportunity in shaping seaport competition. *Environment & Planning A*. 43 (7): 1674–1692.

Lefebvre, H. (1991 [1974]). *The Production of Space*. Trans. D. Nicholson-Smith. Cambridge, MA: Blackwell.

Monios, J. (2017). Policy transfer or policy churn? Institutional isomorphism and neoliberal convergence in the transport sector. *Environment and Planning A*. 49 (2): 351–371.

Monios, J., Wilmsmeier, G. (2012). Port-centric logistics, dry ports and offshore logistics hubs: Strategies to overcome double peripherality? *Maritime Policy and Management*. 39 (2): 207–226.

Monios, J., Wilmsmeier, G. (2015). Identifying Material, Geographical and Institutional Mobilities in the Global Maritime Trade System. In: T. Birtchnell, S. Savitzky and J. Urry (eds.), *Cargomobilities: Moving Materials in a Global Age*. Abingdon: Routledge. pp. 125–148.

Ng, A.K.Y., Pallis, A. A. (2010). Port governance reforms in diversified institutional frameworks: Generic solutions, implementation asymmetries. *Environment & Planning A*. 42 (9): 2147–2167.

Notteboom, T., de Langen, P., Jacobs, W. (2013). Institutional plasticity and path dependence in seaports: Interactions between institutions, port governance reforms and port authority routines. *Journal of Transport Geography*. 27: 26–35.

Notteboom, T. E., Rodrigue, J.-P. (2005). Port regionalization: Towards a new phase in port development. *Maritime Policy & Management*. 32 (3): 297–313.

Offe, C. (1984). 'Crisis of Crisis Management': Elements of a Political Crisis Theory. In: J. Keane (ed.), *Contradictions of the Welfare State*. Cambridge, MA: MIT Press. pp. 35–64.

Paget-Seekins, L. (2015). Bus rapid transit as a neoliberal contradiction. *Journal of Transport Geography*. 48: 115–120.

Peck, J. (2001). Neoliberalizing states: Thin policies/hard outcomes. *Progress in Human Geography*. 25 (3): 445–455.

Rodrigue, J.-P. (2006). Transport geography should follow the freight. *Journal of Transport Geography*. 14 (5): 386–388.

Sánchez, R. J., Wilmsmeier, G. (2010). Contextual Port Development: A Theoretical Approach. In: P. Coto-Millán, M. A. Pesquera and J. Castanedo (eds.), *Essays on Port Economics*. ISBN 9783790824247. New York: Springer. pp. 19–44.

Sánchez, R. J., Wilmsmeier, G. (2011). Liner Shipping Networks and Market Concentration. In: K.P.B. Cullinane (ed.), *International Handbook of Maritime Economics*. Cheltenham: Edward Elgar. pp. 162–206.

Sheller, M. (2015). Mobilizing Transportation, Transporting Mobilities. In: J. Cidell and D. Prytherch (eds.), *Transport, Mobility and the Production of Urban Space*. New York: Routledge. pp. 12–18.

Sheller, M., Urry, J. (2006). The new mobilities paradigm. *Environment & Planning A*. 38 (2): 207–226.

Smith, N. (2005). Neo-critical geography, or, the flat pluralist world of business class. *Antipode*. 37 (5): 887–889.

Wilmsmeier, G., Hoffmann, J. (2008). Liner shipping connectivity and port infrastructure as determinants of freight rates in the Caribbean, maritime economics & logistics. 10 (1–2): 130–151.

Wilmsmeier, G., Monios, J. (2015). The production of capitalist 'smooth' space in global port operations. *Journal of Transport Geography*. 47: 59–69.

Wilmsmeier, G., Monios, J. (2016). Institutional structure and agency in the governance of spatial diversification of port system evolution in Latin America. *Journal of Transport Geography*. 51: 294–307.

Wilmsmeier, G., Sánchez, R. J. (2017). Economies of scale in the liner container shipping industry: Challenging the beliefs – port management implications in decoupled supply and demand market conditions. Forthcoming.

4 How people green the port

Kristianne Hendricks and Peter Hall

Introduction

Here are two stories which illustrate that something profound is shifting in the political, relational and contingent ways in which cargo mobilities are constructed and shaped.

In 1998, the Regina Maersk, then the world's largest container ship, was sent on a tour of North America ports, with an arrival in the Port of New York and New Jersey "staged to send a message to port officials and politicians along the Eastern seaboard" that "[t]he advent of mega containerships made upgrading of existing port infrastructure necessary" (van Ham and Rijsenbrij, 2012: 159). The 6,000-plus TEU Regina Maersk was not the first post-Panamax containership, and this was not the first time adjacent ports had been forced to compete with each other to attract cargo. As Brian Slack observed in 1993, "Ports are becoming pawns in a game of commerce that is global in scale, and on a board where the major players are private corporations whose interests rarely coincide with the local concerns of the port administrations" (Slack, 1993: 358). Nor, of course, was Regina the end of the matter; seemingly never-ending economies of scale in container shipping have allowed steamship lines to blast past the new-Panamax level with the latest generation containerships designed to carry 20,000-odd TEUs.

Such exercises in naked bargaining power, but also the less visible processes of corporate restructuring and alliance formation, terminal lease renewal and infra-structure investment have reinforced the view that the fortunes of ports, and the localities that host them, are first and foremost shaped by decisions taken by and within the maritime and continental transportation industries. They echo the ways that railroads were able capture ports in in an earlier era (Fogelson, 1993). In other words, this is evidence for assertions that the key agents constructing and shaping cargo movements are transport industry actors. Consistent with both traditional transport geography and some contemporary network analyses, this perspective suggests that decisions are first taken within and about ocean and landside net-works, and then ports are left to respond or be bypassed (Rodrigue et al., 2009; Graham and Marvin, 2001). Transcontinental industries shape route choices, leaving local actors, including port labourers, at the mercy of these external forces.

Contrast the story of Maersk with that of coal, where in the past five years, local governments and communities on the west coast of north America have competed aggressively against each other to avoid this cargo flow – that is, not to host coal export facilities. This was not always the case. Since at least the 1960s (Bowden, 2012), successive rounds of development in East Asian economies have been associated with waves of coal export terminal development in ports from northern British Columbia to Southern California. These include such experiments as the Los Angeles LAXT terminal, which opened in 1997, stopped operating in 2003 and, finally, closed in 2006. In the 1980s, a similar terminal in Portland opened and closed, while the Ridley Island Terminal in Prince Rupert has operated since 1984, but with its uneven fortunes very much tied to the boom-bust cycle of this resource industry. The most successful modern coal terminal on the west coast of North America, Westshore Terminal at Robert's Bank south of Vancouver, enjoys something of a first mover advantage, having started in the late 1960s, although it too never became as large as originally planned.

Coal is a commodity that is subject to shifting fortunes, and certainly some of the current resistance to these port terminal developments is informed by past experiences. Coal's place in a warming world is also both uncertain and controversial. Yet what changed in the recent round was that local coalitions in traditional port cities – from the Oakland City Council in California, to Whatcom County in Washington, to New Westminster in British Columbia – were passing motions against the export of coal. And in some places, they were backed by local branches of the ILWU (International Longshore and Warehouse Union). Whether or not these locality-based coalitions are ultimately successful remains to be seen, but it is clear that the location of port facilities – certainly for controversial commodities like coal, but increasingly for container terminals as well – depends on the ability of proponents to manufacture agreement within the communities impacted by port work. This is especially the case in democratic nations, but is observed in some Chinese port cities where local authorities are under pressure to reduce the environmental externalities of port activity (Wang, 2014).

Social and environmental license, broadly construed, is an increasingly important element in maritime decision making: not only on the ocean but also intensely in port locations, and so it has emerged as a key concern of shipping interests. In short, the ways in which maritime industry actors are able to secure the political and public support required to build/expand and operate terminals are shifting from a context in which they can simply play one port off against another, to one that is more complex. Increasingly, maritime actors need to construct support, working with the regions in which they seek to locate, rather than separately from them. This is not to say that the macro-scale exercise of bargaining power revealed in the Regina Maersk story has ended, rather that the coal story demonstrates that understanding the developmental trajectories ports also demands consideration of the micro-scale processes implicating local actors. A *mobilities* perspective which emphasizes the flow-shaping roles of institutions, politics, culture, and the particularities of place, is especially useful in this regard (Sheller and Urry, 2004).

Port workers have featured on both sides of the cargo-attraction and -rejection debates. We argue that the role of port workers as simultaneously representative of maritime and other transport interests, as well as being members of local communities and polities, has positioned them as central intermediaries in the port greening process. Hence, in order to understand how cargo mobilities in a warming world are shaped by and through particular port places and transport actors, we need to understand how dockworkers mediate the acceptance or rejection of particular cargo regimes. In this analysis, we explore the role of port workers in shaping maritime cargo flows in relation to port greening initiatives. To define port greening, we build on the work of Dahlstrom (2011), where the term green describes "all efforts to consume, produce, distribute, promote, package, and reclaim products in a manner that is sensitive or responsive to ecological concerns" (p. 5). Applied to seaports, port greening then indicates the actions of port actors towards improving the long-term eco-sustainability of seaports.

We look at the role dockworkers play in terminal development and operations through the lens of greening practices on the docks. In doing this, we focus on the social implications which come into play, rather than examining environmental concerns of the port, such as emissions, sediment disruption or habitat destruction. We explore the construction of local spatialities, jurisdictions and exclusions in the intimate connections between dockworker and city, and explore how support and/or opposition to greening practices enable dockworkers to shape the greening of the port through the practices they choose to embrace, reject or modify. We conclude that maritime mobilities need to pay more attention to the collective actions labour.

Labour and port geographies

As demonstrated in the case of coal, the 'blind shipping' of any type of cargo is increasingly difficult in some locations. Local actors are demanding that ports pay increasing attention to the environmental impacts of the goods they ship through their communities. Statements meant to distance the ports from the products moving through them, indicating that "we only move the goods, we do not control what is being moved" are increasingly being rejected by these actors, while global pressures to green businesses – that is, to bring a focus on ecological sustainability to the forefront of business practices – are on the rise. Maritime actors, not exempt from these pressures, have responded through the greening of their practices, and port authorities have introduced policies, procedures and environmental clauses within the leases they grant. Comtois and Slack (2007) demonstrated that there was an industry-wide commitment to maritime greening, though admittedly at difference paces throughout the world. Through their work, the authors brought a focus on the best practices at the time, demonstrating that sustainability had become an 'essential factor' in the restructuring of maritime industries (Comtois and Slack, 2007: 6). Dockworkers are on the frontline of implementing these measures. Through their adoption, modification or rejection of these measures, they play an important role in shaping the flow patterns of goods as they move through the ports, affording dockworkers with some ability to shape port geographies.

Greening and improved environmental performance in the port, as a relatively new focus, sets an arena through which we can observe how dockworkers shape the port. Using Vancouver as a case study, we have interviewed dockworkers, port authority agents and other stakeholders to explore these ideas. Located on Canada's west coast, the Vancouver Fraser Port Authority, popularly known as the Port of Vancouver (and before that as Port Metro Vancouver), seeks to be "the world's most sustainable port" (VFPA, 2016). As Canada's largest port, moving 138 million of Canada's 306.5 million tons of cargo in 2015 (ACPA, 2016), the port's 27 marine terminals are important to the national economy. Most dockworkers are not employed in a terminal-specific manner; rather, the British Columbia Maritime Employers Association (BCMEA) dispatch them to the terminals. While the BCMEA acts as an intermediary between the various employers and waterfront employees, active registration with one of the ILWU Canada locals as either a casual or a member is required to be dispatched for work. The main locals in the Vancouver area include Local 520 (port authority workers), Local 500 (dockworkers at the Burrard Inlet terminals) and Local 502 (dockworkers on the Fraser River and at Deltaport). Training, which in practice is conducted by existing union members who have learned on the job, is also a function of the BCMEA as part of its responsibility for worker health and safety (BCMEA, 2011).

Dockworkers are not only members of the union but also citizens of the 16 municipalities surrounding the port; hence, they straddle the line between the economic interests of the port and communal aspirations for environmental amenity in the spaces in which they live, play, raise their children and work. As a public agency in a multi-level governance context, the Port of Vancouver attempts to balance its mandate to promote trade with the needs of the community members surrounding their facilities, through community involvement, engagement and investment; the establishment of community liaison committees; and with a focus on aboriginal relations (VFPA, 2016). These relationships have waxed and waned; as in any port city, at times these are highly conflictual, while at other times the port authority has enjoyed the support of surrounding communities as they seek to minimize negative externalities.

The negative externalities of maritime industries, and attempts to mitigate them, have gained growing scholarly attention. Ocean governance and the protection of the environment features in the work of Lister et al. (2015) examining the regulation – or under-regulation – of the maritime industry, to De Lay Fayette's (2008) focus on the social and environmental consequences of shipping through the arctic, to studies questioning the mandate and role of the International Maritime Organization and Port State Control in addressing the environmental concerns of the industry (Shi, 2013; Lister et al., 2015; van Leewen and Kern, 2013). The problem of carriers who attempt to bypass regulations through flags of convenience have been studied (Llinás Negret, 2016; Mitroussi, 2008), as have the contingent working conditions of seafarers (Wu and Winchester, 2005; Rugganan, 2011). Overlooked in most of this, however, are perspectives on port workers, particularly in regards to the ways that waterfront workers – especially dockworkers – act to connect oceanside and landside goods movement.

Historically, dockwork was the heavy, dirty work of the working class living in waterfront regions, where workers utilized physical strength and a mastery of spatial configuration as they transferred materials between land and ship (Levinson, 2006). The advent of containerisation in the mid-50s both changed waterfront work and demonstrated just how critical these labourers are in shaping the geography of trade. The use of containers meant that ships were no longer loaded piecemeal at the dock; rather, manufacturers could load containers on their factories or at warehousing facilities, while new, specialized equipment at the waterfront further reduced the manual requirements of waterfront work. Despite the exponential improvements in the speed and efficiency at which goods could be moved, this shift also meant that the goods no longer required the same handling and storage at the waterfront, which presented a very real threat to waterfront work.

Building on Jamie Peck's (1996) "*Work*-Place," Herod (1998) examined the response to these pressures as they played out on the East Coast of the United States from 1955–1985, where the ILA (International Longshoremen's Association) fought against employers and the International Brotherhood of Teamsters to secure the right to perform tasks previously restricted to the waterfront. Through an analysis of adjustments to jurisdictional boundaries, contract disputes and legal proceedings, Herod shows how on the East Coast, the ILA successfully created a new geographical space – a 50-mile radius around the port – within which container work would be handled by its members. The ILA argued that the ability to load and unload containers away from the waterfront threatened the jobs of dockworkers and thus presented this radius as an essential job preservation initiative (ibid, 1998). Ultimately, the ILA's win directly impacted shippers and manufacturers, forcing them to adjust the locations and activities of distribution and warehousing that were, at least for a time, acceptable to the union. Herod's analysis demonstrated the role that organized labour plays as an agent in constructing patterns of flow and their attendant scalar geographies. This geography of work, however, remains fluid; the standardization which accompanied containerization eventually allowed cargo interests to bypass the ILA's container rules, highlighting the limits on the durability of any particular scalar fix.

Such actions by dockworkers to create protective regulations also create institutional memories which are carefully guarded by union representatives because they simultaneously ensure that dockworkers retain a knowledge of the power they hold collectively, while empowering individual workers to assert agency in the workplace. Through the particularity, irregularity, diversity and danger of the work that is shared by all dockworkers, specific collective cultures have evolved in ports (Hein, 2011). This leads to the identification and adoption of common concerns, and hence demands on employers for responses under the threat of work stoppages. It is this ability to enact change through the collective exertion of pressure through which unions are recognized as being "among the most powerful social movement sectors" (Obach, 2004: 7).

However, where historically ports competed to attract ships due to their unique abilities to handle specific types of cargoes, standardization through containerization resulted in a uniformity across a multitude of ports (Levinson, 2006; Carmichael and Herod, 2012). When coupled with an expansive network of roads and rail, this has enabled shippers to bypass ports. Hence the relative ease with which cargo can be moved from one side of the country to another through this logistics web puts pressure on actors in each port to keep even the threat of labour disruption to a minimum. This pressure is further intensified by the large capital investments required by intermodal systems. In contrast to the pre-containerized world, where equipment costs were low and labour costs high (Levinson, 2006), current shipping requires investments in largely stationary equipment, such as the gantry cranes which grace the horizons of ports around the world, and the landside infrastructures that connect ports to widely dispersed hinterlands. Expensive infrastructure essentially fixes capital in place, locking the port into its location, and limiting its ability to grow or respond to external pressures through relocation (Lillie, 2005). Worker's organizations, although internally strong and cohesive, are fixed or place-bound in much the same way. Both are confronted by a more mobile shipping industry. Under these conditions, maritime employers have strategic choices to make about how to react to the needs expressed by those whose daily work ensures the productivity and efficiency needed to remain competitive.

Of course, this focus on the needs of workers does not always occur, as can be seen in the union negotiations that take place at the end of each union contract. Such negotiations can and do become conflictual as both the employers and unions representatives fight for their own best interests, with the resolution of such conflict highly contingent upon the nature of the legal framework within which they take place. However, negotiations may also reveal areas of potential alignment between the interests of employers and dockworkers; for example, both parties may have a vested interest in ensuring workplace safety. Dockworkers are compelled to safety initiatives as both their lives and livelihoods depend on them, while employers can reduce disruption, legal and other costs which would be incurred by an accident causing injury. Likely areas of contradiction include job loss – dockworkers in Vancouver have been vocal about resisting the job loss which might accompany the automation of container terminals, despite the fact that automation would reduce the likelihood of personal injury on the dock. Nevertheless, the fact that these negotiations between the union and the port employer take place further evidences the importance of the workers, in that they are not simply replaceable.

A lesson from Herod's work is that the ability of a dockworkers' union to establish jurisdictions of work regulation across various geographic scales is a key variable in determining the relative strength of workers in opposing the threat of bypass. In contrast to the ILA which was saw its 50-mile container rule eventually bypassed by trucking and warehouse developments further inland (Herod, 2001), the ILWU on the west coast of north America has pursued a strategy of imposing consistent working conditions in all ports along that coast. To date, they have proven more successful in convincing employers they are able to halt operations in all ports on that coast, effectively halting operations and risking the potential for future business. In order to remain competitive, port employers have had to address many of the demands brought to the bargaining table by the ILWU. Bargaining success gives further credence to individual workers in recognizing the importance of their voice, whether focused on traditional concerns such as guaranteeing work hours (Carmichael and Herod, 2012), or towards environmental concerns such as the pollution of the air due to conveyor belt loading of raw materials into the bulk holds of ships.

City and port: dockworkers as agents of both

Ports are places where transnational actors pursue macro-scale or non-local spatial strategies to enhance goods mobility, but where they intersect with workers, communities and other actors pursuing micro-scale or local spatial strategies to capture the benefits, and to minimize the negative effects of such mobility. Ravetz (2014) presents a model in which we can recognize this intersection as a linkage vital in the evolution of cities towards an idealistic future in which industry, commercial activity and residential aspects of the city mutually reinforce sustainable development. Through a systemic embrace of all the actors within the complex system of the city, Ravetz projects a city free of the disruptions which plague our current system through the establishment of synergistic pathways between the key nodes as in modern cities, and the key actors. While this is certainly utopian, it does demonstrate a vital aspect of maritime mobilities: as important actors, dockworkers and port authorities alike act as synergistic links which shape cargo flows through their participation in trade.

But how does this occur? How are port authorities and dockworkers alike with respect to shaping maritime mobilities? The relatively new policy area of 'port greening' is one in which port authorities are not merely reacting to short-run competitive pressures. In an emerging policy area such as this, and one in which the port is called to respond to a complex mix of local and external pressures, local agencies are responsible for both responding to, and proposing, greening methods (Boschken, 1988; Hall and Jacobs, 2010). One of the ways port authorities have responded to these pressures is to present a strong public profile to the communities surrounding the port. For example, the Port of Montreal has good neighbor committees that promote the social responsibility of the port (MPA, 2015), while the Port of Prince Rupert has an interpretive centre to enable community members to better understand the port (PRPA, 2014). The Port of Vancouver is actively involved in community events throughout the year in an effort to bolster public support. From the sponsoring the FusionFest in Surrey, a festival celebrating the multiculturalism and diversity of culture in the area, to assisting first nations community members in compiling a directory of first nations businesses, to tours for school children learning about the shipping industry, the Port of Vancouver engages with the community in a very visual manner, seeking to maintain a positive public profile for an inherently environmentally damaging industry while simultaneously working to minimize this damage (VFPA, 2016).

While engaging with urban communities helps to send the message that the port is a good neighbor that is dedicated to the integrity of the environment, there are indicators that this commitment goes deeper than simply greenwashing. The staff roster, mission, value statements and website as well as interviews with office staff from ILWU Local 520 revealed that they are all involved in the creation and implementation of sustainability policies and procedures, with a deep pride among workers for this involvement.

The same may not necessarily be said of members of other ILWU Locals 500 and 502 responsible for physical dock work. In the same interview set, dockworkers and union representatives did not demonstrate the same deep awareness of the sustainability plans as the port authority office workers, or of the extensive reporting that the port undergoes. Neither were they aware of the port's membership with Green Marine, a North America–wide initiative for marine industries, where best practices are shared and greening projects are monitored and recorded, with awards provided to those who achieve excellence.

Despite the disconnect between the office and the dock, both the port authority and dockworkers play a similar role in the community though in different forums. Where the port authority presents a public image of the port at official community events and to schools throughout the region, dockworkers represent more personal knowledge of the waterfront. The people that they interact with, their friends and family, are afforded an intimate insight into the industry stories they tell of waterfront work. These stories draw a connection between the city and the waterfront, bringing a deeper meaning to those hearing them. The port authority recognizes the value of stories, as is evident in a series of videos currently being published on YouTube (www.youtube.com/user/PMVUser), and promoted through various social media including Twitter (https://twitter.com/portvancouver) and Facebook (www. facebook.com/Portofvancouver); however, the reach of these stories is limited to those who have already expressed an interest in the port by following these media outlets. When dockworkers tell the same stories to their friends, family members and community acquaintances, on the other hand, they are simply sharing parts of their lives in an ongoing narrative. In sharing their lives, they elicit the responses of their community members, whether verbalized or through body language.

In these responses from the public, shared concerns are found, and dockworkers are in a unique position to act on them. Take, for instance, the story of what is known amongst dockworkers as "the first greening initiative on the waterfront" (Longshore Interview), concerning regulations stating that workers could no longer throw their coffee cups and cigarette butts over the edge of the ships during their breaks. According to longshoremen, who were working at the time these rules were implemented, this was not a 'top-down' initiative passed from head office to the dock, rather grew organically from the dockworkers themselves, and was brought up to the employers by the union. Dockworkers have historically lived most of their lives by the waterfront: they lived, worked and played along the edges of the waterbodies on which ports have been located. In a time when the vastness of the ocean seemed un-spoilable, those living along the shorelines of the Burrard Inlet, in Vancouver, became increasingly aware of the environmental damage which was occurring due to the practice of throwing garbage over the side of the ships, as their beaches became littered with this garbage. Unsatisfied to continue living in this manner, the union workers living in these areas brought their concerns together, and through the workings of the safety committee, presented this practice as damaging and asked that it would cease. The request was granted and put into procedure in collaboration with the BCMEA. While this could be viewed as simply a way of improving the visual aesthetics of their beaches, a passion for the environment was evident in both the voices and comments of the interviewed workers. This passion continued across other topics involving the protection of the environment, such as the labour demand that potash or coal conveyor belts be encapsulated or covered to reduce the amount of dust being emitted, where it could be breathed in by labourers, but also would settle onto the clean laundry drying on lines surrounding the port. Thus, by interacting with both the communities in which they reside and the communities in which they work, dockworkers have played a direct role on the greening of the waterfront as a synergistic link.

Rejection, modification and adoption

The greening of the waterfront is not a new concept; rather, it has been picking up momentum over time (Acciaro et al., 2014). Ports across Canada have engaged with their communities to identify local concerns and have sought to meet these concerns with the implementation of eco-sustainability focused policies and procedures. The Port of Vancouver has offered onshore power to its cruise ship operators since 2009 (Hall et al., 2013). This practice allows ships to cease the use of their auxiliary engines while in port, utilizing landside power instead. This action reduces the amount of sulphur oxides measured in the air where ports berth by as much as 90 percent (Yau et al., 2013) and is increasing in popularity, with ports across Canada either implementing or moving to implement the technology needed to facilitate this. Despite its growing popularity, concerns over shoreside power as a potentially global solution to port emissions do exist. Hall (2010) looks to the source of this power as a key determinant of its usefulness. If the power provided to the ship is generated with the use of coal, for example, and transported along inefficient power lines, then the ultimate outcome may be that more pollution is created in the production and delivery of the power than the use of auxiliary engines would entail.

While shoreside power may be a solution to reduce the local negative effects of shipping emissions that has been widely studied (Lirn et al., 2013; Lai et al., 2011; Hall, 2010; Han, 2010) and expressly shared with the public as a key measure in greening many ports (VFPA, 2016; PRPA, 2014), this is just one of the many greening measures which occur within ports and one which has had a relatively small impact on dockworkers in the past. As the Port of Vancouver works with its terminal operators to establish shore-power enabled berths at its container ships this may change, however presently shoreside power availability is restricted to Cruise Terminals.

When options such as shoreside power are introduced, dockworkers have three ways to respond to the changes in work that may accompany it: rejection, modification or adoption. While ordered differently, these options echo Albert Hirschmann's notion of "Exit, voice, and loyalty" (1970). Hirschman posits that workers respond to change by leaving the workforce operation (exit), attempting to change the workplace (voice) or embracing chance and demonstrating an allegiance to the organization providing the work (loyalty). Hirschman's key insight, confirmed in numerous empirical studies including port studies, is that when workers have a 'voice', they become part of the solution (de Langen and Visser, 2005). Dockworkers typically do not have an exit option; instead, we offer rejection as the analogous reaction to unwanted change. Dockworkers, and their union collectives, are agents through which both voice (modification) and loyalty (adoption) are practiced.

In the Vancouver region, dockwork and membership in ILWU Locals are a highly competitive and coveted, offering excellent pay and job stability. A worker seeking a position on the waterfront cannot simply approach an employer and sell his/her labour; rather, they must move through the union, which first requires being hired as a casual worker. Interviews with ILWU members indicate that after 10 to 12 years of 'casual' work, the individual then becomes eligible to become a member of the union (Longshore Interview). It should be noted that the term 'casual' does not denote an unavailability of work or ineligibility for training. The seniority system in place within the union also extends to those on the casual list, guaranteeing training opportunities according to a hierarchy established through hours of work. As casuals, the accumulation of hours requires that workers present themselves as ready to work for each of the daily available shifts. Additionally, the union has won the right to complete the work in all of the region's terminals, whether auto, bulk, break bulk or container, and as such the incentive to exit from one organization with the ability to carry out similar work within a different organization is greatly restricted. As seniority is gained then, and particularly once union membership has been achieved, a complete 'exit' by an individual within the workforce becomes an undesirable option. 'Loyalty' then becomes a connection to the union, rather than to the employers, and 'voice' is achieved primarily through the collective actions of the union.

Through the collective action of the union, 'exit' takes the form of 'rejection'. Fearful of job loss, union members come together and demand that jobs be protected, or the union will collectively exit the workforce in the form of a strike. If port greening initiatives take place in such a way as to threaten the job security of waterfront workers or if the needs of the workers are completely overlooked in the planning and implementation of greening policies, procedures and the implementation of new technologies, the likelihood of rejection increases. In Vancouver, plans to develop a fully automated new terminal at Deltaport could face this type of reaction from dockworkers, requiring either alternate work or additional training to ensure that union members will not feel the threat of potential job loss to ensure that work-stopping job action does not take place.

In reducing the potential for rejection, and the work stoppages which would result, port authorities and employers can respond by giving waterfront workers a 'voice', effectively enabling modification. Modification on the waterfront can take two forms. It could be in the form of collective action between employers and union to reach an agreement. This could take place, for example, through investments in the training that dockworkers would need to operate the computer programs needed to run an automated port from a location which might be completely removed from the site. Alternately, if no existing union members are able to operate new equipment, for example with the need for electrical engineers to connect ships to shoreside power sources safely, an agreement might be made to allow these personnel to be hired from outside of the union on the condition that they become members of the union.

It is also possible for modification to take the form of individual resistance. In Vancouver, interviews demonstrated that this form of resistance does occur, for example, in that some dockworkers choose convenience over the greening effects of anti-idling policies and thus do not turn off their trucks while awaiting the loading or unloading of their containers. Personal modifications can also take place in the choice to throw recyclables into the trash, or by ignoring posted speed limits which are in place to maximize the energy efficiency of the engines being used. Alternately, a dockworker working with bulk goods may not effectively spray down the load in effort to save time, in effect increasing the likelihood of dust contamination.

It is important to note, however, that not all modifications are those which detract from the potential greening of the port. Tradesmen and women on the docks see all forms of product, as well as all forms of waste, due to the fluid nature of their work as they move from port area to port area maintaining, adjusting and repairing machines. As they move between terminals, they are able to see – and react to – variances between terminals which suggest "lack-luster control for waste management" (Longshore interview), concerns which have then been brought to terminals through the union resulting in increased environmental attention. In this same interview, the dockworker also emphasized the role of the union trades members in demanding that conveyor belts be covered to improve the quality of air in which they were working. Another dockworker recounts the role of the union in the literal greening of the port through the push to plant trees along a key truck route which leads from the port through a residential area to the city and hinterlands beyond. In addition to bringing colour to the otherwise dull, busy roadway, the dockworker expressed that trees would eliminate potential parking spots, thus eliminating idling, and, further, the trees would absorb emissions (Longshore Interview).

In addition to dockworkers sharing stories of their involvement in greening the waterfront this sentiment was also shared by terminal management. An upper-level environment manager noted, for example, that rubbish bins on the docks, formerly open containers, were converted to closed bins due to pressures from the dockworkers to reduce the potential for the wind to pick up and spread waste across the dock and beyond. Further, an interview with a manager at BCMEA noted that "longshoremen want what is best for the environment . . . It used to be a dirty job, but now people want to feel that they've provided value" (BCMEA Interview), demonstrating that a commitment to greening the port is both felt among dockworkers and reported to employers.

Within the union then, changes can be agreed upon, or adopted, essentially demonstrating Hirschman's 'loyalty' to the organization through the union. Due to the organization of waterfront labour, where the union is dispersed across various locations and employers do not have control over which workers will arrive at their location, loyalty is predominantly directed towards the union, while adoption is more terminal-location/ employer specific. As with rejection and modification, adoption holds a social element: where workers unite towards a cause, they take ownership of it, and it becomes 'theirs'. In the case of the conveyor belts being covered as a result of pressure by the trades members, interviewees mentioned in passing other factors such as community concerns over dust settling on laundry hung out to dry, and (perhaps more importantly within a business context) customer complaints that bulk products were arriving with unacceptable levels of wind-blown cross contamination. These factors, however, were less important than the pride expressed by workers for the union's involvement in improving the environment both for those working at the terminal and for the surrounding communities.

Where dockworkers then are engaged in the process of greening the port, adoption is more likely to be the ultimate result. Modification may be required either through collaboration between the union and employers or subversively by the workers on the docks, but the risk of rejection can be mitigated in recognizing the role of the union member.

Conclusion

With regards to the greening of the port, a dockworker interview revealed that the

> perception that the port isn't green is far from the truth. There is still lots to do, but look at the air quality of Vancouver compared to the rest- Vancouver has been green for a long while, we stay ahead of the curve.
>
> (Longshore Interview)

As a resident of the city, it is not only the workplace conditions that this worker is reporting on but also the conditions of the city beyond the waterfront. Both the waterfront and the city are important to these workers, who depend on each for their lives and livelihoods. Dock work of the past may have been dirty work, for example, in the hauling of animal hides, or the handling of asbestos without protection (Longshore Interview); however, the need for improvement in port environmental performance has been widely recognized. Just as macro-level influences, such as the Regina Maersk's inaugural tour, play a role in shaping the fortunes of ports, so also do the dockworkers at a micro-level, seeking to maintain an enjoyable living environment for themselves and for their children. The involvement that dockworkers play within their communities can result in a synergistic link between the city and the port.

If we are to understand cargo mobilities, or the actual the ways that goods movements are contingently shaped by social, economic and political processes, then a recognition that dockworkers have long played an important role in shaping the geographies of ports must be considered. Just as the dockworkers of the East Coast were able to utilize legal negotiations to secure their jobs, impacting development of ports in the past, so also will port developments continue to be shaped in the future. As communities react to global warming and embrace a desire for greener industry, port workers may utilize the union to bridge the gap between their concerns and the interests of the port authority through the adoption, modification or rejection of greening initiatives. In these ways, workers both influence the social licence of the port as they project their experiences to the communities around them, while continuing to shape the flow of goods in their responses. Individually and/or as a group, port workers affect the flows of goods through the port, particularly in their embrace – or otherwise – of new technologies. In recognizing the importance of dockworkers and ensuring their voice is heard, developers avoid potential disruptions and stoppages in work.

What happens in ports, and how the social actors of the ports respond, has become part of a new appreciation of mobilities in which stakeholder dynamics are considered rather than stagnating in a transport-centric perspective on the forces shaping patterns of movement.

References

Acciaro, M., Vanelslander, T., Sys, C., Ferrari, C., Roumboutsos, A., Giuliano, G., Siu, J., Lam, L., Kapros, S. (2014). Environmental sustainability in seaports: A framework for successful innovation. *Maritime Policy & Management*. 41 (5): 480–500.

Association of Canadian Port Authorities (ACPA) (2016). Association of Canadian Port Authorities: The leading voice of Canadian ports website. Available at: www.acpa-ports. net Accessed 28 July 2017.

Boschken, H. (1988). *Strategic Design and Organizational Change: Pacific Rim Ports in Transition*. Tuscaloosa: University of Alabama Press.

Bowden, B. (2012). A history of the Pan-Pacific coal trade from the 1950s to 2011: Exploring the long-term effects of a buying cartel. *Australian Economic History Review*. 52: 1–24.

British Columbia Maritime Employment Association (BCMEA) (2011). British Columbia Maritime Employers Association website. Available at: www.bcmea.com Accessed 28 July 2017.

Carmichael, L. L., Herod, A. (2012). Dockers and seafarers: What the politics of spatial embeddedness and geographical scale have meant for union organizing in the European maritime trades. *Labor Studies Journal*. 37 (2): 203–227.

Comtois, C., Slack, B. (2007). *Restructuring the Maritime Transportation Industry: Global Overview of Sustainable Development Practices*. Montreal, QC: Ministère des Transports du Québec.

Dahlstrom, R. 2011. Green Marketing Management. Mason, OH: Cengage Learning.

de Langen, P. W., Visser, E.-J. (2005). Collective action regimes in seaport clusters: The case of the Lower Mississippi port cluster. *Journal of Transport Geography*. 13 (2): 173–186.

De Lay Fayette, L. A. (2008). Ocean governance in the Arctic. *International Journal of Marine & Coastal Law*. 23: 531–566.

Fogelson, R. M. (1993). *The Fragmented Metropolis: Los Angeles, 1850–1930*. Los Angeles: University of California Press.

Graham, S., Marvin, S. (2001). *Splintering Urbanism: Networked Infrastructures, Technological Mobilities and the Urban Condition*. London: Routledge.

Hall, P. V., Jacobs, W. (2010). Shifting proximities: The maritime ports sector in an era of global supply chains. *Regional Studies*. 44 (9): 1103–115.

Hall, P. V., O'Brien, T., Woudsma, C. (2013). Environmental innovation and the role of stakeholder collaboration in West Coast Gateways. *Research in Transport Economics*. 42 (1): 87–96.

Hall, W. J. (2010). Assessment of CO_2 and priority pollutant reduction by installation of shoreside power. *Resources, Conservation and Recycling*. 54: 462–467.

Han, C. (2010). Strategies to reduce air pollution in shipping industry. *The Asian Journal of Shipping and Logistics*. 26 (1): 7–29.

Hein, C. (2011). *Port Cities: Dynamic Landscapes and Global Networks*. New York: Routledge Taylor & Francis Group.

Herod, A. (1998). Discourse on the docks: Containerization and inter-union work disputes in US ports, 1955–1985. *Transactions of the Institute of British Geographers*. 23 (2): 177–191.

Herod, A. (2001). *Labor Geographies: Workers and the Landscapes of Capitalism*. New York: The Guilford Press.

Hirschmann, A. O. (1970). *Exit, Voice, and Loyalty: Responses to Decline in Firms, Organizations, and States*. Cambridge, MA: Harvard University Press.

Lai, K. H., Lun, V.Y.H., Wong, C.W.Y., Cheng, T.C.E. (2011). Green shipping practices in the shipping industry: Conceptualization, adoption, and implications. *Resources, Conservation and Recycling*. 55 (6): 631–638.

Levinson, M. (2006). Container shipping and the decline of New York, 1955–1975. *The Business History Review*. 80 (1): 49–80.

Lillie, N. (2005). Union networks and global unionism in maritime shipping. *Relations Industrielles*. 60 (1): 88–111.

Lirn, T., Wu, Y.C.J., Chen, Y. J. (2013). Green performance criteria for sustainable ports in Asia. *International Journal of Physical Distribution & Logistics Management*. 43 (5–6): 427–451.

Lister, J., Taudal Poulsen, R., Ponte, S. (2015). Orchestrating transnational environmental governance in maritime shipping. *Global Environmental Change*. 34: 185–195.

Llinás Negret, C. F. (2016). Pretending to be Liberian and Panamanian: Flags of convenience and the weakening of the nation state on the high seas. *Journal of Maritime Law & Commerce*. 47 (1): 1–101.

Mitroussi, K. (2008). Employment of seafarers in the EU context: Challenges and opportunities. *Marine Policy*. 32: 1043–1049.

Montreal Port Authority (MPA) (2015). Montreal Port Authority. Available at: www. port-montreal.com Accessed 28 July 2017.

Obach, B. K. (2004). *Labor and the Environmental Movement: The Quest for Common Ground*. Cambridge, MA: MIT Press.

Peck, J. (1996). Work-Place: The Social Regulation of Labor Markets. New York: Guilford Press.

Prince Rupert Port Authority (PRPA) (2014). Port of Prince Rupert. Available at: rupert-port.com

Ravetz, J. (2014). Interconnected responses for interconnected problems: Synergistic pathways for sustainable wealth in port cities. *International Journal Global Environmental Issues*. 13 (2–4): 363–388.

Rodrigue, J.-P., Comtois, C., Slack, B. (2009). *The Geography of Transport Systems*. Abingdon, UK: Routledge.

Rugganan, S. (2011). The role of organised labour in preventing a 'race to the bottom' for Filipino seafarers in the global labour market. *African and Asian Studies*. 10: 180–208.

Sheller, M., Urry, J. (2004). The new mobilities paradigm. *Environment and Planning A.* 38 (2): 207–226.

Shi, Y. (2013). The challenge of reducing greenhouse gas emissions from international shipping: Assessing the international maritime organization's regulatory response. *Yearbook of International Environmental Law.* 23 (1): 131–167.

Slack, B. (1993). Pawns in a game. *Growth and Change.* 24: 579–588.

Vancouver Fraser Port Authority (2016). Port of Vancouver website. Available at: www.portvancouver.com

Van Ham, H., Rijsenbrij, J. (2012). *Development of Containerization: Success through Vision, Drive and Technology.* Amsterdam: IOS Press and Delft University Press.

van Leewen, J., Kern, K. (2013). The external dimension of European Union Marine Governance: Institutional interplay between the EU and the International Maritime Organization. *Global Environmental Politics.* 13 (1): 69–87.

Wang, H. (2014). Preliminary investigation of waterfront redevelopment in Chinese coastal port cities: The case of the eastern Dalian port areas. *Journal of Transport Geography.* 40: 29–42.

Wu, B., Winchester, N. (2005). Crew study of seafarers: A methodological approach to the labour market for seafarers. *Marine Policy.* 29: 323–330.

Yau, P. S., Lee, S. C., Cheng, Y., Huang, Y., Lai, S. C., Xu, X. H. (2013). Contribution of ship emissions to the fine particulate in the community near an international port in Hong Kong. *Atmospheric Research.* 124 (28): 61–72.

Part 2
Economic mobilities

5 Off shore

The sustainable city and its logistical costs

Boris Vormann and Patrick DeDauw

Introduction

Many have hailed the rise of the sustainable city as a story of progress. This powerful narrative of smart and green growth figures the postindustrial waterfront as a symbolic space of transition toward a more environmentally friendly urbanity. In what has become a global investment strategy, formerly derelict logistics hubs have been turned into green esplanades and playgrounds for knowledge economy workers. While this model of reinvention originated in cities of the US Northeast, it has since spread to cities in Europe, East Asia, and West Africa alike, with almost-identical blue-glass skyscrapers, luxury condominiums, and boutique shopping establishments sprouting up overlooking the water from New York City to Buenos Aires, from Hamburg to Lagos. The global mobility of this model for urban redevelopment has, however, itself depended on a set of spatial and economic shifts in the systems of trade and transport that themselves sustain the dream of urban sustainability.

While municipal officials, city-branders, and some urbanists have imagined revamped waterfront spaces across the globe as greenfields of a new public sphere, others point to the ways in which shoreline revitalization projects can lead to gentrification processes and the dissolution and relocation of long-standing communities (Ferreira and Visser, 2007; Wonneberger, 2008; Scharenberg and Bader, 2009). This more critical perspective is warranted, but it cannot stop at the scale of local phenomena of displacement.[1] Once we extend the analytical perspective to broader urbanization processes and their materialization in global networks, as we set out to do, we can understand how the money made through these investments depends on a series of cost shifts at several scales and sites: The space freed up for postindustrial consumption utopias requires particular kinds of industrialization elsewhere. While we recognize the important critique of gentrification as one of a naturalized process of displacement, a focus on the global production networks that tie together urban areas across the planet can render visible laborscapes of exploitation and uneven development that otherwise remain unnoticed and seemingly disconnected in critical analysis. These hidden processes point to a much less sustainable urban future than the redeveloped waterfronts of the world's global and mega cities suggest.

In this chapter, we explore this contradiction between the emergence of utopian urban sites and the sprawling production networks on which they materially depend. Understanding the global mobility of this strategy for repurposing and recapitalizing industrial waterfronts requires an attentiveness both to the mobility of capital in and out of the built environment and to the infrastructure-enabled externalization of costs at various scales. These sets of site-specific and extra-local conditions must coalesce to make this particular vision for urban economic development appealing to the city-boosting politicians and investors who make them happen in the innumerable contexts that they do. That classic examples such as New York City and Dublin's Silicon Docks seem to have so much in common with the megastructures emerging in Ninhua New City, Lagos, and Belgrade is not a sign that this is an inexorable process emerging out of technical change, infrastructural obsolescence, or stages of economic development. Rather, these developments – on vastly different terrains – are the consequence of deliberate strategies and political choices. These office and luxury residential spaces depend not only on one another, as in transnational professional networks, but also directly on spaces and corridors of extraction, production, waste-dumping, and displacement.

Promises of a postindustrial era

New York City's waterfront transformation is the *locus classicus* for the now-proliferating myth of postindustrial urban progress. This sanguine vision was built into the post-1970s crisis reinvention of the city from the outset. In his 2011 book *Triumph of the City*, Edward Glaeser links New York City's "rebirth" after the 1975 fiscal collapse to the city's "entrepreneurial" elites in high-end service industries (2011: 56). This renaissance, in Glaeser's and others' accounts (e.g. Gastil, 2002; Butzel, 2007), has brought a permanent solution to the ailing city; it has turned around and revitalized inner-city neighborhoods – and has led Manhattan to rise like a phoenix from the ashes over the past four decades. This story of progress, which has contributed its fair share to obfuscating the labor struggles on which New York City was built (Greenberg, 2008), has been one epitomized by and enacted on Manhattan's postindustrial waterfront, where the entrance into the postindustrial era was both facilitated and staged. The waterfront served as a particularly dramatic backdrop for deindustrialization and imaginaries of a better future, because its increasing state of dereliction in the 1960s and 1970s became for many the symbol of a broken Fordist system, upon which a more sustainable urban fortune could be built (Vormann, 2015).[2]

While Boston and Baltimore are often cited as the cities where waterfront redevelopment originated, it is New York City where the waterfront became an integral part of a complete turnaround in urban development strategy. In that context, the past as a harbour city became a folkloristic backdrop for the business-led financialization of the city's economic structure and outlook. In addition to a critique of what had been, the mid-1970s crisis presented an opportunity for new coalitions of actors, starting with the Koch administration, to reimagine what Manhattan's waterfront might become. After 1975, new branding campaigns were devised that represented, above all, a look into the glorious pre-Fordist past. In the new context of pro-business restructuring, where locations close to the Central Business District were redeveloped, the push for redevelopment projects on Manhattan's shorelines was based both on the premise of New York City's glorious past as a mercantile global city as well as on the promise of a postindustrial future (Boyer, 1996, 1997; Greenberg, 2008).[3]

Both on New York City's shorelines and in North American and European developments following its example, a common trope has been the distinction of the postindustrial waterfront as a counter-development to the industrial era. On today's urban waterfronts, work is no longer as back-breaking as it used to be; white-collar occupations in commercial offices and service jobs in boutiques, maritime museums, and restaurants dominate the range of industrial occupations of redeveloped shorelines. It is certainly a sign of progress, argues Marc Levinson, that the "armies of ill-paid, ill-treated workers who once made their living loading and unloading ships in every port are no more" (2008: 2). These allusions to the past help us commemorate what seems to have been overcome. Consider as examples in New York City the redevelopments of Battery Park City, the revitalization of a former dock facility in the Gantry Plaza State Park in Queens or, for that matter, Brooklyn Bridge Park, where old industrial piers have been turned into playgrounds and parks. Other examples on both sides of the Atlantic readily come to mind. Think, for instance, of the redeveloped Speicherstadt in Hamburg, Germany, the docklands of London, or the old Port of Montreal. What had been perceived in the local media and in the discourses of local politicians as blighted and polluted landscapes during the 1960s and 1970s, as derelict infrastructure and unsafe sites of hard work, have been turned into spaces that are described as part of these cities' outward representations as more sustainable, more accessible and inclusive, safer, and leisure-oriented.

A global investment strategy

This purported expansion of the public sphere and hopes for a sustainable era have now proliferated across the planet, benefiting not only the civic-minded but also those in search of opportunities for more mundane kinds of profits. The redevelopment of postindustrial waterfronts has become a global investment strategy. Across the Atlantic from New York, it has migrated to the maritime mouth of the cyclically sickly Celtic Tiger, where more blue-green glass towers have sprung up dockside to house the EU headquarters of tech giants such as Google (since 2004), Twitter, Airbnb, and Facebook. Dublin's International Financial Services Centre, and the so-called Silicon Docks, face each other across the river Liffey and are, respectively, the financial accomplices and the on-the-ground *pieds-à-terre* of many of the multinational corporations inverting in Ireland for tax purposes, legal-fiscal relocations that explain Ireland's staggering nominal 26 percent GDP growth in 2015 (Harpaz, 2016). The late-2016 decision by the EU competition bureau to order the payment by Apple of €13 billion in evaded taxes, to comply with Ireland's still paltry nominal corporate tax rate of 12.5 percent, has again highlighted Ireland's peculiar offshore status, both within the EU and globally, and the peculiar turn its national "industrialization by invitation" model has taken in the era of high technology (McDonough, 2016).

These knowledge-industrial location decisions, made possible by bargain-basement tax regimes and the transport and communications technologies that allow for office mobility, in turn enable the profitable reinvestment of capital within the built environment on the once-derelict old port and canal entryway. Despite the halving of housing values in the brutal bursting of the Irish property bubble in 2007, apartment rental prices in the docklands have climbed, as of 2015, 17 percent higher than they were before the crash (Padnaude, 2015), while the city as a whole has seen the temporary crisis of property values transformed into an acute, expulsive crisis of affordable housing (Boland, 2016). This set of interconnected movements shows how the silicon gilding of the Dublin docklands and the massive sums made in the property speculation that came along with it depended not only on the land freed up by shifting shipping geographies within the city but also on direct national-state intervention and the shifting of legal jurisdictions to evade *de jure* redistribution through taxation, shuffling the economic activity of global production networks through legal geographies until it fiscally disappears.

On the other end of Europe's periphery, and on the other side of the European Union's frontier, similar plans have been set in motion and similar postindustrial hopes have been sparked. The Belgrade Waterfront, hailed by some as the biggest construction project in Europe at €3.5 billion, has been at the center of a pitched political controversy since its announcement in 2012, not least because its lead (and sole named) investor, Abu Dhabi-based firm Eagle Hills, has allegedly only promised €300 million (Wright, 2015). One of the biggest social movements Serbia has seen in years has emerged to challenge the development plan following summary evictions (Wright, 2015), untransparent alterations to national building regulations to suit the needs of the project (Lalović et al., 2015), and a bizarre midnight demolition by masked men threatening observers with baseball bats hours after parliamentary election polls closed (Delauney, 2016). The intensity of the state's aid to investors over contrary views of the public interest in this case, and the drama of the forced demolitions, should not distract us too much from what they remind us about gentrification strategies in general: state giveaways of land and tax vacations to spur development have long been part of postindustrial urban development strategies by entrepreneurial city governments attempting to compete for investment dollars (Smith, 1997, 2008).

While one *Guardian* headline quipped that "Belgrade's 'top-down' gentrification is far worse than any cereal cafe," referring to the cartoon villains selling bowls of cereal for upwards of £4 in an historically working-class East London neighbourhood, the sequence of events in the Serbian capital, mere years after the port-adjacent region opened its first cafe, should give us pause (Eror, 2015). The interruption of the "normal" unfolding of the gentrification process, almost as if a form of micro-economic stage-jumping, reminds us that these imitative and competitive urban strategies are consciously implemented projects on the ground.

Investors and state actors are both aware of and attempting to replicate the success of previous examples – on often starkly different terrain.

There remains, of course, the distinct possibility that such projects, as clearly distanced as they are from the purchasing power that surrounds them, may never find buyers on the wider market – particularly given Belgrade's declining demand for office space and relative lack of the classic assets present in many competitive global cities (Lalović et al., 2015). The resulting losses may very well be collectivized as sovereign debt, shifting to the Serbian public a share of the risks well out of proportion with the private benefits that may still accrue to private actors even in the case of a failure (see Harvey, 2010: Chapter 1). Decisive action at the national-state level to facilitate the preconditions for (and to ensure maximum benefit from) such developments does not solely spring from Dublin's and Belgrade's primate-city status within their jurisdictions. As Ireland's state-led sacrifice of taxes and Serbia's deregulatory acrobatics for the waterfront investment plan tell us, local struggles over urban land use fit within, depend upon, and enable larger political visions for reorganizing the geography of economic life at multiple scales.

This politics of winners and losers is the common denominator in and beyond cities that have chosen to take the path of postindustrial waterfront development. The deliberate global reproduction of the waterfront strategy is further underscored by the presence of some of the same specialist actors at its many iterations. A German architecture firm, gmp Architekten, heavily involved in the dockland redevelopment of Hamburg's HafenCity district, was granted the contract for the planning of Nanhui New City (formerly Lingang), a planned city near Shanghai. The Chinese state has since compensated for its failure to develop as a "mini-Hong Kong" – in spite of its success in real-estate sales – by inserting eight universities, drawing 100,000 students to provide a set of productive tenants and users (Shepard, 2016). With Yangshan Free Trade Zone and its deep water port lying just on the development's doorstep, Nanhui New City is evidence of the spread of pre-planned waterfront designs, even in the form of full new cities, to sites even *within* the so-called world's factory. Global production networks and the attempts to propagate the urban and non-urban spaces they enable and require show how investment visions of successful insertion into particular positions within the increasingly scrambled scales at which the global division of labour is organized shape the recreation of the kinds of urban areas considered necessary for its operation.

A massive waterfront development program on land reclaimed from Atlantic erosion has likewise begun construction on the Gulf of Guinea, in the form of Lagos, Nigeria's Eko Atlantic business district, and has depended in its own way on a complex of shifts in costs, activities, and people at many scales. A key component within the state-led restructuring of the city of Lagos, the waterfront project is the capstone of a broader project to gentrify the city itself into a commanding business hub of sub-Saharan Africa, with familiar scenes of slum clearing (including by arson) and massive governmental land grants to private entities (Nwanna, 2015; Okeowo, 2013).

Billed as "Africa's Big Apple", this attempt to recreate the success of New York's transformation on a different economic landscape comes equipped with dedicated underground water, sewage, and energy systems, infrastructural amenities autonomous and absent even from some richer areas in the city (Okeowo, 2013). Further, in June of 2016, the state of Lagos signed an investment deal with the CEO of Smart City Dubai (a quasi-governmental Emirati LLC) to collaborate on the former's transformation into the first Smart City in Africa, "an important centre for innovation in smart technologies, wellness and destination for green tourism" (Ayorinde, 2016). Meanwhile, then-President Goodluck Jonathan's controversial 2015 edict to relocate all port activities involving Nigeria's booming oil and gas industry, including a half-built $500 million deep-water project, away from Lagos and to to-be-dredged ports in eastern Nigeria, closer to the conflict-ridden Niger Delta oilfields, shows how much the restructuring of Lagos depends on the rerouting of the externalities and benefits of extractive and transport activities well beyond the urban scale (Ogah, 2015; Post Nigeria, 2015). However one parses the intricacies of cronyism and regional politicking (Nigerian News Direct, 2016), the decongesting relocation dovetails nicely with the postindustrial, business-class vision for the reinvention of the city.

Almost as though a metaphor, abnormal ocean surges in poor districts have been blamed (Akinrefon, 2012) on the construction of the waterfront sea wall, itself designed to protect Eko Atlantic, and all of redeveloped Lagos, from surges and rising tide levels due to global warming (Adegboye, 2011; Okeowo, 2013). The question of course is, given the many scales at which Lagos is externalizing activities and people necessary to but – unsightly within – its postindustrial vision, who will be left to enjoy the Smart (and dry) Lagos, and who will pay the bill?

Infrastructural regimes beneath and beyond gentrification

The global mobility of postindustrial waterfront redevelopment as an instrument for urban investment strategies since the 1970s requires us to ask some difficult questions about the larger production-transportation-consumption geographies into which it fits. Just as Neil Smith has argued more generally about how coordinated state and investor actions aiming at the class repurposing of urban space we know as gentrification has become a global strategy for capital (2008), the particular waterfront form of this development has spread to many of the many human settlements clustered around water. As we have seen, promises of a better urban future, symbolized by the postindustrial waterfronts, have been articulated in cities in very different social and political contexts to attract (and compete for) tourist and investor capital, often exacerbating existing urban inequalities and seldom implemented as participatory community-led projects.

Doubtless, one obvious problem with the dominant discourses of progress on postindustrial waterfronts is of course that the putative new public sphere is very exclusive. It is clearly shaped with the service of particular classes and "racial" groups in mind. With port facilities and industrial work disappearing from the inner-city waterfront of New York City, for instance, the "tight-knit" communities of the industrial era (Levinson, 2008) have been replaced by highly mobile (whiter) and wealthier white-collar workers and tourists (Pries, 2008: 194). For good reasons, the forced and gradual displacement of poorer and stigmatized populations from these sites and their surrounding areas has thus been a central grounds for criticism (see Vormann and Schillings, 2013). This type of critique is of course just as valid for the displacement of traditional working classes from Dublin's docklands (Kelly, 2014) as it is for state-led development and eviction of tenants and squatters in Lagos, Nigeria (Jimoh et al., 2013; Nwanna, 2015).

These processes of displacement should not be taken lightly and they display very clearly what is wrong with a depoliticized perception of urban change as inexorable and natural. Indeed, discussions about urban futures have been removed from an (assumed) public sphere and relegated to technocrats and experts. Seeing gentrification as a planetary phenomenon (see Brenner and Schmid, 2015) redirects our view to the actual agents and politics of change. As Neil Smith has argued, we need to be cautious even of the language of "revitalization" and "regeneration," so often used also in the context of waterfront developments, because it naturalizes urban processes and "sugar-coats gentrification" so that "the advocacy of regeneration strategies disguises the quintessentially social origins and goals of urban change and erases the politics of winners and losers out of which such policies emerge" (Smith, 2008: 98). In a similar vein, Tom Slater has diagnosed the "eviction of critical perspectives from gentrification research," a discourse that has instead been "appropriated by those intent on finding and recommending quick-fix 'solutions' to complex urban problems" (Slater, 2006: 752). From this perspective, discourses of revitalization on urban waterfronts are symptoms of an increasingly undemocratic society.

But criticizing these transformations of postindustrializing sites across the planet as forms of gentrification is not enough. As we can already infer from the few examples outlined so far, gentrification is only one visible instance of a wider mesh of political-economic projects in which social vulnerabilities are exploited and risks shifted. For us to understand the politics of winners and losers around the postindustrial waterfront, we need to redirect our focus from the symbolic reinvention of the city proper to its spatial reorganization in the context of geographical economic restructuring. We can thus grasp the different dimensions of cost-shifting and displacement effectuated by postindustrial urbanization processes. If we stop at a critique of neighborhood gentrification, as important as it certainly is, the shifting of many other costs within and especially *beyond* the city as a whole will remain invisible to us. Improved waterfronts are not only designed with specific wealthy users in mind, and at the expense of the former residents they expel, but likewise depend upon the ramping up of displaced industrial activities elsewhere, and the flurry of land-clearing, pollution externalities, job casualization, and splintered infrastructural underdevelopment (see Graham and Marvin, 2001) required to take on the necessary city-sustaining functions of the decommissioned Fordist urban port.

As we argue in the remainder of this article, a focus on large-scale infrastructures helps us to rearticulate the terrain on which we pose certain questions about urban change, and thus to formulate a critique. It is crucial to understand how the imbrication of waterfront developments and gentrification projects depends on the actions of national and local states in financing additions to the property market and within broader regulatory and tax regimes. We must adapt our perspective to grasp how decisions about the reorganization of production and distribution function in practice, decisions that created the idled, disinvested land that the waterfront strategy seeks to set into a new kind of economic motion. To end our analysis at the scenes of urban displacement would miss key enabling conditions – likewise political decisions – that underpin these forms of urban development and labor transformation, and thus may lead us to view the cost shifts these developments depend upon within too narrow a spatial terrain.

Indeed, the 1975 New York City fiscal crisis that precipitated its industrial restructuring – which David Harvey has called the "opening shot in the [. . .] restoration of class power" following the Fordist compromise (2006: xxii) – was a symptom of a larger systemic change in the way that goods are produced, distributed, and consumed. In many ways, it is the scaling-up of production networks that has produced the conditions of possibility for the new postindustrial waterfront to emerge. The containerization of trade was an important, albeit often neglected aspect of these larger changes and has facilitated global production networks that depend on frictionless supply chains and efficient container ports. This logic of seamless flow often became paramount in local concerns and contestations (Hesse, 2013). The ensuing relocation of expanded container port activities (needing deeper water and more space) downstream to Brooklyn and, more importantly, to Newark and Elizabeth, New Jersey, opened up former industrial port spaces in downtown Manhattan for redevelopment, regeneration, and the branding of a new image of the city that would reflect the ascent of the new service and knowledge-based economy.

A change in economic regimes has resulted in a changed use of the urban waterfront from a place of production to one of cultural consumption, and this is precisely the attempted development we have traced through different examples across the planet. More specifically, once we broaden our perspective we realize that the spatial and infrastructural realignment of New York City was a correlate of the transition from Fordist mass production – where industrial activity was located in the inner-city for technological and political reasons – to flexible accumulation and global, just-in-time production networks.

The spatial unbundling of production processes was facilitated precisely through a new *infrastructural regime* – a historically and geographically specific set of networked mobility infrastructures – based, essentially, on containerization and the rise of new IT technologies as well as on political reforms on scales other than the local that provided the necessary legal and regulatory frameworks. In this transition to facilitate global production networks, the costs of producing, distributing, and consuming goods have been redistributed. While the postindustrial waterfront has risen as the site of a questionable new public sphere and promises of the good life, costs have been relocated both within and beyond the global city.

The postindustrial waterfront's hidden costs

However postindustrial these consumption spaces may appear, they of course rest on globalized infrastructures that enable manufacturing activities to be distributed far from each other and from their markets. Concurrent with an increased exploitation of global economic unevenness to link sites of cheap labor with consumers at the point of sale, sea traffic has skyrocketed – and has reshaped the face of urban logistics. On a global scale, the movement of shipping containers more than tripled from 1970 to 2007, and in the two decades following 1990, world container throughput has increased sixfold (UNCTAD, 2011: 86). In this process, a new systemic logic of frictionless circulation has come to dominate urban and regional planning, requiring deeper harbours, quicker intermodal forwarding, and greater volume than older urban agglomerations could provide, and these suburban relocations of restructured port functions have also transformed lives far from the gentrifying city center (see Vormann, 2015; Wachsmuth, 2016).

Massive undertakings of cost-shifting in the transition from Fordism to post-Fordist global production networks have taken place on multiple dimensions and scales, from intra- to inter-city, from regional to planetary. Some costs were shifted immediately at the moment of transition in the 1970s; others have been externalized more permanently and passively over the decades to follow. If, on the postindustrial waterfront, the hard work of the pre-container breakbulk era seems to have faded into the past, working conditions in the container ports and the deregulated transportation industries do not speak of a better present, and hardly foreshadow a brighter future. These cost shifts cascade not only through the city itself but also up and down supply chains, allowing for the reorganization of the regional economies and urban spaces they link and those they bypass. As we have stressed, these are not the outcomes of natural processes, but of connected political decisions.

An important way to reduce transportation costs has been the deregulation of transportation industries. This included the privatization of many ports as well as the deregulation of trucking, shipping, and the railroad industries. While the number of longshoremen and railroad workers has decreased significantly since the 1980s, and while the occupations of North American and Western European seafarers have to a large extent been passed on to crews from countries in the Global South and Eastern Europe with lower labor standards and who specialize in their export, such as the Philippines, Indonesia, China, and Russia, the number of truck drivers within the United States has steadily risen due to deregulation and a series of advantages of road transportation vis-à-vis rail freight, most notably speed, flexibility, and price (Madar, 2000: 3; Rodrigue et al., 2009).

In the United States, all these measures to reduce transportation costs and facilitate seamless circulation were implemented by the state in a series of legislative changes in the 1970s and 1980s, and constitute a complementary set of policies to the free trade agreements that followed in subsequent years (Vormann, 2015). These measures were replicated elsewhere because the dominant position of the United States in global production networks helped to push labor practices into other national contexts. Transnational arbitrage between labor markets has pushed the costs of cheap transportation to those least able to refuse them.

The port-trucking industry is a particularly blatant example of the deliberate relocation of costs within the supply chain that has occurred in this process. Deregulation policies in the United States have lowered entry barriers, fragmented the labor force of the port-trucking industries, and led to risky, contingent, and low-paid work for independent contractors (Belzer, 2000; Bensman, 2009). By intensifying competition and shifting responsibilities after the Motor Carrier Act of 1980, the fluctuations of the shipping business – and risks of overcapacity or shortages associated with it – have been relegated to the workers through the establishment of per-load, short-term contracts (Viscelli, 2016). The costs of overcapacity, of sitting on idled capital, are paid by the individual contractor in waiting time and performing social reproduction during incomeless periods, and externalized from the firm, who no longer has to pay permanent employees through periods of overcapacity who have nothing economically productive to do. These externalized labor costs are matched by substandard labor policies in the Global South, often hierarchically dominated by big-box stores and retailers in the north, able to enter arm's-length contracts with suppliers in China.

Further, the new infrastructural regime of just-in-time containerized trade has led to a displacement of waterfront workers: both physically, from inner-city waterfronts to the container port on the edge of postindustrial urban agglomerations, and numerically, having been reduced by as much as 60 percent in some countries from 1970 to the mid-1980s through automation (Bonacich and Wilson, 2008: 177). More metaphorically, formerly decently paid and protected jobs in the transportation industries have been replaced by highly flexible, "independent" jobs (Bensman, 2009; Bensman et al., 2012). In this process, to which we will return shortly, costs and risks of the supply chain have been shifted down to current and laid-off transportation workers. It is worth noting in parenthesis that through the subsequent decreases in transportation costs, processes of economic restructuring and territorial deindustrialization have been reinforced, equally undermining the leverage of unions in other industries and thereby extending the externalization of costs to other spheres of society.

One might argue that these examples of cost-shifting are overly specific. One might equally be tempted to insist that the negative impacts of containerization on manufacturing industries in the United States belong to the past and are not worthy of scholarly and public attention today. But the impacts of the logistics revolution go deeper than that – and they shape the politics of the present.

On a more abstract level, the bottlenecks of trade have been realms of contestation and historical strongholds of union activism (Mitchell, 2011). It is not a coincidence, then, that the breaking up of resistance on the industrial waterfront by means of containerization resulted in the breakdown of labor organizations in the transportation industries and had repercussions in other sectors and industries. But pushing the costs onto other labor regimes is just one aspect of externalization to keep trade cheap. Another transnational cost-factor that clearly transcends the borders of North Atlantic states is shipping pollution and its impact on port-adjacent communities, industrializing countries, and future generations.

State action might seem more passive today than it was in the formative decades of the 1970s and 1980s, but its consistent *non*-regulation of environmental and social externalities from the transportation industries is essential to the functioning of global production networks. In fact, non-regulation by the state has led to some very tangible consequences that affect some more than others. With the tripling of trade and traffic since the mid-1970s, port-adjacent communities and those communities who live near the new major transportation corridors have become hotspots of unregulated environmental pollution. Inhabitants from Newark and Elizabeth, NJ, communities close to North America's most important port on the East Coast, the Port of New York and New Jersey, are disproportionately exposed to carcinogenic diesel fumes – and are largely non-white populations who earn less than a fifth of the incomes of residents on the postindustrial waterfronts of Lower Manhattan (WHO, 2012; Bloch et al., 2010).

These port-adjacent communities could be seen as the postindustrial waterfront's "twin"; the changes in these places are both related effects of deindustrialization, but while, in the New York case, Manhattan's shorelines attracted investment due to their proximity to economic and political power elites, Elizabeth and Newark have suffered disinvestment and decline. Likewise, on a global scale, the massive increase in shipping traffic has left heavy-traffic shipping corridors like the Horn of Africa absorbing the costs of pollution while reaping very few of the benefits (Cowen, 2014). Perhaps more than any other global region, East Asia has been affected by the global increases in shipping emissions. The health effects of this pollution have caused thousands of deaths (Liu et al., 2016), presenting to us the darkest side of postindustrial urbanization on a hyper-industrialized planet.

The importance of the political

There is a clear mismatch between the narrative of sustainable progress and the realities of these postindustrial cities as nodes in broader global production networks – one that is even missed by more critical accounts. While processes of marketization have led to seemingly more sustainable, leisurely, and safe places on the postindustrial waterfront – sites of high visibility that have come to be regarded as representative of the city as a whole – this utopian discourse obfuscates the infrastructures and networked mobility spaces (Graham, 2001) that are necessary to maintain these sites and makes it easy to forget the unevenness and externalities of urbanization processes that stretch beyond city limits and offshore, across and into the ocean.

Given sizable environmental and social externalities, the notion of having arrived in a postindustrial era, a utopia of a leisurely, secure and sustainable system is a misrepresentation of social relations. Rather than resolving the pathologies, the risks and liabilities of the industrial age, the costs of the new accumulation regime have simply been relocated in a new infrastructural context. Poverty and pollution have been relegated away from the cities' most visible sites to other places within and outside the city.

The postindustrial platforms on the waterfront are built on seas of infrastructure and externalized costs. These two spaces – the logistics hubs and the postindustrial city – are two sides of the same coin. Their emergence as unequal twins is not a matter of technological determinism and external flows of globalization, however, but of deliberate state action and decisive inaction. While the waterfront has become the emblematic trademark of many a city, its logistics spaces fell into oblivion and became highly functional spaces realigned in order to facilitate reliable, flexible and cost-efficient trade. In a move from the Fordist regime of accumulation toward global production networks, city spaces have been recast to suit the logic of seamless supply chains and just-in-time production. Functional urban elements may well be reorganized in the transition from one economic order to another but they do not simply vanish. In this article, the focus on infrastructure has helped us view globalization processes in international trade not as apolitical, universal processes, external to the city, but as historically specific, geographically situated, and produced on the ground.

The questions that we can pose from such a perspective are fundamentally questions of legitimacy and accountability. In the new context of global production networks, a small number of actors have been able to externalize their costs and impose them on wide sections of society, particularly on its lower strata, with the help of the state. Not only are some better off – those who are "Richer, Smarter, Greener, Healthier, and Happier" (Glaeser, 2011) – but some are actually losing. In this sense, decisions about which types of social relations should be enabled through infrastructure and supported by the state should be subject to democratic, not technocratic debate. That is, the globe-trotting path of this strategy for remobilizing land and infrastructure made idle by a set of political and economic decisions to shift costs within global transport and production networks does not attest to it being a natural or inevitable outcome of dynamic property markets on the ground, nor of globalizing technological change in itself, but of often state-led decisions about who will pay for costs, how, and where.

These multiple movements – in space, in time, and across balance sheets – enable each other, but not in any simple Newtonian sense. They are as much social and political as they are geographical and economic. The displacement of people and ways of life, through sudden demolitions and formal resettlement, through the slow attrition of rising rents and quality-of-life policing, through abandonment by industrial flight and infrastructural neglect; the shifts in land use and land ownership, as immoveable land circulates through the property market and capital moves in and out of flipped buildings, pushing property values up and down; the unbundling and reshuffling of sites and channels of extractive, productive, and distributive activities – these are achieved through a series of interlocking political projects of creating and shaping infrastructure, the "matter that enable the movement of other matter" (Larkin, 2013: 239). The cumulative effects of these infrastructural projects sink certain social and geographical relations into the ground, enabling certain movements and disallowing others, accumulating pools of wealth in some hands and tailing ponds in others.

Strategies for making the most of idled or underperforming assets within the shifting sands of capitalist geography travel too, often bringing with them and depending upon cost shifts up and down the supply chain. Such strategies may not, and likely cannot, work everywhere, as conscious imitation bumps up against unevenness, institutional heterogeneity, dissensus and resistance, and competition on the ground. While entrepreneurs and governments turn to building glistening new waterside developments even on land far from classic ports, simply to recreate the glowing feel of previous successes for investors, they are no less part of this larger historical and geographical set of cost shifts that unevenly distribute the clean lifestyle of sustainability far from the worn-out places that sustain it. By taking such a multiscalar and infrastructural perspective, we can see that the politics of winners and losers emerging from these postindustrial waterfront projects neither begins nor ends at the water's edge.

Notes

1 Our work resonates with inroads made by scholars that take the perspective of planetary urbanization to address the shortcomings of sustainable city debates, notably Angelo et al. (2016).
2 The institutions and socio-spatial arrangements of the Fordist era were viewed in public discourses, for instance, in comment sections and articles of local newspapers, as the main culprits for the derelict state of the waterfront (Vormann, 2015). As eminent port city scholar Brian S. Hoyle put it, the downstream movement of the container port resulted in a "vacuum, an abandoned doorstep, a problematic planning zone [. . .] and a zone of pronounced dereliction and decay where once all had been bustle and interchange and activity" (Hoyle, 2000: 397). The disappearance of industries and port activities, in turn, sharpened an acute sense of crisis and an urge for redevelopment.
3 South Street Seaport, for instance, which imitates a pre- to early industrial 19th century neighborhood, and which was completed as a project in the 1980s, unites this binary fiction. At once pointing toward a glorious past and toward a time yet-to-come as a site of new white-collar work in a service-oriented future, this double move, so dominant in many of the revitalization campaigns of waterfronts on the North American continent, has served to render Fordist industrialism into an illegitimate intermezzo (Vormann, 2014, 2015).

References

Adegboye, K. (2011). Developer Denies Claim that Eko Atlantic wall contributed to ocean surge. *Vanguard*, 20 September 2011.

Akinrefon, D. (2012). PDP asks FG to halt sand filling of Lagos beach. *Vanguard*, 21 August 2012.

Angelo, H., Wachsmuth, D., Cohen, D. (2016). Expand the frontiers of urban sustainability. *Nature*. 536: 391–393.

Ayorinde, S. (2016). Lagos signs historic smart city deal with Dubai. *Lagos State Government Centre of Excellence*, 21 June 2016. Available at: http://akinwunmiambode.com/lagos-state-government-signs-historic-smart-city-deal-with-dubai/

Belzer, M. H. (2000). *Sweatshops on Wheels: Winners and Losers in Trucking Deregulation*. Oxford: Oxford University Press.

Bensman, D. (2009). Port trucking down the low road: A sad story of deregulation. 20 July 2009. Available at: www.demos.org/publication.cfm?currentpublicationID=9DCA474F-3FF4-6C82-5517F7989318548B Accessed 27 January 2010.

Bensman, D., Smith, R., Marvey, P. (2012). The big rig: Poverty, pollution, and the misclassification of truck drivers at America's ports. National Employment Law Project. Available at: http://smlr.rutgers.edu/DavidBensman/News/BensmanDriver_Survey_Report%201%2023%2009.pdf. Accessed 28 July 2017.

Bloch, M., Carter, S., McLean, A. (2010). Mapping America: Every city, every block. Available at: http://projects.nytimes.com/census/2010/explorer Accessed 28 July 2017.

Boland, V. (2016). Ireland: Too many houses in the wrong place. *The Financial Times*, 21 June 2016. Available at: www.ft.com/content/ba41c19e-3478-11e6-ad39-3fee5ffe5b5b

Bonacich, E., Wilson, J. B. (2008). *Getting the Goods: Ports, Labor, and the Logistics Revolution*. Ithaca, NY: Cornell University Press.

Boyer, M. C. (1996). *The City of Collective Memory: Its Historical Imagery and Architectural Entertainments*. Cambridge and London: MIT Press.

Boyer, M. C. (1997). Cities for Sale: Merchandising History at South Street Seaport. In: M. Sorkin (ed.), *Variations on a Theme Park: The New American City and the End of Public Space*. 8th ed. New York: Hill and Wang. pp. 181–204.

Brenner, N., Schmid, C. (2015). Towards a new epistemology of the urban. *City*. 19 (2): 151–182.

Butzel, A. K. (2007). Foreword. In: S. Seccombe (ed.), *Lost Waterfront: The Decline and Rebirth of Manhattan's Western Shore*. Bronx, NY: Fordham University Press/Friends of Hudson River Park. pp. 5–6.

Cowen, D. (2014). *The Deadly Life of Logistics: Mapping Violence in Global Trade*. Minneapolis: University of Minnesota Press.

Delauney, G. (2016). Controversy surrounds Belgrade waterfront development. *BBC News*, 21 June 2016. Available at: www.bbc.com/news/business-36576420

Eror, A. (2015). Belgrade's 'top-down' gentrification is far worse than any cereal cafe. *The Guardian*, 10 December 2015. Available at: www.theguardian.com/cities/2015/dec/10/belgrade-top-down-gentrification-worse-than-cereal-cafe

Ferreira, S., Visser, G. (2007). Creating an African riviera: Revisiting the impact of the Victoria and Alfred waterfront development in Cape Town. *Urban Forum*. 18 (3): 227–246.

Fu, M., Jin, X., Shang, Y., Shindell, D., Faluvegi, G., Shindell, C., He, K. (2016). Health and climate impacts of ocean-going vessels in East Asia. *Nature Climate Change*. 6: 1037–1042.

Gastil, R. (2002). *Beyond the Edge: New York's New Waterfront*. 1st ed. New York: Princeton Architectural Press.

Glaeser, E. L. (2011). *Triumph of the City: How Our Greatest Invention Makes Us Richer, Smarter, Greener, Healthier, and Happier*. New York: Penguin Press.

Graham, S. (2001). Flow city. *DISP*. 144: 4–11.

Graham, S., Marvin, S. (2001). *Splintering Urbanism. Networked Infrastructures, Technological Mobilities and the Urban Condition*. New York: Routledge.

Greenberg, M. (2008). *Branding New York: How a City in Crisis Was Sold to the World*. New York: Routledge.

Harpaz, J. (2016). World economies watch as Ireland reaps 26% GDP windfall on tax inversions. *Forbes*, 18 July 2016. Available at: www.forbes.com/#23a02bf22254

Harvey, D. (2006). *The Limits to Capital*. London: Verso.

Harvey, D. (2010). *The Enigma of Capital: And the Crises of Capitalism*. Oxford: Oxford University Press.

Hesse, M. (2013). Cities and flows: Re-asserting a relationship as fundamental as it is delicate. *Journal of Transport Geography*. 29: 33–42.

Hoyle, B. S. (2000). Global and local change on the port-city waterfront. *Geographical Review*. 90 (3): 395–417.

Jimoh, H. O., Omole, F. K., Omosulu, S. B. (2013). An examination of urban renewal exercise of Badia East of Lagos State, Nigeria. *International Journal of Education and Research*. 1 (5): 1–14.

Kelly, S. (2014). Taking Liberties: Gentrification as Neoliberal Urban Policy in Dublin. In: A. MacLaran and S. Kelly (eds.), *Neoliberal Urban Policy and the Transformation of the City*. Springer, VS: Wiesbaden. pp. 174–188.

Lalović, K., Radosavljević, U., Đukanović, Z. (2015). Reframing public interest in the implementation of large urban projects in Serbia: The case of the Belgrade waterfront project. *Facta Universitatis* (Architecture and Civil Engineering). 13 (1): 25–46.

Larkin, B. (2013). The politics and poetics of infrastructure. *Annual Review of Anthropology*. 42: 327–343.

Levinson, M. (2008). *The Box: How the Shipping Container Made the World Smaller and the World Economy Bigger*. 9th ed. Princeton, NJ: Princeton University Press.

Liu, R. et al. (2016). Ambient Air Pollution Exposures and Risk of Parkinson Disease. *Environmental Health Perspectives*. 124: 1759–1765.

Madar, D. (2000). *Heavy Traffic: Deregulation, Trade, and Transformation in North American Trucking*. Vancouver: University of British Columbia Press/Michigan State University Press.

McDonough, T. (2016). Ireland's bad apples. *Jacobin*, 9 September 2016. Available at: www.jacobinmag.com/2016/09/ireland-tax-haven-apple-inversion-eu

Mitchell, T. (2011). *Carbon Democracy: Political Power in the Age of Oil*. London and New York: Verso.

Nigerian News Direct (2016). Atiku's firm in $500m investment controversy. *Nigeria News Direct*, 29 February 2016.

Nwanna, C. (2015). Gentrification in Nigeria: The Case of Two Housing Estates in Lagos. In: L. Lees, H. B. Shin and E. López-Morales (eds.), *Global Gentrifications: Uneven Development and Displacement*. Bristol: Policy Press. pp. 311–328.

Ogah, D. (2015). Controversy trails directive on oil, gas cargo diversion, LADOL relocation. *The Guardian Nigeria*, 7 June 2015. Available at: https://guardian.ng/business-services/controversy-trails-directive-on-oil-gas-cargo-diversion-ladol-relocation/

Okeowo, A. (2013). A safer waterfront in Lagos, if you can afford it. *The New Yorker*, 20 August 2013. Available at: www.newyorker.com/business/currency/a-safer-waterfront-in-lagos-if-you-can-afford-it

Padnaude, A. (2015). Tech Workers Flock to Dublin's Silicon Docks. *The Wall Street Journal*, 28 May 2015. Available at: www.wsj.com/articles/tech-workers-flock-to-dublins-silicon-docks-1432822827

Post Nigeria (2015). Courts reverse FG's N500million oil project relocation. *Post Nigeria*, 16 May 2015. Available at: www.post-nigeria.com/courts-reverse-fgs-n500million-oil-project-relocation/

Pries, M. (2008). *Waterfronts im Wandel. Baltimore und New York*. Stuttgart: Franz Steiner Verlag.

Rodrigue, J.-P., Comtois, C., Slack, B. (2009). *The Geography of Transport Systems*. London and New York: Routledge.

Scharenberg, A., Bader, I. (2009). Berlin's waterfront site struggle. *City*. 13 (2–3): 325–335.

Shepard, W. (2016). One way that China populates its ghost cities. *Forbes*, 19 January 2016. Available at: www.forbes.com/sites/wadeshepard/2016/01/19/one-way-that-china-populates-its-ghost-cities/

Slater, T. (2006). The eviction of critical perspectives from gentrification research. *International Journal of Urban and Regional Research*. 30: 737–757.

Smith, N. (1997). *The New Urban Frontier: Gentrification and the Revanchist City*. London and New York: Routledge.

Smith, N. (2008). New Globalism, New Urbanism: Gentrification as Global Urban Strategy. In: N. Brenner (ed.), *Spaces of Neoliberalism: Urban Restructuring in North America and Western Europe*. Malden: Blackwell. pp. 80–103.

United Nations Conference on Trade and Development, UNCTAD (2011). *Review of Maritime Transport*. New York and Geneva: United Nations Publication.

Viscelli, S. (2016). *The Big Rig: Trucking and the Decline of the American Dream*. Oakland, CA: University of California Press.

Vormann, B. (2014). Infrastrukturen der globalen Stadt. Widersprüche des urbanen Nachhaltigkeitsdiskurses am Beispiel Vancouvers. *Zeitschrift für Kanada-Studien*. 63: 62–86.

Vormann, B. (2015). *Global Port Cities in North America: Urbanization Processes and Global Production Networks*. New York and London: Routledge.

Vormann, B., Schillings, S. (2013). The vanishing poor: Frontier narratives in New York City's gentrification and security debates. *Critical Planning*. 20: 145–165.

Wachsmuth, D. (2016). Infrastructure alliances: Supply-chain expansion and multi-city growth coalitions. *Economic Geography*. 93 (1): 44–65.

Wonneberger, A. (2008). Notions on Community, Locality and Changing Space in the Dublin Docklands. In: W. Kokot, M. Gandelsman-Trier, K. Wildner and A. Wonneberger (eds.), *Port Cities as Areas of Transition: Ethnographic Perspectives*. Bielefeld: Transcript. pp. 47–73.

World Health Organization, WHO (2012). IARC: Diesel engine exhaust carcinogenic. Press Release. 213. Lyon, France, 12 June 2012.

Wright, H. (2015). Belgrade waterfront: An unlikely place for Gulf petrodollars to settle. *The Guardian*, 10 December 2015. Available at: www.theguardian.com/cities/2015/dec/10/belgrade-waterfront-gulf-petrodollars-exclusive-waterside-development

6 Costs and benefits of mobility

The case of Chinese seafarers

Lijun Tang and Gang Chen

Introduction

This chapter discusses issues of mobility related to seafarers. Seafarers are mobile primarily because of their workplace – ships, which transport cargo from one port to another across seas and oceans. Their mobility is further enhanced by the fact that rather than confined to the national fleet, many seafarers work on ships flying foreign flags and owned and managed by foreign shipping companies. This enhanced mobility is related to the practice commonly known as flagging out in the shipping industry, which allows ship owners/managers to register their ships in Flag of Convenience (FOC) countries, such as Liberia and Panama, and to employ seafarers from any labour supply countries without restrictions and on short-term contracts. As such, this enhanced mobility results in widespread temporary employment in shipping. When seafarers are hired on a short-term basis, their employment becomes precarious, and they may have to move frequently to the next contract, maybe with a different employer. This can be understood as employment mobility. In the first two sections, drawing up existing literature, we discuss the first two types of mobility and the negative effects on seafarers. The remaining parts discuss some consequences of employment mobility through examining the social security coverage of Chinese seafarers.

Mobile workplace

As merchant ships sail at sea, seafarers have to be away from home as well as from land for a period of time, which results in intermittent separation from their families. The separation period can be between a few weeks to more than a year, depending on many factors, such as types of ships, and seafarers' rank and nationality.

Working at sea means seafarers are confined to their ships and suffering from social isolation (Sampson and Thomas, 2002). Furthermore, shipboard working environment is full of hazards, such as noise, vibration, ship movement, heavy machinery, steel structure, and long working hours; when things go wrong in the middle of vast oceans, such as bad weather, illness, and engine failure, it is difficult to get help from the outside world, and seafarers have to rely on themselves.

Unsurprisingly, the safety record of the shipping industry has been a concern of the stakeholders (Bloor et al., 2000). For example, Danish research suggested that Danish fleet seafarers were about six times more likely to die from occupational accidents compared with Danish workers ashore in modern days (Hansen, 1996; Borch et al., 2012).

Being confined to ships and cut off from the rest of the world, seafarers have limited means to communicate with their families ashore and are unable to participate in family activities (Tang, 2007). Consequently, they are likely to miss many important family and social events, for example, children growing up, and celebrations of birthdays and festivals. This exacerbates the sense of social isolation on ships.

More importantly, working at sea and intermittent separation poses problems for intimate and personal relationships. According to Baumeister and Leary (1995), intimate relationships entail both physical proximity as well as frequent and pleasant interactions in a continuous and shared temporal framework. Sharing time together is believed to be good for relationships, and in fact, the most enjoyable time for couples has been reported to be leisure time spent together (Sullivan, 1996). For seafarers and their spouses, intermittent separation makes longing for each other's company a painful but frequent experience (Tang, 2012). Furthermore, seafarers' intermittent absence also means that they are not able to spend time with their friends, which makes it difficult for them to sustain friendships at home (Thomas, 2003). As a consequence, seafarers often feel socially isolated when they are home.

From the perspective of seafarers' spouses, apart from longing for their beloved ones, they also suffer from a series of problems related to seafarers' absence. They have to manage everything at home without support from their spouses. Also due to separation, seafarers' spouses feel that they live different lifestyles and have different experiences from other women whose partners work ashore. As a consequently, they tend to separate themselves from others and felt that non-seafaring people could not fully appreciate and understand their situation, which in turn leads to socially isolation (Tang, 2007; Thomas, 2003).

Due to these problems, seafaring is not regarded as an attractive vocation. People from developed countries are reluctant to find a career at sea and ship managers there have to look elsewhere for alternatives (Grey, 1991; Wallis, 2009). In fact, the number of seafarers from OECD countries has reduced dramatically since the 1970s. This reduction is also related to flagging out and the rise of the global seafarer labour market, to which we turn next.

Mobile capital

The second type of mobility is related to flagging out. Until around the late 1960s, the majority of ship owners registered their ships in home countries and employed domestic seafarers. As much of the maritime business was operated and owned by ship owners from the advanced economies, such as the United Kingdom, Japan and Norway, these States were widely known as the Traditional Maritime Nations

(TMN) which generally imposed high standards for admitting ships in their registries and maintained stringent regulatory practices (Alderton and Winchester, 2002). However, from the mid-1960s, flagging out started to gain momentum, as the transfer of assets to a FOC provided several benefits for ship owners. First, the regulatory framework of FOCs offered ship owners a set of relaxed regulatory requirements, thus lowering labour, safety and environment standards in the industry. Second, it brought about a competitive cost advantage, such as low registration fees and tonnage tax (DeSombre, 2006). Furthermore, FOCs did not impose any restriction on the nationality of seafarers, the ship owners increasingly began to employ low-wage seafarers from new labour supply nations, such as from the East European, East and South-East Asian countries. This enabled consolidation of economic advantage by engaging in increased cross-border activity and exploitation of various resources. It also gives rise to a global seafarer labour market (Alderton et al., 2004; ILO, 2001).

The global labour market leads to enhanced mobility of seafarers. Needless to say, this enhanced mobility is driven by the mobility of shipping capital which aims to cut cost and maximize profit. As such, while mobile shipping capital brings much needed job opportunities to newly emerging seafarer supply countries, it also has negative impacts on the working and employment conditions in the industry. To save running costs, ship owners/managers increasingly employ cheaper seafarers from new labour supply nations on short-term contracts, which serves to end the practice of permanent employment. Research evidence shows that the 'majority of seafarers worked on contracts covering a single voyage or tour of duty', which was typically between 5 and 12 months, but some were for longer, and employers thus have no obligation towards the seafarers' future employability (ILO, 2001: 64; see also Kahveci and Nichols, 2006).

Accompanying the structural change of the industry is technological advancement (ILO, 2001). Ship operations have become more automated, which led to significant reductions in crew size. Adoption of new technology, however, is not necessarily globally synchronized. Morris and Donn (1997) examined the relationship between new technology and industrial relations in US and Australian shipping. They found that strong resistance from maritime unions coupled with public policies protecting and subsidising national fleets made fleet modernisation in the 2 countries about 15 to 20 years lagging behind other OECD countries. This finding suggests that when they were strong, national maritime unions played an important role in protecting seafarers' jobs. However, Morris and Donn also noted that as US and Australian governments leaned towards neoliberalism economic policies in the 1980s, maritime trade unions could no longer resist technological changes in shipping. Furthermore, the rise of FOCs has dwindled national fleets of OECD countries significantly, which also weakens the influence of national unions. As such, the average crew size of Australian merchant navy fleet was reduced from 35 in 1982 to 16 in 1994 (Morris and Donn, 1997).

Technological innovations have also made ships sail faster and greatly reduced port turnaround time (Kahveci, 1999). In one typical port, the data suggested that vessel berth time on average was cut from 138.50 hours in 1970 to about 15.75 in

1998 (Kahveci, 1999). Even though technology makes some ship operations less demanding, it can hardly replace manpower in berthing and un-berthing operations. Reduction in crew size and turnaround time means that there are fewer people but less time to do the same amount of work, which inevitably results in work intensification (ILO, 2001; Kahveci, 1999). Thus it is not surprising that fatigue has been a serious concern in the industry for many years and subject to extensive research and discussion (Smith, 2007).

The earlier discussion does not imply that protecting seafarers' rights and improving working and employment conditions have been overlooked. The International Transport Workers' Federation (ITF) provides union support to the seafarers at the global level, and it has been working at the transnational level successfully, bargaining for seafarers' wages by negotiating with seafaring unions in TMN and in new labour supply nations (Lillie, 2005). In 2006, the International Labour Organization adopted the Maritime Labour Convention (MLC) to protect seafarers and promote decent work in this sector. It imposes regulatory requirements on issues related to working and living conditions on ships, employment conditions, and welfare and social security. In 2013, the convention came into force globally. The effect of MLC enforcement on labour standards, however, remains to be seen.

As mentioned, the global seafaring labour market is characterized by precarious employment, which can be regarded as employment mobility. Research in land-based industries indicates that employers in general do not buy social insurance for temporary and contracted labour (Smith, 2015). This question arising here is what problems employment mobility might pose on the MLC implementation. In remaining sections of this article, we address this question using the case of Chinese seafarers as an example.

Mobile employment

The case of Chinese seafarers

China is a major seafaring labour supply country and at the same time controls a large national fleet. According to the most recent BIMCO Manpower Report (2015), China has become the top seafarer labour supply country with 243,635 seafarers, followed by the Philippines with 215,000 seafarers. Other major seafarer supply countries are Indonesia (143,702), Russia (87,061), India (86,084), and Ukraine (69,000). However, according to Chinese official statistics (MSA, 2016), in 2015, a total number of 638,990 Chinese held valid seafarer certificates,[1] and 133,326 of them worked on foreign ships. The majority of Chinese seafarers are still from relatively richer coastal provinces, such as Shandong, Jiangsu, Zhejiang, Fujian, and Guangdong, though some inland provinces, such as Hubei and Henan, also produce a large number of seafarers (MSA, 2016).

Over the last three and half decades or so, the employment of seafarers has undergone significant transformations in China. First, Chinese seafarers started to work on foreign ships in 1979, and the following decades witnessed a growing number of them deployed overseas. Second, the transition from a planned economy to a market one which started in the early 1980s opened the market for private shipping companies and crewing agencies to crop up and grow. As a result, employment of seafarers has been diversified. Third, when the employment market was monopolized by state- or local-government-owned shipping companies, Chinese seafarers were employed for life and their welfare was looked after by their employers. With the deepening of the market reform, seafarers' employment was gradually changed to contract based. Thus, in the 1990s, seafarers working at state- or local-government-owned shipping companies had permanent or long-term contracts, while those working for private ship owners and crewing agencies were likely to have short-term contracts, three to five years, for example. At the same time, a group of 'freelance' seafarers also appeared in the labour market who secure employment through crewing agencies on contracts covering a tour of duty only. Therefore, the employment of Chinese seafarers is no longer universally fixed for life to state-owned companies, and a range of employment practices co-exist and compete with each other today. Needless to say, seafarers are more mobile when their contract length is shorter as they are more likely to change employers frequently.

Research evidence in the early 2000s suggested that working on foreign ships was much more attractive than on the national fleet as the former offered higher salaries and more job opportunities (Wu, 2004). Consequently, many seafarers employed by state-owned shipping companies wanted to break free from their employers in order to work for crewing agencies. This resulted in a rapid increase in the number of freelance seafarers who worked for crewing agencies on tour-of-duty contracts (Wu et al., 2006). State-owned shipping companies, however, did not want to lose their workforce. To retain seafarers, they were reported to control their seafarers' certificates (Wu et al., 2006; Zhao, 2011): when seafarers are on leave, their company would collect their certificates to make sure that they would not be able to work for other companies. Nevertheless, it is fair to say that Chinese seafarers increasingly choose to be highly mobile for better pay and job opportunities.

It is also important to note that the changes related to seafarers' employment take place in the bigger context of the transformation of employment relations in China. Until the early 1990s, workers were in general employed permanently without contracts. In 1996, the *Labour Law* came into force, which introduced a labour contract system. The main purpose of this contract system was to 'smash the iron rice bowl', which referred to life-long employment. Gradually, permanent employment is replaced with one that is contract based, even though some contracts are open-ended.

In 2008, China's new *Labour Contract Law* (LCL) came into effect, providing more protections for labour. It requires all workers to have a written contract and stipulates that an open-term labour contract is deemed in effect if an employee has successfully concluded two consecutive fixed-term contracts or has worked for the employer for one year without a written contract. It also requires employers to contribute to their employees' social insurance, and social insurance should be included in the employee's labour contract. There are five types of social insurance, all of which are predominantly provided through employers: pensions, medical, unemployment, work injury, and maternity insurances. Both employers and employees are required to make financial contributions to the social insurance programs. Another important employment-based benefit, the housing provident fund, was established in 1994 to help employees establish personal housing fund accounts and increase housing affordability as housing became privatized and housing prices rose drastically. The administration and financing of the housing provident fund are similar to those for the social insurance programs, with both employers and employees making regular payments.

According to this LCL, seafarers should have contracts and their employers should make contributions to their social insurance. As such, in terms of welfare and social security, the LCL arrangement would satisfy the requirements of MLC 2006. In this context, an examination of the LCL implementation in relation to Chinese seafarers will shed light on the implementation of MLC, and problems associated with the LCL implementation are likely to be encountered by MLC implementation, as they are similar in terms of requirements on employment conditions.

In relation to this issue, a study of Chinese seafarers' rights and protection was conducted in 2014. A total number of 37 shipping and crewing companies from five provinces, Fujian, Hubei, Guangdong, Liaoning, and Henan participated in the study, and the managers were interviewed between June and October of 2014. The next section reports some findings from these interviews. It is worth noting here that these accounts are from managers' perspective.

Social insurance and mobility

To make sense of issues related to seafarers' social security, it is necessary to explain the common seafarer employment practices in China. This is because the data suggests that seafarers' social insurance coverage is closely linked to their employment status.

The separation between operation management and crew management is commonplace in shipping. Ship managers crew their ships through either in-house crew management departments or third-party crewing agencies. This practice results in a supply chain of crewing service. The companies participated in this study represent an entire chain. On top of the chain are shipping companies whose ships are manned through either in-house crew management arms or third-party crewing agencies or a combination or both. Apart from manning their own fleet, many of the in-house crew management arms also provide crewing service to third-party shipping companies. Those that provide crewing service directly to third-party shipping companies can be seen as occupying the second tier in the supply chain. A few big crewing agencies also subcontract some service to smaller crewing agencies who are on the bottom tier of the supply chain.

Among the 37 companies participating in the study, apart from one shipping company that does not employ seafarers directly but outsources crewing service from agencies, the rest of the 36 companies are engaged in crew management.

For convenience, both in-house crew management arms and third-party crewing agencies are referred to as crew management companies.

It is common that crew management companies employ and differentiate between two groups of seafarers. The first group are commonly referred to as 'company-owned' seafarers. They are employed on medium-term contracts, and the contract length varies, ranging from three to six years. Upon the completion of the first contract, 'company-owned' seafarers can have open-ended contracts if they so choose. In a sense, this group of seafarers form the relatively stable pool of workforce. The second group can be regarded as temporary workforce, consisting of seafarers employed on tour-of-duty contracts. They are commonly known as self-employed or freelance seafarers in the spot labour market. The ratio between the two groups varies among these companies. While some companies outsource less than 10 percent of their workforce from the spot market or next tier agencies, one crewing agency 'owns' only 20 percent of their workforce on medium-term contracts.

In general, crew management prefer to keep officer seafarers on medium-term contracts, while outsource ratings from next tier agencies or the spot labour market. According to the managers interviewed, this is because there is a shortage of officers and an oversupply of ratings in the market. As bigger crewing agencies tend to outsource ratings, there are also subcontractor agencies specialized in providing ratings. One subcontractor participated in this study keeps only 20 percent of their workforce on medium-term contracts, while outsourcing the other 80 percent from the spot market.

What are the differences between the 'company-owned' workforce and the temporary one from the perspective of companies? The main difference is costs. One cost that can be saved by outsourcing is leave pay. For 'company-owned' seafarers on medium-term contracts, the company needs to pay them an 'at service' salary when they are working at sea and leave pay when they are taking leave ashore. By contrast, if a company outsources crewing service from a third-party agency or the spot market, the company only needs to pay seafarers for the period working on ships.

Another cost that can be saved is social insurance fees. According to the interviewed companies, they buy social insurance for all those 'company-owned' employees to fulfil the legal obligation under the LCL. If they outsource crewing service, they shift this legal obligation down the supply chain to the next tier crewing agencies or freelance seafarers. Again, the next tier agencies only buy social insurance for their 'company-owned' pool of workforce. For freelance seafarers temporarily employed from the spot market, while some companies make it clear that they pay a social insurance subsidy into seafarers' salaries, others do not, but leave the social insurance matter to the seafarers themselves. In a sense, freelance seafarers tend to be treated as self-employed, and as they are employers of themselves, they are responsible for their own social insurance.

In fact, social insurance, if paid in full and in proportion to income, is quite expensive. One company complained that social insurance was a heavy financial burden to them, up to 42.2 percent of crewing costs, which meant that seafarers

Table 6.1 A typical example of social insurance that state companies buy for employees

Social insurance type	Employee contribution (as percentage of salary)	Company contribution (as percentage of salary)	Total
Pension	8%	20%	28%
Medical insurance	2%	14%	16%
Unemployment insurance	1%	2%	3%
Work injury insurance	0	0.8%	0.8%
Maternity insurance	0	0.2%	0.2%
Housing provident fund	15%	15%	30%
Total	26%	52%	78%

could only get 57.8 percent of what their employer paid into their accounts. Table 6.1 is a breakdown of different types of social insurance that a typical state company employee would have. It shows that the employee would contribute 26 percent of his/her salary into social insurance and that the employer would contribute another 52 percent. In total, an employee's social insurance is worth 78 percent of his/her salary.

Therefore, if companies do not arrange social insurance for freelance seafarers, they are more able to offer a higher salary. In fact, interviewees mentioned that freelance seafarers in spot market preferred that their temporary employers paid them a higher salary instead of buying social insurance for them. Employers are happy to do that. As such, freelance seafarers in the spot market in general are not covered by social insurance, but their salaries are higher than others who are.

There is another issue related to social insurance. Although all interviewed companies stated that they bought social insurance for 'company-owned' seafarers, they took different approaches to adjust the ratio between social insurance and seafarer salary. State-owned big companies choose to buy full social insurance for their employees, but pay a lower salary. By contrast, other companies may choose to buy social insurance of the lowest possible standard and pay a higher salary to seafarers. Inevitably, complaint about the lower salary by seafarers at state-owned big shipping companies is commonplace. According to these companies, they face the huge challenge of losing their workforce to other crewing companies and the spot market where seafarers enjoy a higher salary. They complained that they had become the seafarer training base for others. Once they had trained seafarers up, these seafarers would want to leave for higher salaries.

It is fair to say that social insurance serves to differentiate and segment the seafaring labour market in China. On one end, state-owned companies provide more stable employment, full social insurance coverage, but lower salary. On the other, freelance seafarers are highly mobile and take precarious employment for a higher salary with no social insurance.

Costs and benefits

The earlier discussion suggests a tension between salary and social insurance. Salary is more visible because it is immediately available and can be used at present. As a contrast, the benefit of social insurance is less visible, as it helps mitigate future risks and takes effect in future. For current or short-term gains, seafarers may choose a higher salary with lower or no social insurance coverage. Although it is a legal obligation for companies to buy social insurance for their employees, they nevertheless cater for seafarers' demand in order to attract sufficient workers.

Wu et al.'s (2006) data suggested that the number of freelance seafarers grew rapidly between 2000 and 2004, from 4,000 to more than 30,000. As seafarers were unsatisfied with the salary offered by state-owned companies, once they had completed their first contracts, many of them chose to leave these companies and become freelancers. Although no recent data about the number of freelance seafarers are available, it is reasonable to assume that a large proportion of seafarers are now freelance.

High mobility carries risks, which are manifested more visibly when occupational injury or death occurs at sea. Even though maritime safety has been improving continuously (Allianz, 2012), seafaring remains a relatively dangerous occupation (Hansen, 1996; Roberts and Marlow, 2005; Borch et al., 2012). Therefore, occupational health and safety incidents on ships do happen from time to time, and happen more frequent than in other workplaces. In one participating crew management company which employed about 2,600 seafarers, about 10 cases of work-related illness, injury, death occurred each year, and they tried to contain the accident rate below 0.5 percent. According to the manager, their 'company-owned' seafarers were covered by ship owners' P&I (protection and indemnity insurance) clubs, personal accident insurance bought by the crew management company, and social insurance, and by contrast, freelance seafarers were protected only by the first two and did not have social insurance. In this situation, if accidents occurred, the needs and expectations of victims in the first group and their families could be satisfied by compensation, but for freelance seafarers, it was be a different story and for a few times accidents had led to conflicts between seafarers and the crew management company. This problem also existed in other companies.

To be sure, lack of social insurance can also lead to other problems which may not be concerns of management companies and therefore were not mentioned by managers during the interviews. For example, without pension, freelance seafarers may not have a stable income when they reach retirement. Furthermore, when they get sick while not working on ships, they are not covered by medical insurance.

This is not to suggest that despite the lower salary, state-owned companies are better because they fulfill the obligations without discount regarding their employees' social security. The point here is that LCL implementation is not problem free. Even though it is a legal requirement under the LCL that employers should arrange and contribute to social insurance of employees, in practice it is often avoided in relation to freelance seafarers. Lured by higher salaries and immediate gains, seafarers take risks and disregard possible future consequences of not having social insurance. Employers take advantage of and cater for freelance seafarers' risk behavior in order for successful recruitment from the spot market. In other words, no or low social insurance has become a competitive edge serving to attract the flow of seafarers. When accidents happen, however, treatment and compensation can become a headache for both employers and employees.

Conclusion

By its very nature, working at sea is an occupation associated with mobility. The globalization of the shipping industry has enabled the mobility of shipping capital. Partially due to this double mobility, the workforce at sea is increasingly and predominantly drawn from the developing regions, such as the Philippines, China, South Asia, and Eastern European countries. Accompanying this transformation is the rise of precarious employment. All forms of mobility have consequences for seafarers' well-being.

In this context, the MLC 2006 has been adopted and come into effect with the aim to protect seafarers' rights and well-being. It regulates working and living conditions on ships, employment conditions, and welfare and social security.

In China, the LCL, which has been in force since 2008, similarly requires employers to arrange and contribute to employees' social insurance. The compliance, however, varies. State-owned companies, for political reasons, may comply with regulation in full, but other companies may lower the standards or avoid it completely so that they are able to offer higher salaries to seafarers. In this way, social insurance may serve to segment the labour market and be used to create a competitive edge in recruitment. Lured by a higher salary in the spot market, seafarers break away from medium-term or open contracts with former employers to become freelance and embrace employment mobility, resulting in a mobile workforce without social insurance.

This article examines the issue based on managers' accounts only. From seafarers' perspective, there are perhaps more issues cropping up. Nevertheless, this does not blur the main issue here – that is, mobility may make LCL implementation problematic in China. This message may also be relevant to the implementation of MLC, because the global seafaring labour market is characterized by employment mobility. Crew management's pursue for cost cutting and seafarers' pursue for immediate gains may make MLC implementation problematic especially in relation to social security.

Note

1 It is unknown why there is a big discrepancy between the BIMCO figure and the MSA one. One contributory factor could be that while some people hold valid certificates, they do not work at sea any more.

References

Alderton, T., Bloor, M., Kahveci, E., Lane, T., Sampson, H., Thomas, M., Winchester, N., Wu, B., Zhao, M. (2004). *The Global Seafarer: Living and Working Conditions in a Globalised Industry*. Geneva: International Labour Office.

Alderton, T., Winchester, N. (2002). Globalisation and de-regulation in the maritime industry. *Marine Policy*. 26: 35–43.

Allianz (2012). Safety and shipping 1912–2012: From titanic to costa concordia. Available at: www.agcs.allianz.com/assets/PDFs/Reports/AGCS_safety_and_shipping_report.pdf Accessed 28 July 2017.

Baumeister, R. F., Leary, M. R. (1995). The need to belong: Desire for interpersonal attachment as a fundamental human motivation. *Psychological Bulletin*. 117: 497–529.

Bloor, M., Thomas, M., Lane, T. (2000). Health risks in global shipping industry: An overview. *Health, Risk and Society*. 2 (3): 329–340.

Borch, D. F., Hansen, H. L., Burr, H., Jepsen, J. R. (2012). Surveillance of deaths onboard Danish merchant ships, 1986–2009. *Occupational and Environmental Medicine*. 63 (1): 7–16.

DeSombre, E. R. (2006). *Flagging Standards: Globalization and Environmental, Safety, and Labour Regulations at Sea*. Cambridge, MA: MIT Press.

Grey, M. (1991). Hong Kong shipowner to train Chinese cadets: Wah Kwong to teach seafarers from C. Lloyd's list, 26 June.

Hansen, H. L. (1996). Surveillance of deaths onboard Danish merchant ships, 1986–1993: Implications for prevention. *Occupational and Environmental Medicine*. 53: 269–275.

ILO (2001). *Impact on Seafarer's Living and Working Conditions of Changes in the Structure of the Shipping Industry*. Geneva: International Labour Office.

Kahveci, E. (1999). *Fast Turnaround Ships and Their Impact on Crews*. Cardiff University: SIRC.

Kahveci, E., Nichols, T. (2006). *The Other Car Workers: Work, Organisation and Technology in the Maritime Car Carrier Industry*. New York: Palgrave Macmillan.

Lillie, N. (2005). Union networks and global unionism in maritime shipping. *Relations Industrielles/Industrial Relations*. 60 (1): 88–111.

Morris, R., Donn, C. (1997). New technology and industrial relations in United States and Australian shipping. *New Technology, Work and Employment*. 12 (2): 136–145.

MSA (2016). Statistical information of seafarers. Available at: www.mot.gov.cn/2016wan gshangzhibo/2016zhuanti3/xiangguanlianjie/201606/P020160624526276061516.pdf Accessed 1 March 2017.

Roberts, S. E., Marlow, P. B. (2005). Traumatic work related mortality among seafarers employed in British merchant shipping, 1976–2002. *Occupational and Environmental Medicine*. 62: 172–180.

Sampson, H., Thomas, M. (2002). The social isolation of seafarers: Causes, effects, and remedies. *International Maritime Health*. 54 (1–4): 58–67.

Smith, A. (2007). *Adequate Crewing and Seafarers' Fatigue: The International Perspective*. Cardiff University: Centre for Occupational and Health Psychology.

Smith, V. (2015). Employment Uncertainty and Risk. In: S. Edgell, H. Gottfried and E. Granter (eds.), *The Sage Handbook of the Sociology of Work and Employment*. London: Sage. pp. 367–384.

Sullivan, O. (1996). Time co-ordination, the domestic division of labour and affective relations: Time use and the enjoyment of activities within couples. *Sociology*. 30 (1): 79–100.

Tang, L. (2007). The 'presence' of the absent seafarers: Predicaments of seafarer-partners. SIRC Symposium, Cardiff University, Cardiff, July 2007.

Tang, L. (2012). Waiting together seafarer-partners in cyberspace. *Time & Society*. 21 (2): 223–240.

Thomas, M. (2003). *Lost at Sea and Lost at Home: The Predicament of Seafaring Families*. Cardiff University: SIRC.

Wallis, K. (2009). Japan owners launch China joint training centre. Lloyd's List, 19 August 2009.

Wu, B. (2004). Participation in the global labour market: Experience and responses of Chinese seafarers. *Maritime Policy & Management*. 31 (1): 69–82.

Wu, B., Lai, K. H., Cheng, T. E. (2006). Emergence of 'new professionalism' among Chinese seafarers: Empirical evidence and policy implications. *Maritime Policy & Management*. 33 (1): 35–48.

Zhao, Z. (2011). The human resource strategies of Chinese state crewing agencies with special reference to labour export and the experience of Chinese seafarers. PhD Thesis. Cardiff University. Available at: www.sirc.cf.ac.uk/Uploads/Thesis/Zhao.pdf

7 'Cruise to the Edge'

How 1970s prog-rock dinos found a safe haven on the cruise ship

Markus Hesse

Introduction

The cruise industry represents a striking case of *mobilities*, situated in between tourism and travel, leisure and consumption, ocean navigation and port-urban issues. It is characterised by strong growth rates and offers big potentials for the maritime and shipping industries. As a consequence, the cruise industry has gained increasing attention in recent times. Cruise operations are also associated with negative externalities in terms of energy consumption, air pollution and massive urban impacts, generated by herds of tourists invading the often historical setting at the port of calls. In terms of movement and mobilities, cruise trips offer a strange mix of mobility (on sea, at land) and custody (on the ocean ship). Most importantly, the cruise industry has a certain draw for the modern consumer which appears to be increasingly popular: besides the sports and leisure, shopping and eating overkill offered on board, passengers are brought to remote places such as resorts and ocean beaches, port cities and private islands, thus finding certain a *space* that allows them to escape from the peculiarities of daily life.

In addition to that, as event tourism has grown significantly in recent years, cruise tours also offer customers relief in terms of *time*: by organising specific journeys that are reminiscent of the passengers' own past. The product comprises musical events with bands that were popular at times when many fans – the now wealthy baby boomers – grew up. This is also the subject of interest to this chapter, which focuses on the '*Cruise to the Edge* (CttE)' – a programme that sees the 1970s British progressive rock heroes *Yes* at centre stage. *CttE* is but one of many high-profile, event-based products offered by the tourism industry in general and the cruise industry in particular. *CttE* started in 2013, and its fourth edition was taking place in February 2017. *CttE* is used to take various musicians on board of the cruise liner, mostly from classic rock and pop music line-ups, thus representing a sort of 'heritage rock' that is reminiscent of a past to which the consumers are connected via a specific nostalgia. While *Yes* were considered innovative more than 40 years ago, the band's classical repertoire is still appreciated by a hard-core community of fans, many of whom are now middle-aged or retired, wealthy and with plenty of time and disposable income for leisure, so they build an ideal target group for event-based tourism. During the few days of their cruise, they enjoy music, good company and a feeling of the times when they were young.

CttE is a perfect case of the commodification of increasingly mobile life styles, and fan cruises change our traditional understanding of bands' touring, as artists join their (mobile) audience in the separate, exclusive space of the cruise ship (Figure 7.1). The market potential of such packages seems huge, and while container transhipments may stagnate with the ups and downs of global trade, the cruise industry offers growth potentials for shipping lines, ports and port cities, by exploiting increasingly sophisticated maritime value chains. Thus both the socio-cultural and the economic features of cruise tourism can be understood

Figure 7.1 Advertising flyer for the 2015 edition of the cruise

Illustration used by permission/Cruise to the Edge

as a key component of emerging *maritime mobilites*. In this context, the chapter also confronts the place-based emphasis pursued by recent studies of the creativity economy in general and the music industry in particular, with movement and mobility, which can be considered central to the rock cruise phenomenon.

The remainder of this chapter is organised as follows. Following the introduction, Section 2 discusses the context of mobilities studies, tourism and the variegated geographies of music and thus conceptualises the subject matter. Section 3 gives an overview of recent developments in the cruise industry as a fast-growing segment of maritime industries, thus building the socio-economic framework of this market segment. Section 4 provides some evidence on rock cruises as a particular case of event-based tourism in the cruise industry. This section also introduces the 1970s progressive rock band *Yes* and their landmark record *Close to the Edge*, whose persistent popularity can be seen as a template for the development and marketing of the *CttE* cruises. Finally, Section 5 critically interprets the products and practices associated with the rock cruise, as this practice combines movement and mobilities with custody; also, it is concerned with the commodification of leisure in the context of popular music as cultural heritage and the exploration of future market segments of cruise tourism, which can be considered a vital part of maritime mobilities.

Mobilities, tourism and shifting geographies of music

Since the late 1990s/early 2000s the debate about the 'new mobilities paradigm' has contributed significantly to a new, enhanced understanding of the role that movement and various forms of mobilities (plural) have played and continue to play for what is considered to be late-modern society. As Sheller and Urry (2016: 11–12) have put it in their review of ten years plus on the new mobilities paradigm, these studies have revealed the constitutive role of movement – of all kinds of subjects – for social practices, lifestyles, social relationships and institutions. *Constitutive* in this respect means that mobility is neither a mere by-product of social practice nor something one would wish to avoid (such as commuting times), but that it enables social practices, is about to become a purchase in itself and is also a requirement for activities that are sensitive of access. The authors also emphasised that new mobilities are not simply about a world that is becoming overall more mobile, but that both the *potentials* and *constraints* of mobility are more finely regulated than they have ever been – i.e., by the help of new information technologies, logistics concepts, surveillance practices, etc. This applies both to the area of passenger mobility and to goods movement. As the new mobilities research is inspired by social sciences, cultural studies, anthropology and the like, it turns out to be rather distinct from traditional approaches in transport sciences, engineering or transport geography.

The field of tourism can be considered a template case of practiced mobilities, not only due to the sheer magnitude to which travel and tourism as mass phenomena have grown in recent decades but also given the qualitative changes that were associated with this development and the various ways how tourism is inscribed in places or personal lives (see e.g. Wilson, 2012; Rickly et al., 2016; Tesfahuney and Schough, 2016). Newer developments such as city tourism, bundled packages of distance shopping, gambling and entertainment, cruise trips or other theme concepts add to the broad variety of tourism-based value chains. However, mobilities studies have only partly contributed to the study of tourism, without providing full coverage of the subject matter. Likewise, tourism geographies have proliferated already some time ago, particularly in the post-war period (Hall and Page, 2012). The last set of actual progress reports on this topic was published almost a decade ago (see Gibson, 2008). It is the core tourism industry and related research that is pushing forward here more directly than academic disciplines have done so far. Obviously, issues such as tourism behaviour, destinations and markets have developed rather rapidly and so have they changed in recent times. Most interestingly, there are some explicit linkages between mobilities and tourism studies, as there is a 'mobile turn' (Hall and Page, 2012: 15) noted in the field of tourism as well. This is related to the rising interest in the flows of people (such as migration) or the flow of information (e.g. when booking travels) and the role of movement as a requirement for travel. The preference of consumers for having more frequent but shorter holiday trips has been shifting the attention to mobilities as well. The idea of encounter with the unknown, the 'other', the not so ordinary part of life still represents an essential of tourism practices, and it is likewise a fundamental experience of mobility. This applies both to contexts where encounter is sought for – following a sort of socialising attitude – and a reflection of holiday travels being driven by escapism.

A second point of departure of this chapter is music – a habit, a socio-cultural practice, a collective endeavour which is either practiced or consumed, one that can't be underestimated in its cultural, societal and economic importance. Music has gained much interest recently as to the geographical contexts within which it is produced and reproduced, most notably spurred by research on creativity. This debate actually followed what was introduced earlier as the geography of music, consisting of a variety of topics, approaches and cases of study (cf. Carney, 1998). These include the regional origin of certain music (e.g. reggae music from the Caribbean); the evolution of musical styles such as Motown from Detroit, Michigan, or country music originating from Nashville, Tennessee; the links made between Liverpool and the Mersey Beat, or between Grunge and Seattle; the diffusion of musical directions such as jazz switching between the East and West coasts of the United States; the association of music with spatial trajectories such as migratory flows or communication networks; and musical genres that inhibit a political message, such as punk music in the mid- and late-1970s, or particular sorts of aggressive audio that tends to accompany nationalist and right-wing activists' political articulation.

Carney (1998) has noted the importance of place for musical production, which at later stages was also included in meticulous studies pursued in the context of creativity. The musical economy is relevant here for different reasons: On the one hand, it represents an established segment of both higher culture and its popular variant, whose commodification and mass consumption made it very important economically. On the other hand, the production, distribution and valuation of music have been subject to radical transformation in times of digitalisation and virtualisation. New strategies of creating value have substituted for the traditional interaction of artists, audience, music industry and the media. Particularly, the production and distribution of music are increasingly evolving from self-made patterns, which take place in distinct but changing social milieux and creative scenes, also in symbolic contexts and constellations. What was previously emerging at spatially fixed entities such as a recording studio is now increasingly going to be mobilised, which is mainly due to the role of mobile digital devices and software-based equipment. This observation seemingly fits with the renaissance of the touring activity of popular music groups, which has seen a revival since the 2000s. Being on the road, having the musical and recording equipment in the board cases and sharing ready-made concert audios with the fan base brings new forms of encounter with the audience – another round of mobilisation of musical production and performance. As research inspired by the mobilities paradigm tends to go beyond the place-based emphasis that creativity studies have often pursued, it can contribute significantly to the study of music in variegated spatio-temporal settings. The rock cruise is a template case that indicates this potential.

Enclaved consumption and mobility: the rise of the cruise industry

The cruise ship sector represents an increasingly popular way of spending holidays abroad, and it is also an emerging business model that promises steady growth and new prospects for the cruise industries, for port cities and for associated fields of economic development. While the maritime agenda was dominated for some time by the interest of shipping companies, terminal operators and port authorities in the long-standing growth of container shipments, the current focus is on the cruise ship industry and related branches such as tourism. The modern cruise ship, the glossy incarnation of a place to be that offers everything everywhere, and lacks nothing, epitomises the desire for movement and mobility, and embodies the promise of total consumption in a clean environment. This image of the contemporary cruise as an 'omnitopia' (Bennett, 2016) stands in certain contrast with the working conditions of a mostly globally hired staff and is also linked to severe environmental problems such as toxic emissions and the periodic overflow of ancient cultural sites and historic cities by thousands of passengers at the ports of call (Lamers et al., 2015). Cruise trips are clearly as controversial as they are popular.

The customer market for cruise trips has been flourishing for a while now, with accelerated growth measured by numbers of passengers, cruises and destinations observed in recent years. According to the *Cruise Lines International Association* (*CLIA*), the global cruise ship market comprised a total of about 23 million passengers by 2015, a volume that had more than tripled since 2000 (cf. Rodrigue and Notteboom, 2013). The geographical distribution of the countries of origin of the cruise customers is still uneven, with almost half of all passengers coming from the United States (11.28 m), followed by Germany, the United Kingdom and

Australia in the range of one to two million passengers per annum. Concentration also applies to the destination markets for cruise trips, of which the Caribbean (34.7 percent) and the Mediterranean (19.4 percent of all cruise trips) are the most popular (data by CLIA, as of 2015). The global fleet of cruise ships is divided between ocean- and river-going vessels, the former comprising 279 out of the total of 448 ships, while 169 generally smaller ships are dedicated to river cruises.

The leading cruise markets tend to be distinct from traditional shipping markets: while commercial shipping is thought of as being derived from trade activities, the cruise business seems to be created, on the basis of successful pricing, branding and marketing strategies in an environment of global tourism, particularly in the most wealthy nations as mentioned earlier (Coggins, 2014; Rodrigue and Notteboom, 2013). Also, as Rodrigue and Notteboom (2013) have argued, the cruise industry's market is unique in that the cruise ship is not only the vessel but also the destination – a notion that fits perfectly with the new mobilities perspective of movement that is being inscribed into social practice. The growth of the industry clearly exacerbates tensions between the variegated geographies of origins, destinations and itineraries that are included here. The peculiar relation between spaces and flows that is inherent to the cruise ship business model also allows operators to situate their portfolio between routes, ports of calls and an optimal allocation of passenger flows. Thus the value chains in the cruise ship industry and related service sectors can be more extensively exploited than before.

Specialisation and diversification strategies of the cruise industry are probably one of the secrets behind its recent success story. Among the standard products offered on board of a cruise liner, perhaps as important as the dining options, are the sports and entertainment. On-board entertainment in the form of a variety of crowd-pleasing options is an essential requirement for market success. Moreover, it also offers potentials for further marketisation and diversification of the cruise adventure, putting particular target groups on the screen of the cruise liner. This has unfolded in the development of specialised offers to music aficionados who are going abroad to see, and listen to, their idols – not in clubs or concert halls, but on the ocean ships, combined with the cosy atmosphere of a sunny holiday trip. The most famous case of such rock cruise trips is the '*CttE*', with the 1970s prog-rockers *Yes* at centre stage.

Yes, retro rock music and the 'Cruise to the Edge'

'*Cruise to the Edge' (CttE)* borrows from the progressive rock group *Yes* and their template 1972 record '*Close to the Edge*'. It has meanwhile unfolded as a business model that assembles bands from the late 1960s/early 1970s or even later for a less-than-a-week rock cruise to the Caribbean, where fans get the opportunity for a concert-plus experience. This experience often includes meet-and-greet events with the artists and a selected number of musical performances in a small stage/club setting that is more intimate than the standard concert hall of today. While theme-oriented cruises are on the market for some time now, apparently the *Pink Floyd* concert cover event *A Great Gig in the Sea* from 2009 was the first really popular rock cruise (Reynolds, 2011: xx). Since 2013, *CttE* is headlining on a regular basis, and it is no coincidence that reference was made to the *Close to the Edge* album by *Yes*, which likely helped with the branding and selling the rock cruise. *Yes* got started back in 1968 and helped a musical genre called progressive rock to evolve – a unique combination of rock, folk and classical styles that aimed at expanding musical borders significantly. The group became a successful touring band and were well known for opulent stage designs and light concepts that framed their two- or three-hour long concerts quite well. The fantasy drawings by artist Roger Dean for stage and album designs complemented the entirely new, 'progressive' package with which the music was sold. *Close to the Edge* was album number five in the band's long history. The record was first released in 1972, and as the title track occupied the entire A-side of the record (with only two songs on the B-side), this indicated already the change to longer pieces of music that became favoured not only by *Yes* but also by many other progressive bands (Covach, 1997). *Close to the Edge* was and still is thought of as the band's masterpiece. The album reached number three on the *Billboard* charts in the US and number four on the UK album charts (Welch, 2008), and according to a poll among readers of the special interest website *progarchives.com*, it is considered one of the template albums of the prog-rock era at all.

Close to the Edge also certainly marked a career peak for the band. Not unlike progressive music in general, *Yes* found itself under attack by the mid-1970s, when Punk and New Wave gained momentum and artistic credibility, undermining established musical genres at the time. Subsequent prog releases (such as *Yes's* 1977 *Going for the One*, or the band's 1980s blockbuster 'Owner of a Lonely Heart') tried to adapt to the changing musical taste of the times. Nevertheless, the band remained active despite frequent personnel changes, and *Yes* is still touring and recording, receiving support by a small but strong fan base. However, recent recordings no longer prove to be musically original and innovative, and thus the band has failed to attract broader interest among listeners, particularly among younger generations. As musical creativity seems to be lacking, the core community of aficionados consists of those adolescents who were musically socialised with *Yes* at the time when the band was at its creative peak, which was probably the case in the late 1960s or the first half of the 1970s. Different from other template prog-bands, which were not only keeping their creativity at high levels but sought for constant change (see, e.g., King Crimson whose style and line-up has evolved since the 1970s), *Yes* was primarily attached to what was perceived as its trademark style. Also, as the band members are getting older (with bassist Chris Squire's passing in 2015 marking the end of the original line-up), it is interesting to note that the last new recruitments of the band targeted rather young singers who had practiced in *Yes* cover bands. Ironically, fresh blood enabled the band to bring new life to the rather old material.

Yes's small but still existing fan base, which now mostly comprises aging baby boomers who grew up with the band's early music, made *Yes* an ideal headliner for a new concert experience: the rock cruise. In 2013, the '*CttE*' was offered for the first time, just a year after the first '*Monsters of Rock Cruises*' took off. From the same organiser, other cruise packages have booked headliners such as *Def Leppard* (1980s metal) or the *Moody Blues* (late 1960s soft rock). The 2013 *CttE* took place from 25 to 29 March, sailing from Fort Lauderdale, Florida, USA to the Caribbean. While *Yes* was the only headliner, the set-list had a combination of prog icons such as ex-*Genesis* guitarist Steve Hackett, ex-*ELP* drummer Carl Palmer, the late *King Crimson/Asia*-veteran John Wetton or *Nektar*, and more recent performers such as *Ambrosia, Glass Hammer, IOEarth* or *Zebra*. The 2017 edition of *CttE* was the fourth and took place on 7 to 11 February, cruising the Caribbean between Tampa, Florida, and Cozumel, Mexico, including an optional pre-cruise party on February 6. The line-up of this *CttE* was much more ambitious and comprehensive than the first has been, having booked *Yes*, 1980s stadium-rockers *Kansas*, Steve Hackett, John Wetton (who had to pull off for health reasons and meanwhile passed away in February 2017) and Mike Portnoy (ex-drummer from post-rockers *Dream Theater* and *Transatlantic*). These headliners were accompanied by 19 other acts in a broad range of prog rock, classic rock, post-rock, metal and related sub-genres.

While previous rock cruises used the MSC shipping line's '*Divina*', with a capacity of 4,345 passengers and approximately 1,400 crew, the current cruise liner is the Royal Caribbean International's '*Brilliance of the Seas*'. The ship has a carrying capacity of only 2,500 passengers and about 850 crew members on board. Pools and whirlpools, a rock-climbing wall, mini-golf course, basketball court and jogging track are provided for sports and leisure purposes. Besides a variety of dining rooms and a casino, 16 bars and lounges are suited for presenting musical entertainment. The cruise ticket includes a four-night trip across the Caribbean, all meals, the use of the fitness centre, pools and the like and access to all concert events. Tickets are offered in different categories, between $1,100 for a standard double cabin and $3,000 for an 'owner's suite', which also includes a 'VIP Experience', which consists of lodging in a special suite (with a balcony) and provides access to photo experiences, showroom performances, assigned seating, a VIP cocktail party (likely with musicians being in attendance) and certain VIP gifts and credentials.

The relatively intimate setting compared to the usual concert hall obviously offers a certain add-on to cruise passengers, so they might be keen on the possibility of chatting with their heroes, etc. In its Q&A section, the organiser promises, "All artists will be joining you for the full cruise, and performing onboard the ship." Also, many of the artists "will be doing formal photo sessions, which will be announced, in more detail, as we get closer to sailing." In a BBC-coverage of the 2013 *CttE*, ex-*ELP* drummer Carl Palmer is quoted as follows: "They're on holiday, cruising with their favourite band. That's what they get out of it. There we are in the morning and you can see us having breakfast." More recently, a diary consisting of five pieces on the 2017 *CttE* provided by Ira Kantor on the online music-mag Elmormagazine.com gives good insight on the personal interactions between bands and audience. This encounter may increasingly attract more customers to such form of concert-plus experience, thus making it a significant selling point of the rock cruise (Kantor, 2017).

Likewise, a report in the *Premier Guitar* magazine (Jeffers, 2014) about the 2014 *CttE* illustrates this close encounter of the musical kind. Having commenced with a classical concert review, the report delves into a description of the musical gear of selected artists, presents some of them as 'storytellers' (mostly bringing anecdotes to the audience that relate to their 1970s adventures), then closes with an interview of a musician and picking some quotes from the stage about the rock cruise and artists' appreciation. According to Jeffers (2014: 2–3), this is how a usual day on the rock cruise liner looks like:

> As the ship glided away from the Port of Miami, guests settled into what would be their home at sea for the next five days. Sporting black Cruise to the Edge T-shirts for the blackout-themed disembarkation party, the fans gathered to hear Saga kick off the music festivities on the Pool Stage. The central and highest performance area on the ship, the Pool Stage featured two-tiered concert seating, lawn chairs, hot tubs, and plenty of island-style booze concoctions. The music went from sun up to, well, almost sun up. A typical morning might include breakfast at the Manitou buffet, followed by some sunning or a dip in the pool while the first performers welcomed you into the day. Inside the ship, there were a half dozen stages and more things to see than there was time to see them. The Atrium stage provided a nice focal point in the middle of all the activity, and bands had the opportunity to play a variety of shows: a larger concert, an intermediate lounge show, and a stripped-down acoustic or Q&A/ meet-and-greet event in a setting reminiscent of Inside the Actor's Studio.

While the performing artists are at centre stage of the rock cruise, the core of its value chain is the organiser, which is likely to be an experienced player of the music industry. In the case of the rock cruises named earlier, it is *On the Blue*, by self-description the world's leader in classic rock cruises, staying in the business for about 20 years now. The company usually books the artists and charters the cruise ship, whose capacity is then sold to customers. Based on a report in the *Music Connection* magazine (Feterl, 2014), the company does not need to spend much money on advertising and marketing. "Social media has revolutionized marketing for us. The Monsters of Rock audience was pretty much built on Facebook, and now 60%–70% are repeat passengers," a company representative claimed. This also allows an easy reach to international customers – *CttE* often attracts passengers from up to 25 different countries for their cruises. The crucial part of marketing, however, is picking the right fan base, for which the small communities of long-term, hard-core aficionados of prog rock seem to be ideally suited. According to the same report, the company confirms the age of the target groups: "While the Monsters of Rock demographic is 20–60, the average age is 45, and CttE and The Moody Blues Cruise average 45–60 year-olds". Customer satisfaction, however, is not guaranteed. A lengthy comment placed by a 'superfan' in a forum of rock cruise passengers complains about a bad experience with the *Moody Blues* cruise, summing up a list of disappointments, particularly since what was sold as a VIP cabin with two queen beds turned out to be a tiny little cabin with different but small beds. For these fans, the uncomfortable stay on board was accompanied by an unfriendly crew, which was hardly concerned with the customers' problems, but had difficulties to deal with a sold-out ocean liner. Other complaints about the 2013 *CttE* on cruisecritic.com came from passengers who had simply booked tickets for the cruise without realising they would be in the company of a large number of fans of loud rock music. However, a large majority of the passengers probably do enjoy the unique combination of cruise holidays with intimate rock concerts, meet-and-greet events and merchandising/shopping that brings them in touch with the idols of their youth and thus provides a strong sense of nostalgia.

Interpreting the rock cruise between past and present, mobilities and custody

The emerging theme-based cruise tourism represents a stimulating case of maritime mobilities that adds to our understanding of the spatio-temporalities of movement and mobilities across the sea. In this context, the festival ship is more than just an ocean vessel that brings tourists to the places of their desire: It represents an artefact that helps variegated forms of mobilities and of immobilities to emerge, and it is geographically relevant as the cruise-related routing, scheduling and logistics practices provide a complex set of space-time arrangements that explore and exploit sea and land in new ways. In such a complex setting, change is imminent and multi-dimensional, for which authors such as Cresswell (2010) or Ducruet and Zaidi (2012) have, though in different contexts, already introduced the term 'constellations'. In the case of theme-oriented cruise tourism, the particular mobility or maritime constellation means that it represents a complex package consisting of various components that are tightly knit together: most notably i) the cruise businesses and their maritime strategies and operations, ii) the cruise ship as a hybrid of a travel means and a destination, iii) passengers and their leisure interest and practices and iv) the localities – cruise ports and destination areas – whose network builds the architecture of the cruise trip. These locations are profiting from the business, and they are simultaneously affected by cruise tourism.

While the main aim of maritime businesses is moving commodities, vessels and containers for the purpose of enabling material trade, cruise ships are involved in what Hasty and Peters (2012: 669) have coined the 'tourist trade'. Its mission is not necessarily about transport from A to B only, although the sea provides an important setting of water, sky, sunset and the like. Here, most important is the passage, the gift of travel time, which offers a range of activities to be undertaken on board of the ship. Hence the cruise ship essentially acts as a "floating resort (or a theme park)" (Rodrigue and Notteboom, 2013: 33) that carries all facilities that are usually needed to establish a destination worth to visit. As a consequence, the cruise-based maritime mobilities also include, necessarily, a certain amount of immobility that occurs when being on board of the ocean liner – most notably during the passage between two ports of call, when the passenger is stuck on board and can't leave the cruise ship. While becoming subject to *cruising* (Merriman, 2016) or *drifting* (Peters, 2015), the passenger is destined to act as a customer and trigger on-board sales and other commercial activities. This part of the passage reflects the 'moorings', the importance of stillness, stuckness and waiting

(Cresswell, 2012) that always contradicts the act of movement and the related desire of the traveller to move on.

Even though the modern cruise liner represents a floating resort that appears increasingly sophisticated in terms of entertainment, encounter and dispersion, there are, however, concrete destinations that are to be served by the ship, both for logistical reasons (loading and unloading resources and materials) and to ensure the pleasure and entertainment of the disembarking customers. Ross Dowling's edited volume *Cruise Ship Tourism* (2006), which is one of the few standard works dealing quite comprehensively with this subject matter, includes a small case study chapter that is devoted to the island of Cozumel, off the coast of Yucatan in the Mexican part of the Caribbean (Sorensen, 2006). Cozumel is among the top three spots of cruises across the region and worldwide, not least since its coastal environment provides a highly demanded diving location. Cozumel, which also served as the destination of the 2017 *CttE*, has experienced tremendous growth over the past decades. Sorensen's case study illustrates the imprint and the challenges that the cruise trips bring to the physical and socio-economic setting of their destination. These are at least threefold: firstly, the construction of piers and terminals creates the new landing infrastructure that facilitates the cruise vessels' operations. Secondly, the property of becoming a cruise tourism destination provides an enormous growth of passengers and crew that stop by on the island, which was estimated for the season 2014/2015 to score about 2.5 m for passengers and 0.5 m for crew members (in contrast to a population of roughly 80,000). Thirdly, economic life gets increasingly dependent from, and controlled by, foreign cruise lines. Although tourists, crew and cruise lines themselves generate a significant amount of spending, a majority of these economic gains may benefit the distant operator, and less so the local destinations' communities (see Sánchez and Wilmsmeier, 2012: 5). Thus the relationship between tourism and local development remains critical: "Cozumel's unprecedented growth rate is centred around the cruise product, and the economy was quickly dominated by foreign firms" (Sorensen, 2006: 358). While knowing "how to manage tourism and its inevitable crowds" (ibid) is considered to be the key to success, the fast pace of recent development of the island may explain that the impact of the cruise business on local culture and the local economy is hotly debated. Sheller (2009) confirms such endemic problems of the tourism economy in the Caribbean against the background of state re-scaling, where shifting mobilities (of capital, labour force, tourist flows and the like) evolved to play a key role.

Moving vessels, containers and cruise ships has become a big business based on circulation. The maritime mobilities of the rock cruise are no exception here, and they are nested in the same contradiction between economic development and preservation, between local interest and (often) global exploitation. However, they can only be fully understood by emphasising some peculiarities from the demand side, which add to the success of this business model in specific ways. Most rock cruises, including the *CttE*, have in common that they do not only offer entertainment while travelling to distant territories but also offer a journey to different life times of the customers. In this sense, the rock cruise is part of a broader societal phenomenon, the attraction of popular music of the past among the respective generations. This trend evolved some decades ago when nostalgia started to affect the entire consumer-entertainment complex, including musical performance, its commodification and technological reproduction. Simon Reynolds (2011) voluminous study 'Retromania' has probably provided the most comprehensive account of the trend back to the appreciation of music of the yesteryears, which is by far not a new phenomenon, but for him is already indicative for the late 1950s/early 1960s. The mass production and commodification of music by the related industries have helped this phenomenon to spread more widely since the 1970/1980s. The same applies to technological changes such as the shift from vinyl LPs to CDs, and the associated re-release of popular music oeuvres and their back catalogues since the mid-1980s, which have spurred this development indeed further.

Rock cruises have evolved in the course of Retromania as they are not only somehow relating to 'the past' but also linked to developments that happened in living memory of a particular target group. Also, retro involves an element of exact recall, which is enabled by the ready availability of archived documentation (photographic, video, music recordings, Internet) allowing for the precise replication of old styles. Retro also generally involves the artifacts of popular culture, and a final characteristic of the retro sensibility is that it does not idealise or sentimentalise the past, but seeks to be amused and charmed by it (Reynolds, 2011: xxx). As the appreciation of the past gained certain momentum particularly with regard to popular music, this phenomenon found certain recognition in the humanities and social sciences, framing it as 'heritage rock' (Bennett, 2009; Brandellero and Janssen, 2014). This debate not only points at the rising appreciation of popular culture but also emphasises they ways in which pieces of past times can become truly iconic. What initially started as an expression of counter-culture became part of a widely accepted mainstream decades later, being re-positioned and aestheticised as 'classic'. This is most importantly a generational phenomenon, based on the cultural hegemony of the baby-boomer generation. According to Bennett (2009: 486), they represent one of very first generations (if not the first) that grew up in a fully mediatised and consumerised society. This does not necessarily mean that young listeners would not adore old performers, as Bennett (2008) put it in the neat observation that "things they do look awful cool". However, the very large majority of retro-aficionados belong to the "grey-haired globetrotters" (Frye, 2015) – a target group that seems well suited for the rock cruise, as it shares a certain musical taste while getting older and, at the same time, has significant purchasing power. Among the listeners of rebel music, getting older was once something conceived of as to be avoided in any instance ("I hope I die before I get old", *The Who – My Generation*, 1965). As the rock cruise demonstrates, the legacy of popular music has now transcended to heritage and allows for making huge economic gains in the cultural industries, event production and certainly tourism. The cruise ship provides the appropriate setting to exploit these variegated space-time frames, packaged in a particular combination of land and sea, travel and consumption, mobilities and immobilities.

Maybe the role and the potential of the music cruise liner are best expressed in Bennett's understanding of the term 'omnitopia' – it is seen as a space offered by "extravagant floating cities" that "package a vacation where you can be everywhere and nowhere simultaneously" (Bennett, 2016: 51). One may add to the "where" – to these various spatialities of the entertainment ship – also different times – that is, the issue of 'when', which is particularly packaged and sold on the rock cruise. However, if the question of space and place is becoming less relevant for the product that is offered here, then it is also increasingly difficult to argue about the economic gains and benefits provided to destination regions. Such benefits would only justify these regions to adapt to the business model of modern tourism if certain returns from infrastructure expansion and assets provision would remain locally, which seems unlikely given the fluidity and volatility of the floating resorts. Thus certain forms of mobilities also contribute to weakening the link between spaces and flows, making the cruise ship becoming a spatial fix, while destinations and ports of call tend to be situated at the disadvantaged end of the value chains.

References

Bennett, A. (2008). 'Things they do look awful cool': Ageing rock icons and contemporary youth audiences. *Leisure/Loisir*. 32 (2): 259–278.

Bennett, A. (2009). 'Heritage rock': Rock music, representation and heritage discourse. *Poetics*. 37: 474–489.

Bennett, M. (2016). Competing with the sea: Contemporary cruise ships as omnitopias. *Performance Research*. 21 (2): 50–57.

Brandellero, A., Janssen, S. (2014). Popular music as cultural heritage: Scoping out the field of practice. *International Journal of Heritage Studies*. 20 (3): 224–240.

Carney, G. (1998). Music geography. *Journal of Cultural Geography*. 18 (1): 1–10.

Coggins, A. O. (2014). The globalization of the cruise industry: A tale of ships. *Worldwide Hospitality and Tourism Themes*. 6 (2): 138–151.

Covach, J. (1997). Progressive Rock, 'Close to the Edge', and the Boundaries of Style. In: J. Covach and G. Boone (eds.), *Understanding Rock: Essays in Musical Analysis*. New York: Oxford University Press. pp. 3–31.

Cresswell, T. (2010). Towards a politics of mobility. *Environment & Planning D: Society and Space*. 28: 17–31.

Cresswell, T. (2012). Mobilities II: Still. *Progress in Human Geography*. 36 (5): 645–653.

Ducruet, C., Zaidi, F. (2012). Maritime constellations: A complex network approach to shipping and ports. *Maritime Policy & Management*. 39 (2): 151–168.

Feterl, A. (2014). Festival ships: Rockin' all way to the bank. *Music Connection*, 19 March 2014. Available at: www.musicconnection.com/festival-ships-rockin-bank/ Accessed 9 October 2017.

Frye, A. (2015). Capitalising on the Grey-haired Globetrotters: Economic aspects of increasing tourism among older and disabled people. ITF-Discussion Paper 11–2015. Paris: OECD/ITF.

Gibson, C. (2008). Locating geographies of tourism. *Progress in Human Geography*. 32 (3): 407–422.

Hall, C., Page, S. (2012). From the Geography of Tourism to Geographies of Tourism. In: J. Wilson (ed.), *The Routledge Handbook of Tourism Geographies*. London: Routledge. pp. 9–25.

Hasty, W., Peters, K. (2012). The ship in geography and the geographies of ships. *Geography Compass*. 6 (11): 660–676.

Jeffers, T. (2014). Cruising to the edge. *Premier Guitar*, 27 May 2014. Available at: www. premierguitar.com/articles/20878-cruising-to-the-edge Accessed 9 October 2017.

Kantor, I. (2017). Cruise to the edge diary, days 1–5. Available at: www.elmoremagazine. com Accessed 9 and 15 February 2017.

Lamers, M., Eijgelaar, E., Amelung, B. (2015). The Environmental Challenges of Cruise Tourism: Impacts and Governance. In: C. M. Hall, S. Goessling and D. Scott (eds.), *The Routledge Handbook of Tourism and Sustainability*. London: Routledge. pp. 430–439.

Merriman, P. (2016). Mobilities II: Cruising. *Progress in Human Geography*. 40 (4): 555–564.

Peters, K. (2015). Drifting: Towards mobilities at sea. *Transactions of the Institute of British Geographers*. 40 (2): 262–272.

Reynolds, S. (2011). *Retromania: Pop Culture's Addiction to Its Own Past*. London: Macmillan.

Rickly, J., Hannam, K., Mostafanezhad, M. (eds.) (2016). *Tourism and Leisure Mobilities: Politics, Work and Play*. London: Routledge.

Rodrigue, J. P., Notteboom, T. (2013). The geography of cruises: Itineraries, not destinations. *Applied Geography*. 38: 31–42.

Sánchez, R., Wilmsmeier, G. (2012). *The Costa Concordia Disaster and the Cruise Industry: An Analysis of Risks and Challenges in Latin America and the Caribbean: FAL Bulletin 306, 2/2012*. Santiago, Chile: Published by the Economic Comission for Latin America and the Caribbean (ECLAC).

Sheller, M. (2009). The new Caribbean complexity: Mobility systems, tourism and spatial rescaling. *Singapore Journal of Tropical Geography*. 30 (2): 189–203.

Sheller, M., Urry, J. (2016). Mobilizing the new mobilities paradigm. *Applied Mobilities*. 1 (1): 10–25.

Sorensen, H. (2006). Cozumel: The Challenges of Cruise Tourism. In: R. Dowling (ed.), *Cruise Ship Tourism*. Oxfordshire: CABI. pp. 350–359.

Tesfahuney, M., Schough, K. (eds.) (2016). *Privileged Mobilities: Tourism as World Ordering*. Cambridge: Scholars Publishing.

Welch, C. (2008). *Close to the Edge: The Story of Yes*. London: Music Sales.

Wilson, J. (ed.) (2012). *The Routledge Handbook of Tourism Geographies*. Routledge: London.

Part 3

Sustainable mobilities

8 Ballast water and harmful aquatic organism mobilities

Matej David and Stephan Gollasch

Introduction

Commercial vessels are built to transport various types of cargo or passengers. In case a vessel is not fully laden, additional weight is needed to ensure the vessel's seaworthiness, for example, to compensate for increased buoyancy which can result in the lack of propeller immersion in water, inadequate transversal and longitudinal inclination or other stresses on the vessel's hull and structure. The material used for the addition of weight to the vessel is referred to as ballast. In former times, ballast material was solid, but after iron was used as basic vessel building material (in the middle of the 19th century) loading of water in cargo holds or tanks was used as ballast, which was demonstrated to be easier and more efficient. Even when a vessel is fully laden ballast water operations may be needed due to (a) a non-equal distribution of cargo on the vessel, (b) adverse weather and sea conditions, (c) an approach to shallower waters and (d) the fuel consumption during the voyage. As a result, vessels depend fundamentally on ballast water for safe navigation and operations as a result of their design and construction (David, 2015).

It is wide accepted that the transfer of non-indigenous species across biogeographic barriers is among the greatest threats to the world's oceans and seas and ballast water was identified as one of the prime vectors of this global issue (e.g., Elton, 1958; Carlton, 1985; Wiley, 1997; Gollasch et al., 2002; Bax et al., 2003; Bailey et al., 2005; Vila et al., 2010; Davidson and Simkanin, 2012). Manifold unwanted impacts are caused by introduced species. Some impacts are more environmental, including changes of species biogeography (e.g., Sorte et al., 2010), biodiversity modifications, introduction of predators, bloom-forming harmful algae, parasites and disease agents. Others include economic problems of marine resource users, such as loss in fisheries, fouling of industrial water pipes and on fishing and aquaculture gear (e.g., Leppäkoski et al., 2002). Even negative impacts on human health are reported as, e.g., harmful algae causing amnesic, diarrhetic or paralytic shellfish poisoning and *Vibrio cholerae* were found in ballast water (e.g., Hallegraeff and Bolch, 1991; Rigby and Hallegraeff, 1994; Bauer, 2006; Kotaki et al., 2000; Ruiz et al., 2000; van den Bergh et al., 2002). In total approximately 300 harmful algae species are known of which ca. 80 species produce toxins causing shellfish poisoning, which also affects sea food consumers (Hallegraeff et al.,

2003; Granéli et al., 2012). Already more than 20 years ago, it was suggested that the increase in harmful algae blooms occurrences may be related to ballast water movements of such species (Hallegraeff and Bolch, 1991; Hallegraeff, 1993). Over this time period, as an example of increased frequencies of algal blooms, the ichthyotoxic algae *Prymnesium* spp. spread from Asia westwards resulting now in occurrences in the Americas (Granéli et al., 2012). Also, algal bloom events were increasingly recorded since the 1970s with almost daily episodes in the west central Atlantic in the 1990s (McGinn, 1999). Other coastal waters, such as San Francisco Bay (USA) and Port Philips Bay (Australia), inhabit today more than 200 and 150 non-indigenous and cryptogenic species, respectively. Several of those species are harmful algae which are locally very abundant documenting the drastic changes caused by introduced species (Cohen and Carlton, 1995; Hewitt et al., 2004). Altogether more than 1,000 aquatic non-indigenous species are known from Europe (Gollasch, 2006; Vila et al., 2010). However, their monetary impact is difficult to quantify (van den Bergh et al., 2002). Comprehensive studies concluded that the estimated annual damage and/or control costs of introduced aquatic non-indigenous species is $14.2 billion in the USA alone (Pimentel, 2005). Costs for repair, management and the mitigation of such species in Europe come to more than 1.2 billion Euros annually (Shine et al., 2010).

Noting the obvious problems caused by introduced species the International Conference for the Prevention of Pollution from Ships in 1973 adopted the Resolution on the "Research into the Effect of Discharge of Ballast Water Containing Bacteria of Epidemic Diseases" (IMO, 1973). This Resolution requested the International Maritime Organization (IMO) and the World Health Organization to "initiate studies on that problem on the basis of any evidence and of proposals which may be submitted by any Government". It took a while for a considerable and global exchange of views until IMO's Marine Environment Protection Committee started to develop a globally applicable marine policy instrument to cope with this problem in the early 1990s (IMO, 1993).

After more than 20 years of ballast water related work at IMO eventually the International Convention for the Control and Management of Ship´s Ballast Water and Sediments (BWM Convention) was adopted in February 2004 (IMO, 2004). The BWM Convention sets global standards on ballast water management (BWM) requirements (Gollasch et al., 2007), while at the same time regional and local specifics have to be considered for the effective implementation of the BWM Convention (David and Gollasch, 2008; Bailey et al., 2011a) and regional policies play an important role to support a more effective implementation of international instruments (Pavliha, 2010).

The BWM Convention will enter into force on 8 September 2017 (IMO, 2016), when all new vessels flying the flag or calling to a port of a State that has ratified the BWM Convention will need to comply with the BWM Convention requirements. A number of countries worldwide have chosen to implement BWM requirements in a national approach already before the entry into force of the BWM Convention. Most national requirements are based on the IMO Ballast Water Exchange Standard (IMO BWM Convention, Regulation D-1), but some countries also refer to the Ballast Water Performance Standard (IMO BWM Convention, Regulation D-2) and a minority of countries in addition refer to land-based ballast water reception facilities (David et al., 2015a).

Ballasting and deballasting process

Ballast water operations are usually conducted in the port as opposite to the cargo operations – i.e., when a vessel would load cargo, ballast water would be discharged and the opposite. A vessel may conduct ballasting and deballasting also during navigation or at the anchorage, depending on the vessel type, weather and sea conditions and vessel operations (David, 2015).

Ballast water is loaded on board a vessel by gravity into ballast tanks below the water line, or by pumping water into ballast tanks or cargo holds used for ballast. Nevertheless, all the water may be taken on board by pumping, instead of using the gravity method. The ballast tanks are filled in a predetermined sequence, depending on the type of the vessel and the ongoing cargo operation. The ballast tanks are usually filled up to their maximum capacity; however, this does not apply to fore-peak and after-peak tanks which are usually filled partially to provide for adequate vessel longitudinal inclination – i.e., trim.

Deballasting is conducted in the opposite way by gravity to discharge ballast water from ballast tanks or cargo holds used for ballast above the water line, or by pumping out the ballast water from ballast tanks or cargo holds used for ballast below the water line. Nevertheless, all the ballast water may be discharged into the surrounding environment by pumping, instead of using the gravity method (David, 2015).

When tanks are being emptied some point in time ballast pumps loose suction. Hence there may be some 5 to 10 percent remaining water in the tanks after the discharge, which may be further emptied only by using stripping pumps. All ballasting and deballasting activities are the responsibility of the chief officer who usually plans and leads ballasting and deballasting activities as part of providing for the vessel's stability.

In the case of loading a heavy cargo – e.g., metal rolls, steel, iron, ore, carbon, oil, a vessel will – when enough cargo is available, load such cargo until she gets immersed to her maximum draught. This means that the vessel will discharge all ballast except the quantity unable to be discharged, and where appropriate, the quantity needed for trimming and heeling. When vessels load light cargoes – e.g., grains, timber, paper, vehicles, containers, more cargo volume is used and less ballast is needed to compensate the cargo operation (David, 2015).

For instance, tanker vessels carrying heavy oil or vessels specialized for the carriage of orange juice, as a rule return to the port of loading empty and therefore require larger quantities of ballast water for safe navigation. Differently, a general cargo and container vessel will when in operation be partially loaded – i.e., at the next port of call some cargo will be discharged and some loaded. These vessels would consequently at the same time carry ballast water from different ports. When a significantly greater quantity of cargo is discharged than loaded, it may be assumed that ballast water will be required on board and vice versa (David et al., 2012).

However, when a vessel loads a light cargo, her maximum deadweight capacity will not be exploited, because the limiting factor becomes the volume available to store the cargo and not the cargo weight. A typical example is that of loading timber on deck, and this may also be the case when heavier containers would be loaded on top of lighter containers or on the upper deck of a car carrier (David, 2015).

These situations show that the ballast water operations are related to different vessel types, vessel construction, cargo operations and weather conditions. However, there are no clear limits among all these factors, but the decision on ballast water operation is under the discretion of the chief officer and direct control of the captain, who is responsible for the vessels stability and safety (David et al., 2012; David, 2015).

In the past global ballast water discharges were assessed or quoted by, e.g., 10 billion tonnes by Gollasch (1998) and 3.5 billion tonnes by Endresen et al. (2004). At the time that these assessments were conducted, the world seaborne trade amounted to around 5 billion tonnes of cargo per year – i.e., in 1995, it was 4.6 billion tones, and in 2000, it was 5.8 billion tonnes (UNCTAD, 2006). The more recent assessment conducted by David (2015) considered the world international seaborne trade in 2011 relevant for ballast water discharges amounted to about 9.3 billion tonnes of cargo. Thus the global ballast water discharges from all vessels engaged in the international seaborne trade in 2013 would be about 3.1 billion tonnes. The estimated amount of global ballast water discharges appeared much lower than some earlier estimations, especially considering that the global cargo transport was much higher. Nevertheless, it is important to understand that the quality of ballast water is more of a concern for the recipient environment than the quantity – i.e., the transfer of harmful aquatic organisms and pathogens present in the discharged ballast water is crucial to result in a harmful consequences due to unwanted impacts of such organisms (Hayes, 1998; Hewitt and Hayes, 2002; Bailey et al., 2011b; Briski et al., 2012; Ruiz et al., 2013; David et al., 2013, 2015b).

Transfer of species with ballast water

The transfer of organisms occurs both unintentionally (e.g., with ships) or intentionally (e.g., aquaculture, scientific research). In shipping, aquatic organisms are transferred with ballast water, in tank sediments and attached to the ships' hull, sea chests or inside ballast tanks on the tank walls. Ballast water studies conducted in different parts of the world proved that ships facilitate a substantial amount of aquatic organisms transfers across natural boundaries (Carlton, 1985; Williams et al., 1988; Gollasch, 1996; Macdonald and Davidson, 1997; Gollasch et al., 2000a, 2000b; Olenin et al., 2000; Ruiz et al., 2000; Gollasch et al., 2002; Gollasch et al., 2003; David et al., 2007). It has also been confirmed that human pathogens are being transferred with ship's ballast water (McCarthy and Khambaty, 1994; Ruiz et al., 2000; Casale, 2002).

Likely, the first biological study in which it was suspected that shipping is a vector of non-native species introductions was published more than a century ago. Ostenfeld (1908) reported the Asian phytoplankton species *Odontella (Biddulphia) sinensis* after its massive occurrence in the North Sea in 1903. Since then ballast water was assumed to be the introduction vector for many species, but the first ballast water sampling study to confirm these assumptions was carried out only 70 years later by Medcof (1975), followed by several others (Carlton, 1985; Williams et al., 1988; Hallegraeff and Bolch, 1991; Locke et al., 1991; Gollasch, 1996; McCollin et al., 1999; Hamer et al., 2000; Murphy et al., 2002; David et al., 2007). Another phytoplankton species, which likely was introduced by ballast water, the diatom *Coscinodiscus wailesii*, was found in the North Sea also because it caused a bloom in the 1970s. This resulted in some problems for fisheries by clogging fishing nets with extensive mucus (Boalch and Harbour, 1977).

Various ballast water studies have reported large numbers and densities of species in ballast samples. Taxa found range from unicellular algae to fish (Gollasch et al., 2002; David et al., 2007). It was estimated that up to 7,000 are moved daily around the world (Carlton, 2001). However, "only" 2,700 species are believed to have an invasion history (Gollasch et al., 2002; Hewitt pers. comm.). In Europe alone more than 1,000 aquatic non-native species were found in coastal and adjacent waters (Streftaris et al., 2005; Gollasch, 2006).

Ballast water may contain organisms that are small enough and sufficiently resistant to survive the ballasting, transport and deballasting process. These could be viruses and bacteria, phytoplankton, fragments of macroalgae and other plants as well as small invertebrates and fish, etc. Small fish up to 15 cm in length were also found in ballast tanks as well as eggs and resting stages of animals and plants. Further, that ballast water and the sediment that it contains, is one of the main (if not the main) transfer vectors of potentially toxic phytoplankton species, such as dinoflagellates (see the aforementioned) (Hallegraeff, 1993; Gollasch et al., 2002; David et al., 2007).

A "successful" introduction of a species into a new environment depends on a number of factors. The main factors among these are as follows:

- survival of the species in transit and during ballast water pumping processes;
- biological characteristics of the introduced species;
- biotic and abiotic conditions in the new environment, including:

  - climate and salinity conditions,
  - the number of introduced species;
  - the number of natural enemies in the new environment; and
  - the quantity of available food.

If all parameters are right, a self-sustaining population may be formed in the new environment, which subsequently may become established. In some circumstances, species also become invasive in their new environment, depending mostly on the conditions in the new environment. This process was termed "chain of events for a successful species introduction" (Carlton, 1985; Hayes, 1998).

There are many different terms and definitions used to describe introduced species and their impacts – e.g., exotic, alien, non-indigenous, allochthonus, non-native, foreign, introduced, invasive, infested, pest. Many different explanations and definitions for each of these terms exist, and there is no common agreement in the scientific community or in regulative/management/policy. Some of the main terms in use are as follows.

Introduced (or non-indigenous species) are:

> any species transported intentionally or accidentally by a human-mediated vector into aquatic habitats outside its native range. Note: Secondary introductions can be transported by human-mediated or natural vectors.
>
> (ICES, 2005)

> Any individual, group or population of a species, or other viable biological material, that is intentionally or unintentionally moved by human activities beyond its natural range or natural zone of potential dispersal, including moves from one continent or country into another and moves within a country or region; includes all domesticated and feral species, and all hybrids except for naturally occurring crosses between indigenous species.
>
> (EPA, 2001)

An invasive species is:

> a species that threatens the diversity or abundance of native species; the ecological stability of infested ecosystems; economic activities (e.g., agricultural, aquacultural, commercial, or recreational) dependent on these ecosystems; and/or human health. Synonyms: harmful, injurious, invader, noxious, nuisance, pest, and weed.
>
> (EPA, 2001)

Harmful aquatic organisms and pathogens are:

> aquatic organisms or pathogens which, if introduced into the sea including estuaries, or into fresh water courses, may create hazards to the environment, human health, property or resources, impair biological diversity or interfere with other legitimate uses of such areas.
>
> (IMO, 2004)

The adverse effects generated by the introduced species can be classified into main categories:

- negative effects on the environment and biodiversity – e.g., predation, parasitism, competition for food and space, introduction of new pathogens, influence on the genepool, alterations of the natural environment;
- human health concerns – e.g., risk of cholera and other diseases transfers, human pathogens generated by toxic algal blooms;

- economic losses – e.g., aquaculture, commercial and recreational fishing, tourism, industrial use of water, municipal waterworks, supply of potable water and power plants;
- rarely positive affects are known in case the introduced species is, e.g., a new resource of income for fishermen or other stakeholders.

Sampling of ballast water is a prime method to prove that potentially harmful organisms are discharged into the environment via shipping. Since the early 1970s, ballast water sampling studies resulted in the assumption that ballast water is one of the most important sources for the introduction of aquatic species (Medcof, 1975; Williams et al., 1988; Carlton and Geller, 1993; Hallegraeff, 1993; Macdonald and Davidson, 1997; Hay et al., 1997; Gollasch, 1998; Ruiz et al., 2000; Wonham et al., 2001; Murphy et al., 2002).

In the EU, different ballast water studies have been conducted. In total, >1,600 samples were collected on >575 vessels. The diversity of species found included bacteria, fungi, protozoans, algae, invertebrates of different life stages including resting stages and fish. Crustacean, molluscan and polychaete invertebrates, as well as algae comprise the majority of species found (Gollasch et al., 2002; David et al., 2007).

Several among these introduced species generate negative consequences while relatively few invasions have had significant (almost catastrophic) and seemingly irreversible impacts (e.g., Hayes and Sliwa, 2003). Some of the most known cases that have been related to ballast water transfer are the zebra mussel *Dreissena polymorpha* to the Great Lakes (Hebert et al., 1989; Carlton and Geller, 1993), the comb jelly *Mnemiopsis leidyi* to the Black Sea (GESAMP, 1997) and *Asterias amurensis* to Australia (Rossa et al., 2003). It is interesting to note that the zebra mussel spread from its area of origin (Black and Caspian Seas) across Europe and reached Western Europe before 1850s. However, the species continued to spread and reached central Europe (France and northern Italy) until 1950s and 2000s. The ongoing spread of this species over centuries is also reflected in the German common name of this species. It is called "Wandermuschel", which means wandering or hiking mussel. The first appearance in Ireland was in the mid-1990s (Minchin et al., 2002). It may well be that the spread of the species in Europe is related to natural spreading capabilities due to larval drift with water currents. This would explain that it took more than 150 years for the species to spread to its current distribution. However, movements with ballast water cannot be excluded. This situation is different in the USA. Here it was first identified in 1988 (Lake St Clair, near Detroit) (Hebert et al., 1989), although it was probably established already since 1986. As natural spread of this freshwater species across the Atlantic is impossible, the only remaining transport vector is ballast water and this assumption is also supported by the fact that it was found near ports and/or typical ballast water discharge zones.

The comb jelly, after it became introduced to the Black and Caspian Seas, was also recorded from the Baltic and North Seas (Ivanov et al., 2000; Vinogradov et al., 2005; Javidpour et al., 2006; Van Ginderdeuren et al., 2012). It later became clear by genetic analysis that multiple species introductions occurred in Europe (Reusch et al., 2010). In contrast, the *A. amurensis* case is unique, as this species was (so far) not found anywhere else outside its natural range area, other than in Australia (Rossa et al., 2003).

A case worth mentioning because it threatened numerous human lives is the introduction of the cholera agent to coastal US waters in 1991 when it was detected in the ballast water of a ship docked in the Port of Mobile in the Gulf of Mexico, Alabama (USA). The causative agent of cholera, *Vibrio cholerae*, was also found in local aquaculture products (e.g., oysters). During a standard inspection, the US Food and Drug Administration isolated *Vibrio cholerae* 01 from the stomach content of a fish caught in Mobile Bay. The isolated agent was different from the one already present in the bay but was unmistakably similar to the agent typical of Latin America (McCarthy and Khambaty, 1994; Casale, 2002). Further, the cholera epidemic that concurrently broke out in three Peruvian port cities was directly linked to ballast water discharge. The epidemic soon spread throughout South America. In 1991, more than 1 million people were infected, approximately 8,000 succumbing to the disease. By 1994, 10,000 victims of the epidemic were recorded, though it is believed that their number was underestimated due to inappropriate coverage. In the described case, the same causative agent of cholera had previously been recorded only in Bangladesh (Casale, 2002).

In an extensive ballast water sampling campaign conducted in Australia, 80 percent of vessels contained up to 30 culturable diatom species, including the potentially toxic *Pseudonitzschia* that causes Amnesic Shellfish Poisoning (Forbes and Hallegraeff, 2001). Viable cultures of dinoflagellates *Alexandrium catenella, A. tamarense* and *Gymnodinium catenatum* were produced from the ballast water of 5 percent of vessels entering Australia from Japan and Korea (Hallegraeff and Bolch, 1992). Studies of vessels entering British ports confirmed the presence of *Alexandrium minutum* and *A. catenella/tamarense* in 17 percent of ballast water samples (Hamer et al., 2001). In one case, a single ballast tank was estimated to contain as many as 300 million viable *Alexandrium tamarense* cysts (Hallegraeff and Bolch, 1992). The potentially ichthyotoxic dinoflagellate *Pfiesteria* has been confirmed by molecular probes in ballast water entering US ports (Doblin et al., 2002). In conclusion, the presence of potentially harmful marine microalgae in ballast water has been firmly established.

Voyage length critically affects the survival rate of organisms in ballast water. However, the organisms can survive in ballast water for a relatively long time. Some algae, in particular dinoflagellates, can form cysts in the ballast water sediment (see the aforementioned). They may remain viable (in a dormant state) despite unfavourable conditions for a long time (up to several years, if not decades) (Hallegraeff and Bolch, 1992). When the voyage is longer, the risk of the introduction of harmful algae still exists. There are also known cases when organisms have reproduced and expanded their population inside a tank. In a ballast water sampling study, which involved daily samplings, it was observed that most species died during the first few days of the voyage. However, one copepod species may have found favourable conditions as its population increased from a few individuals in the beginning to more than a 1,000 per 100 litres of ballast water at the end of the voyage (Gollasch et al., 2000c). Further, a shipping study undertaken in Germany proved that even after more than three months duration, living organisms were found in the ballast tank (Gollasch, 1996; Gollasch et al., 2000a, 2000b, 2000c).

It is difficult to predict which species may become introduced next. A typical example is provided by the zebra mussel case described earlier. Shipping lanes linking the Caspian and Black Seas with North America and the Great Lakes had existed for decades before a "successful" introduction of the zebra mussel occurred. However, risk assessment approaches were developed to evaluate the risk of future species introductions.

The impacts of the introduced organisms are manifold. They may not only be negative but also be positive for some stakeholders (e.g., introduced prawns for aquaculture or decapods for fishing), may not have harmful effects at all (e.g., just survive in the new environment), or have unwanted (e.g., establish in the new environment, compete for food with native species, introduce changes to ecosystem) or detrimental effects (e.g., displace or eradicate native species). The view of the effects of introduced species is critically dependant on their perception. Researches undoubtedly have shown that each vector which facilitates the introduction of organisms, if present, represents a latent threat to the environment, human health, property or resources. In light of this, economic interests must not supersede these threats.

BWM Convention

The main aim of the BWM Convention is to prevent, minimize and ultimately eliminate the risks to the environment, human health, property and resources which may arise from the transfer of harmful aquatic organisms and pathogens (HAOP) via ships' ballast waters also considering related sediments (IMO, 2004). It is important to note that HAOP in this context are not limited to non-indigenous species, but HAOP include all aquatic species irrespective where they are native so that cryptogenic and harmful native species are also covered. IMO defines BWM as "mechanical, physical, chemical, and biological processes, either singularly or in combination, to remove, render harmless, or avoid the uptake or discharge of Harmful Aquatic Organisms and Pathogens within Ballast Water and Sediments."

As per the basic principles of the BWM Convention vessels (not ports) are required to conduct BWM. However, port ballast water reception facilities are also considered by the BWM Convention as a valid BWM option and these may be located in a port as a land-based facility or installed on a movable barge (David et al., 2015a).

The BWM Convention introduces two different BWM standards:

- Ballast Water Exchange Standard (Regulation D-1, so-called D-1 standard) requiring ships to exchange a minimum of 95% ballast water volume; and
- Ballast Water Performance Standard (Regulation D-2, so-called D-2 standard) which requires that ballast water discharges have the number of viable organisms below the specified limits.

(IMO, 2004)

With the BWM Convention entry into force (see the aforementioned), all new vessels, excluding exempted or excepted ones, will need to comply with the D-2 standard. This may presently be achieved only by treating ballast water with a ballast water management system (BWMS). Vessels constructed before the entry into force of the BWM Convention will need to comply with the D-2 standard in the latest at their first renewal survey of the International Oil Pollution Prevention certificate after the entry into force date of the BWM Convention – i.e., at the latest by 2022 (IMO, 2016; David et al., 2015a). However, at a recent IMO seventieth meeting of the Marine Environment Protection Committee (MEPC) this approach was re-opened for debate, and a final conclusion may only be reached at a future IMO meeting, hopefully, when MEPC reconvenes in July 2017 (IMO, 2016).

Under the BWM Convention, the same requirements may apply to all vessels, which is the so-called blanket approach, or the BWM requirements may vary according to the risk posed by the ballast water intended to be discharged. This means that, under certain circumstances, vessels may be released – i.e., exempted or excepted – from conducting BWM or the opposite – i.e., the required BWM measures may be more stringent in high or extreme risk situations. Specific BWM requirements are especially important in cases when some BWM measures under the blanket approach would not be feasible. This, e.g., refers to limitations to conduct ballast water exchange (BWE) because of geographically specific situations and restricted areas (David and Gollasch, 2008; David et al., 2015a).

One of the most important and critical parts for an effective implementation of the BWM Convention are inspections to reveal possible violations of the provisions of this convention. In addition to paper checks – i.e., inspectors verification of certificates and log books – ballast water may be sampled to ascertain compliance with the requirements. IMO provided relevant general sampling guidance documents (IMO, 2004, 2008, 2013); however, sampling of ballast water has shown to be far from easy, especially when planning to obtain a representative sample, which still remains a challenge (David, 2013; Gollasch and David, 2009, 2010, 2013, 2017). IMO noted the current knowledge gap and agreed on an experience building phase with a trial period for two or three years after entry into force of the BWM Convention (IMO, 2016).

As the ballast water issue was shown to be complex, the implementation of the BWM Convention is also facing several unsolved challenges. Interests of the shipping industry to lessen the financial and operational BWM burden was, and still is, in general supported by the countries with larger merchant fleets flying their flag. This substantially delayed the entry into force of the BWM Convention – i.e., we are now 13 years after its adoption, and it is still not boosting the implementation of measures all-around the world, which puts more of a challenge on the port States that implement appropriate measures. USA for instance introduced more stringent requirements than those stated in the BWM Convention, which adds burden to all vessels that would like to enter USA ports. Furthermore, the difference in geographical and environmental situations make some BWM methods not to be feasible – e.g., (a) BWE is not feasible in enclosed or semi-enclosed areas/ seas, (b) BWMS using electrochlorination may not work in low salinity areas and (c) some ballast water chemical treatment products may not degrade at low temperatures. However, vessels in general operate in very diverse environments and areas, which makes this difficult BWM even more complicated and in several cases simply impossible. It is also still unclear what to do with vessels which are found non-compliant and, consequently, should not discharge such ballast water, but in cases where there is no available alternative discharge area designated or ballast water reception facility are lacking, what would be the alternative solution or mitigation measure to avoid such ballast water discharges?

The present situation stipulates that the BWM issue needs to be approached globally and through regional approaches, and the exchange of experience among countries and regions is essential. The BWM Convention as well may need to be adapted to support the implementation of most efficient BWM measures. However, this instrument can only be re-opened for improvement after its entry into force – i.e. in September 2017.

Maritime transport mobilities and ballast water transfer

Commercial vessels are built for the transport of various cargoes or passengers. According to the latest UNCTAD (2016) report on developments in global maritime transport, the estimated world seaborne trade volumes in 2015 surpassed 10 billion tons, which is according to UNCTAD records a record volume. After the 2008 global market crisis and consequent depression in maritime transports, the world seaborne trade is steadily growing and further growth is foreseen.

However, there is no equal growth among the different areas in the world or among cargoes transported and, consequently, the use of different types of vessels vary. It was noted that the world economy recovered from the market crisis by economical growth in developed economies and a market slowdown in developing countries, as well as in economies in transition. Economical data for 2014 show that the world gross domestic product (GDP) increased. This 2.5 percent increase in 2014 was marginally higher than in 2013, where the GDP was 2.4 percent. Further, the world merchandise trade increased by 2.3 percent, which is 0.3 percent less than in 2013 and below the pre-crisis levels. Consequently, the preliminary UNCTAD estimates of global seaborne shipments have increased by 3.4 percent in 2014, which is the same rate as in 2013 (UNCTAD, 2015). The maritime transport market is directly responding and supporting global market developments, and remains still uncertain and exposed to downside risks. This is because of continued moderate growth in global demand and merchandise trade, the fragile economic recovery in Europe, diverging outlooks on oil production and consumption markets, geopolitical tensions and a potential faster slowdown in developing economies, including a large one as in China. Though maritime transports related to the Chinese market have slowed down, there is South-South trade, which is gaining positive momentum. Furthermore, the expanded Panama and Suez Canals have the potential to influence and reshape the directions of seaborne trade. In addition, the ice depletion due to climate change may enable shipping routes in the Arctic to be used more frequently for commercial shipping. Following the changes on the markets in 2015, the tanker vessels segment recorded its best performance since 2008, while the dry cargo vessels sector growth, including bulk commodities and containerized trade in commodities, did not achieve the expectations (UNCTAD, 2012, 2015, 2016).

Having in mind that the ballast water operations are basically directly related to cargo movements – i.e., ballast water discharges occur in the opposite way of cargo being loaded and the changes on the cargo markets and engagement of different types of vessels – the volume and profile of ballast water transfer changes globally through the time.

Where prime resources are moved from their source to the industry that transforms or uses these – e.g., crude oil, coal and iron ore – with oil tankers and bulk carriers, one-way empty voyages are usual practice; the typical ballast operation would be to ballast vessels to full ballast capacity when the vessel is empty (David, 2015). Hence large volumes of ballast water are being transferred in such cases. Whenever a cargo is available to be carried in the opposite way, at least in part of the voyage, shipping companies use this opportunity to avoid ballast (unpaid) voyages. With this, oil tankers and bulk carriers empty voyages and consequently ballast water transfers in the view of mobilities – i.e., of too little movement or too much, or of the wrong sort or at the wrong time (Sheller and Urry, 2006) – are directly and strongly driven by the global distribution of the donor and recipient areas of prime resource cargoes, and secondly respond to the market changes.

Container vessels usually travel partially loaded and conduct partial loading and discharging cargo operations in almost every port they call; consequently, ballast water operations are partially (smaller volumes) conducted in different ports (David, 2015). In container traffic, there are extensive movements of empty containers, which is of concern for mobilities (Monios and Wilmsmeier, 2015). In terms of ballast water transfers, empty containers are relatively light; hence, they do not represent a weight to trigger ballast water operations. With this, the ballast water transfers with container vessels are primarily generated by cargo demands and offers on global markets. Secondly, in a more local geographical profile, this responds to the organization of the container traffic – i.e., with the existence and distribution of hub and/or secondary container ports or terminals (David et al., 2012; David et al., 2017).

In general cargo traffic, vessels mostly partially load and discharge cargo in same ports, similar to container vessels, and ballast operations are also partially conducted in different ports. General cargo movements follow the market demands and offers; hence, ballast water operations correspond to these. Ro-Ro and passenger vessels rely mainly on permanent ballast, hence rarely load and discharge ballast water from/to the surrounding environment.

Conclusions

Ballast water studies conducted in different parts of the world proved that ships facilitate a substantial amount of aquatic organisms and human pathogen transfers across natural boundaries. Several among these introduced species generate negative consequences while relatively few invasions have had significant (almost catastrophic) and seemingly irreversible impacts. Researches undoubtedly have shown that each vector which facilitates the introduction of organisms, if present, represents a potential latent threat to the environment, human health, property or resources.

Vessels fundamentally depend on ballast water for their safe navigation and operations as a result of their design and construction (David, 2015). Different types of vessels have different ballast water operation profiles. Bulk carriers, tankers and general cargo vessels are those transferring major ballast water volumes, while container vessels have high frequencies of ballast water operations in smaller volumes. The prime factor defining the ballast water movements is cargo movement, where ballast water is regular opposite operation of the cargo operation. Hence, the ballast water operations globally correspond to the cargo movements which are triggered by global market demands and offers, which change geographically over the time. More detailed investigations of maritime transport markets and ballast water movements would give necessary insights in how to lower BWMs and respond to concerns of the mobilities theory.

Acknowledgements

The research leading to part of these results has received funding from the European Community's Seventh Framework Programme (FP7/2007–2013) under Grant Agreement No. [266445] for the project Vectors of Change in Oceans and Seas Marine Life, Impact on Economic Sectors (VECTORS).

References

Bailey, S. A., Chan, F., Ellis, S. M., Bronnenhuber, J. E., Bradie, J. N., Simard, N. (2011b). Risk assessment for ship-mediated introductions of aquatic nonindigenous species to the Great Lakes and freshwater St. Lawrence River. *DFO Canadian Science Advisory Secretariat Research Document*. 2011/104: vi–224.

Bailey, S. A., Deneau, M. G., Jean, L., Wiley, C. J., Leung, B., MacIsaac, H. J. (2011a). Evaluating efficacy of an environmental policy to prevent biological invasions. *Environmental Science & Technology*. 45: 2554–2561.

Bailey, S. A., Duggan, I. C., Jenkins, P. T., MacIsaac, H. J. (2005). Invertebrate resting stages in residual ballast sediment of transoceanic ships. *Canadian Journal of Fisheries and Aquatic Sciences*. 62: 1090–1103.

Bauer, M. (ed.) (2006). *Harmful Algal Research and Response: A Human Dimensions Strategy*. Woods Hole, MA: National Office for Marine Biotoxins and Harmful Algal Blooms, Woods Hole Oceanographic Institution.

Bax, N., Williamson, A., Aguero, M., Gonzalez, E., Geeves, W. (2003). Marine invasive alien species: A threat to global biodiversity. *Marine Policy*. 27: 313–323.

Boalch, G. T., Harbour, D. S. (1977). Unusual diatom off the coast of south west England and its effect on fishing. *Nature*. 269: 687–688.

Briski, E., Bailey, S. A., Casas-Monroy, O., DiBaccio, C., Kzaczmarska, I., Levings, C., MacGillvary, M. L., McKindsey, C. W., Nasmith, L. E., Parenteau, M., Piercey, G. E.,

Rochon, A., Roy, S., Simard, N., Villac, M. C., Weise, A. M., MacIsaac, H. J. (2012). Relationship between propagule pressure and colonization pressure in invasion ecology: A test with ships' ballast. *Proceedings of the Royal Society B.* 279: 2990–2997.

Carlton, J. T. (2001). *Introduced Species in U.S. Coastal Waters: Environmental Impacts and Management Priorities.* Arlington: Pew Oceans Commission.

Carlton, J. T. (1985). Transoceanic and interoceanic dispersal of coastal marine organisms: The biology of ballast water. *Annual Review of Oceanography and Marine Biology.* 23: 313–374.

Carlton, J. T., Geller, J. B. (1993). Ecological roulette: The global transport of non-indigenous marine organisms. *Science.* 261: 78–82.

Casale, G. A. (2002). Ballast water – a public health issue? *GloBallast Programme, IMO London, Ballast Water News.* 8: 4–5.

Cohen, A. N., Carlton, J. T. (1995). Nonindigenous species in a United States estuary: A case study of the biological invasions of the San Francisco Bay and Delta, U.S. Fish and Wildlife Service and National Sea Grant College Program. Connecticut Sea Grant.

David, M. (2015). Vessels and Ballast Water. In: M. David and S. Gollasch (eds.), *Global Maritime Transport and Ballast Water Management – Issues and Solutions: Invading Nature.* Springer Series in Invasion Ecology 8. Dordrecht, The Netherlands: Springer Science + Business Media. pp. 13–34.

David, M., Gollasch, S. (2008). EU Shipping in the dawn of managing the ballast water issue. *Marine Pollution Bulletin.* 56: 1966–1972.

David, M. (2013). Ballast water sampling for compliance monitoring – ratification of the Ballast Water Management Convention. Final report of research study for WWF International. Project number 10000675 – PO1368. Gland, Switzerland.

David, M., Gollasch, S., Cabrini, M., Perkovič, M., Bošnjak, D., Virgilio, D. (2007). Results from the first ballast water sampling study in the Mediterranean Sea – the Port of Koper study. *Marine Pollution Bulletin.* 54: 53–65.

David, M., Gollasch, S., Elliott, B., Wiley, C. (2015a). Ballast Water Management Under the Ballast Water Management Convention. In: M. David and S. Gollasch (eds.), *Global Maritime Transport and Ballast Water Management – Issues and Solutions.* Dordrecht Heidelberg, New York, London: Springer Science + Business Media. pp. 59–88.

David, M., Gollasch, S., Leppäkoski, E. (2013). Risk assessment for exemptions from ballast water management – the Baltic Sea case study. *Marine Pollution Bulletin.* 75: 205–217.

David, M., Gollasch, S., Leppäkoski, E., Hewitt, C. (2015b). Risk Assessment in Ballast Water Management. In: M. David and S. Gollasch (eds.), *Global Maritime Transport and Ballast Water Management – Issues and Solutions.* Dordrecht Heidelberg, New York, London: Springer Science + Business Media. pp. 133–170.

David, M., Gollasch, S., Penko, L. (2017). Identification of ballast water discharge profiles of a port to enable effective ballast water management and environmental studies. *Journal of Sea Research, Special Issue Ballast Water Management.* DOI: 10.1016/j.seares.2017.03.001

David, M., Perkovič, M., Suban, V., Gollasch, S. (2012). A generic ballast water discharge assessment model as a decision supporting tool in ballast water management. *Decision Support Systems.* 53: 175–185.

Davidson, I. C., Simkanin, C. (2012). The biology of ballast water 25 years later. *Biological Invasions.* 14: 9–13.

Doblin, M. A., Drake, L. A., Coyne, K. J., Rublee, P. A., Dobbs, F. C. (2002). Pfiesteria Species Identified in Ships' Ballast Water and Residuals: A Possible Vector for

Introductions to Coastal Areas. In: K. A. Steidinger, J. L. Landsberg, C. R. Tomas and G. A. Vargo (eds.), *Harmful Algae 2002*. St. Petersburg, FL: Florida Fish and Wildlife Conservation Commission, Florida Institute of Oceanography and Inter-governmental Oceangraphic Commission of UNESCO. pp. 317–319.

Elton, C. (1958). *The Ecology of Invasions by Plants and Animals*. London: Methuen.

Endresen, Ø., Behrens, H. L., Brynestad, S., Andersen, A. B., Skjong, R. (2004). Challenges in global ballast water management. *Marine Pollution Bulletin*. 48: 615–623.

EPA (2001). *Aquatic Nuisance Species, Annual Report (2001)*. Washington, DC: United States Environmental Protection Agency.

Forbes, E., Hallegraeff, G. M. (2001). Transport of Potentially Toxic Pseudo-Nitzschia Diatom Species Via Ballast Water. In: J. John (ed.), *Proc. 15th Diatom Symposium*. Koenigstein, Germany: Koeltz Scientific Publishers. pp. 509–520.

GESAMP (1997). Opportunistic settlers and the problem of the ctenophore Mnemiopsis leidyi invasion in the Black Sea. *IMO/FAO/UNESCO-IOC/WMO/WHO/IAEA/UN/ UNEP Joint Group of Experts on the Scientific Aspects of Marine Environmental Protection: Reports and Studies, GESAMP*. 58: 84.

Gollasch, S. (1996). Untersuchungen des Arteintrages durch den internationalen Schiffsverkehr unter besonderer Berücksichtigung nichtheimischer Arten. Diss., University Hamburg; Verlag Dr. Kovac, Hamburg.

Gollasch, S. (1998). *Removal of Barriers to the Effective Implementation of Ballast Water Control and Management Measures in Developing Countries (for GEF/IMO/UNDP)*. London: International Maritime Organization.

Gollasch, S. (2006). Overview on introduced aquatic species in European navigational and adjacent waters. *Helgoland Marine Research*. 60: 84–89.

Gollasch, S., David, M. (2009). Results of an on board ballast water sampling study and initial considerations how to take representative samples for compliance control with the D-2 Standard of the Ballast Water Management Convention. Report of research study of the Bundesamt für Seeschifffahrt und Hydrographie (BSH), Hamburg, Germany.

Gollasch, S., David, M. (2010). Testing sample representativeness of a ballast water discharge and developing methods for indicative analysis. European Maritime Safety Agency (EMSA), Lisbon, Portugal.

Gollasch, S., David, M. (2013). Recommendations for Representative Ballast Water Sampling. Final report of research study of the Bundesamt für Seeschifffahrt und Hydrographie (BSH), Hamburg, Germany. Order Number 4500025702.

Gollasch, S., David, M. (2017). Recommendations for representative ballast water sampling. *Journal of Sea Research, Special Issue Ballast Water Management*.

Gollasch, S., David, M., Voigt, M., Dragsund, E., Hewitt, C. L., Fukuyo, Y. (2007). Critical review of the IMO international convention on the management of ships' ballast water and sediments. *Harmful Algae*. 6: 585–600.

Gollasch, S., Lenz, J., Dammer, M., Andres, H. G. (2000a). Survival of tropical ballast water organisms during a cruise from the Indian Ocean to the North Sea. *Journal of Plankton Research*. 22: 923–937.

Gollasch, S., Macdonald, E., Belson, S., Botnen, H., Christensen, J., Hamer, J., Houvenaghel, G., Jelmert, A., Lucas, I., Masson, D., McCollin, T., Olenin, S., Persson, A., Wallentinus, I., Wetsteyn, B., Wittling, T. (2002). Life in Ballast Tanks. In: E. Leppäkoski, S. Gollasch and S. Olenin (eds.), *Invasive Aquatic Species of Europe: Distribution, Impacts and Management*. Dordrecht: Kluwer Academic Publishers. pp. 217–231.

Gollasch, S., Rosenthal, H., Botnen, H., Crncevic, M., Gilbert, M., Hamer, J., Hülsmann, N., Mauro, C., McCann, L., Minchin, D., Öztürk, B., Robertson, M., Sutton, C., Villac,

M. C. (2003). Species richness and invasion vectors: Sampling techniques and biases. *Biological Invasions*. 5: 365–377.

Gollasch, S., Rosenthal, H., Botnen, H., Hamer, J., Laing, I., Leppäkoski, E., MacDonald, E., Minchin, D., Nauke, M., Olenin, S., Utting, S., Voight, M., Wallentinus, I. (2000b). Fluctuations of zooplankton taxa in ballast water during short-term and long-term ocean-going voyages. *International Review of Hydrobiology*. 85 (5–6): 597–608.

Gollasch, S., Rosenthal, H., Botnen, J., Hamer, H., Laing, I., Leppäkoski, E., Macdonald, E., Minchin, D., Nauke, M., Olenin, S., Utting, S., Voigt, M., Wallentinus, I. (2000c). Survival rates of species in ballast water during international voyages: Results of the first workshops the European Concerted Action. First National Conference on Bioinvasions, MA, Massachusetts Institute of Technology (MIT), MIT Sea Grant Program, Center for Coastal Resources, Cambridge, MA, 24–27 January, 1999. Conference proceedings, J. Pederson (ed.), pp. 296–305.

Granéli, E., Edvardsen, B., Roelke, D. L., Hagström, J. A. (2012). The ecophysiology and bloom dynamics of Prymnesium spp. *Harmful Algae*. 14: 260–270.

Hallegraeff, G. M. (1993). A review of harmful algal blooms and their apparent global increase. *Phycologia*. 32: 79–99.

Hallegraeff, G. M., Anderson, D. M., Cembella, A. D. (eds.) (2003). *Manual on Harmful Marine Microalgae: Monographs on Oceanographic Methodology*. Paris: United Nations Educational, Scientific and Cultural Organization.

Hallegraeff, G. M., Bolch, C. J. (1991). Transport of toxic dinoflagellate cysts via ship's ballast water. *Marine Pollution Bulletin*. 22: 27–30.

Hallegraeff, G. M., Bolch, C. J. (1992). Transport of dinoflagellate cysts in ship's ballast water: Implications for plankton biogeography and aquaculture. *Journal of Plankton Research*. 14: 1067–1084.

Hamer, J. P., Lucas, I.A.N., McCollin, T. A. (2001). Harmful dinoflagellate resting cysts in ships' ballast tank sediments; potential for introduction into English and Welsh waters. *Phycologia*. 40: 246–255.

Hamer, J. P., McCollin, T. A., Lucas, I.A.N. (2000). Dinofagellate cysts in ballast tank sediments: between tank variability. *Marine Pollution Bulletin*. 40 (9): 731–733.

Hay, C., Handley, S., Dogdshun, T., Taylor, M., Gibbs, W. (1997). Cawthron's Ballast Water Research Programme Final Report 1996–97. Cawthron Institute, Cawthron Report No. 417, New Zealand, Nelson. p. 144.

Hayes, K. R. (1998). Ecological risk assessment for ballast water introductions: A suggested approach. *ICES Journal of Marine Science*. 55: 201–212.

Hayes, K. R., Sliwa, C. (2003). Identifying potential marine pests – a deductive approach applied to Australia. *Marine Pollution Bulletin*. 46: 91–98.

Hebert, P.D.N., Muncaster, B. W., Mackie, G. L. (1989). Ecological and genetic studies on Dreissena polymorpha (Pallas): A new mollusc in the Great Lakes. *Canadian Journal of Fisheries and Aquatic Sciences*. 48: 1381–1388.

Hewitt, C. L., Campbell, M. L., Thresher, R. E., Martin, R. B., Boyd, S., Cohen, B. F., Currie, D. R., Gomon, M. F., Keough, M. J., Lewis, J. A., Lockett, M. M., Mays, N., McArthur, M. A., O'Hara, T. D., Poore, G.C.B., Ross, D. J., Storey, M. J., Watson, J. E., Wilson, R. S. (2004). Introduced and cryptogenic species in Port Phillip Bay, Victoria, Australia. *Marine Biology*. 144: 183–202.

Hewitt, C. L., Hayes, K. R. (2002). Risk Assessment of Marine Biological Invasions. In: E. Leppäkoski, S. Gollasch and S. Olenin (eds.), *Invasive Aquatic Species of Europe: Distribution, Impact and Management*. Dordrecht, The Netherlands: Kluwer Academic Publishers. pp. 456–466.

ICES (2005). ICES Code of Practice on the Introductions and Transfers of Marine Organisms 2005. International Council for the Exploration of the Sea, Copenhagen, Denmark. p. 30.

IMO (1973). International Convention for the Prevention of Pollution from Ships (MARPOL). Final Act of the International Conference on Marine Pollution 1973, Resolution 18. IMO, London.

IMO (1993). *Guidelines for Preventing the Introduction of Unwanted Aquatic Organisms and Pathogens from Ships' Ballast Water and Sediment Discharges: IMO Assembly Resolution A.774(18)*. London: International Maritime Organization.

IMO (2004). *International Convention for the Control and Management of Ships' Ballast Water and Sediments, 2004: International Maritime Organization, 13 February 2004*. London: International Maritime Organization.

IMO (2008). Guidelines for ballast water sampling (G2), IMO Resolution MEPC.173(58). International Maritime Organization, London.

IMO (2013). International Convention for the Control and Management of Ships' Ballast Water and Sediments, 2004, Guidance on ballast water sampling and analysis for trial use in accordance with the BWM Convention and Guidelines (G2), BWM.2/Circ.42. International Maritime Organization, London.

IMO (2016). *Report of the Marine Environment Protection Committee on Its Seventieth Session: MEPC 70/18*. London: International Maritime Organization.

Ivanov, V. P., Kamakin, A. M., Ushivtzev, V. B., Shiganova, T., Zhukova, O., Aladin, N., Wilson, S. I., Harbison, G. R., Dumont, H. J. (2000). Invasion of the Caspian Sea by the comb-jellyfish Mnemiopsis leidyi (Ctenophora). *Biological Invasions*. 2 (3): 255–258.

Javidpour, J., Sommer, U., Shiganova, T. (2006). First record of Mnemiopsis leidyi A. Agassiz 1865 in the Baltic Sea. *Aquatic Invasions*. 1 (4): 299–302.

Kotaki, Y., Koike, K., Yoshida, M., Chu, T. V., Nguyen, T.M.H., Nguyen, C. H., Fukuyo, Y., Kodama, M. (2000). Domoic acid production in Nitzschia sp. (Bacillariophyceae) isolated from a shrimp-culture pond in Do Son, Vietnam. *Journal of Phycology*. 36: 1057–1060.

Leppäkoski, E., Gollasch, S., Olenin, S. (2002). *Invasive Aquatic Species of Europe: Distribution, Impact and Management*. Dordrecht: Kluwer Academic Publishers.

Locke, A., Reid, D. M., Sprules, W. G., Carlton, J. T., van Leeuwen, H. C. (1991). Effectiveness of mid-ocean exchange in controlling freshwater and coastal zooplankton in ballast water. *Canadian Technical Report. Fisheries and Aquatic Sciences*. 1822: 1–93.

Macdonald, E. M., Davidson, R. D. (1997). Ballast water project, Final report. FRS Marine Laboratory, Aberdeen.

McCarthy, S. A., Khambaty, F. M. (1994). International dissemination of epidemic Vibrio cholera by cargo ship ballast and other non-potable waters. *Applied and Environmental Microbiology*. 60 (7): 2597–2601.

McCollin, T. A., Hamer, J. P., Lucas, I.A.N. (1999). Marine organisms transported in ships' ballast water. Final Report to Report to Ministry for Agriculture, Fisheries and Food, UK.

McGinn, A. P. (1999). Safeguarding the Health of Oceans. In: J. A. Peterson (ed.), *World Watch Paper 145*. World Watch Institute, Washington, DC. p. 87.

Medcof, J. C. (1975). Living marine animals in a ships' ballast water. *Proceedings of the National Shellfisheries Association*. 65: 54–55.

Minchin, D., Lucy, F., Sullivan, M. (2002). Zebra Mussel: Impacts and Spread. In: E. Leppäkoski, S. Gollasch and S. Olenin (eds.), *Invasive Aquatic Species of Europe: Distribution, Impacts and Management*. Dordreicht, the Netherlands: Kluwer Academic Publishers. pp. 135–146.

Monios, J., Wilmsmeier, G. (2015). Identifying Material, Geographical and Institutional Mobilities in the Global Maritime Trade System. In: T. Birtchnell, S. Savitzky and J. Urry (eds.), *Cargomobilities: Moving Materials in a Global Age*. Abingdon: Routledge. pp. 125–148.

Murphy, K. R., Ritz, D., Hewitt, C. L. (2002). Heterogeneous zooplankton distribution in a ship's ballast tanks. *Journal of Plankton Research*. 24 (7): 729–734.

Olenin, S., Gollasch, S., Jonushas, S., Rimkute, I. (2000). En-route investigations of plankton in ballast water on a ships´ voyage from the Baltic Sea to the open Atlantic coast of Europe. *International Review of Hydrobiology*. 85: 577–596.

Ostenfeld, C. H. (1908). On the immigration of Biddulphia sinensis Grev. and its occurrence in the North Sea during 1903–1907. *Medd Komm Havunders Ser Plankton*. 1 (6): 1–46.

Pavliha, M. (2010). New European Maritime Policy for Cleaner Oceans and Seas. In: N. A. Martínez Gutiérrez (ed.), *Serving the Rule of International Maritime Law: Essays in Honour of Professor David Joseph Attard*. London, New York: Routledge. pp. 22–31.

Pimentel, D. (2005). Aquatic nuisance species in the New York state canal and Hudson river systems and the great lakes basin: An economic and environmental assessment. *Environmental Management*. 35 (1): 1–11.

Reusch, T.B.H., Bolte, S., Sparwek, M., Moss, A. G., Javidbour, J. (2010). Microsatellites reveal origin and genetic diversity of Eurasian invasions by one of the world's most notorious marine invader, Mnemiopsis leidyi (Ctenophora). *Molecular Ecology*. 19: 2690–2699.

Rigby, G. R., Hallegraeff, G. M. (1994). The transfer and control of harmful marine organisms in shipping ballast water: Behaviour of marine plankton and ballast water exchange on the MV 'Iron Whyalla'. *Journal of Marine Environment and Engineering*. 1: 91–110.

Rossa, D. J., Johnsona, C. R., Hewitt, C. L. (2003). Variability in the impact of an introduced predator (Asterias amurensis: Asteroidea) on soft-sediment assemblages. *Journal of Experimental Marine Biology and Ecology*. 288: 257–278.

Ruiz, G. M., Fofonnoff, P. W., Ashton, G., Minton, M. S., Miller, A. W. (2013). Geographic variation in marine invasions among large estuaries: Effects of ships and time. *Ecological Applications*. 23 (2): 311–320.

Ruiz, G. M., Rawlings, T. K., Dobbs, F. C., Drake, L. A., Mullady, T., Huq, A., Colwell, R. R. (2000). Global spread of microorganisms by ships. *Nature*. 408: 49–50.

Sheller, M., Urry, J. (2006). The new mobilities paradigm. *Environment & Planning A*. 38 (2): 207–226.

Shine, C., Kettunen, M., Genovesi, P., Essl, F., Gollasch, S., Rabitsch, W., Scalera, R., Starfinger, U., ten Brink, P. (2010). Assessment to support continued development of the EU Strategy to combat invasive alien species. Final Report for the European Commission. Brussels: Institute for European Environmental Policy (IEEP).

Sorte, C.J.B., Williams, S. L., Carlton, J. T. (2010). Marine range shifts and species introductions: Comparative spread rates and community impacts. *Global Ecology and Biogeography*. 19: 303–316.

Streftaris, N., Zenetos, A., Papathanassiou, E. (2005). Globalisation in marine ecosystems: the story of non-indigenous marine species across European seas. *Oceanography and Marine Biology, An Annual Review*. 43: 419–453.

UNCTAD (2006). Review of maritime transport (2006). Report by the UNCTAD secretariat. New York and Geneva: United Nations.

UNCTAD (2012). Review of maritime transport (2012). Report by the UNCTAD secretariat. New York and Geneva: United Nations.

UNCTAD (2015). Review of maritime transport (2015). Report by the UNCTAD secretariat. New York and Geneva: United Nations.

UNCTAD (2016). Review of maritime transport (2016). Report by the UNCTAD secretariat. New York and Geneva: United Nations.

van den Bergh, J.C.J.M., Nunes, P.A.L.D., Dotinga, H. M., Kooistra, W.H.C.F., Vrieling, E. G., Peperzak, L. (2002). Exotic harmful algae in marine ecosystems: An integrated biological – economic – legal analysis of impacts and policies. *Marine Policy*. 26: 59–74.

Van Ginderdeuren, K., Hostens, K., Hoffman, S., Vansteenbrugge, L., Soenen, K., De Blauwe, H., Robbens, J., Vincx, M. (2012). Distribution of the invasive ctenophore Mnemiopsis leidyi in the Belgian part of the North Sea. *Aquatic Invasions*. 7 (2): 163–169.

Vila, M., Basnou, C., Pyšek, P., Josefsson, M., Genovesi, P., Gollasch, S., Nentwig, W., Olenin, S., Roques, A., Roy, D., Hulme, P. E., DAISIE Partners (2010). How well do we understand the impacts of alien species on ecosystem services? A pan-European cross-taxa assessment. *Frontiers of Ecology and Environment*. 8: 135–144.

Vinogradov, M. E., Shushkina, E. A., Lukasheva, T. A. (2005). Population dynamics of the ctenophores Mnemiopsis leidyi and Beroe ovata as a predator-prey system in the near-shore communities of the Black Sea. *Oceanology*. 45 (1): S161–S167.

Wiley, C. J. (1997). *Aquatic Nuisance Species: Nature Transport and Regulation*. Ed. F. M. D'Itri. Ann Arbor: Zebra Mussels and Aquatic Nuisance Species.

Williams, R. J., Griffiths, F. B., Van der Wal, E. J., Kelly, J. (1988). Cargo vessel ballast water as a vector for the transport of non-indigenous marine species. *Estuarine, Coastal and Shelf Science*. 26: 409–420.

Wonham, M. J., Walton, W. C., Ruiz, G. M., Frese, A. M., Galil, B. S. (2001). Going to the source: Role of the invasion pathway in determining potential invaders. *Marine Ecology Progress Series*. 215: 1–12.

9 Mobilities of waste, value and materials in the shadow of the maritime transport system

A case study of the Pakistani ship-breaking industry

Lars Bomhauer-Beins and Anke Strüver

Introduction

In the today's globalised world, more than 90 percent of the continuously expanding and fast-growing freight market is realised by vessels such as bulkers, cargo and container ships (ICS, 2015). The rapid economic expansion ensures that the world commercial fleet, the transportation capacity, the total tonnage and the value of the global maritime trade grow continuously. In 2015, the total world fleet comprised 89,464 vessels with a total tonnage of 1.75 billion dwt and an expansion rate of 3.5 percent (UNCTAD, 2015: 30). The permanent expansion rate, however, outstrips the demand for the transportation of cargo. The result is an economic disequilibrium at the shipping market with impacts on freight volume and profitability (Hellenic Shipping News, 2013).

As all other commodities, ships have a limited life cycle. Normally, the life cycle of vessels ends after 20 to 30 years of operation (NSP, 2015a: 4), and then they are demolished and replaced. A tough competition on the global freight market, depending on cargo capacities, attrition and technical innovations, can influence the life cycle of vessels. Instead of an expensive, environmentally friendly and professional (waste) disposal in countries of the Global North, end-of-life vessels are sold directly or across third parties to ship-breaking yards in the Global South, primarily on the Indian subcontinent. Breaking, dismantling, scrapping and/ or demolition of ships is – from an economic perspective – very profitable. The process allows the re-use of various ship elements, such as steel scrap. Since the early 1960s, the related ship-breaking industry has played a crucial role for the economies on the Indian subcontinent.

Every year, hundreds of end-of-life vessels are sent to the beaches of the Indian subcontinent, where they are broken down mostly by manual work. In 2015, a total of 768 end-of-life vessels (with a scrap volume of 20.4 million Gross Tonnage (GT)) were sent to the ship-breaking yards worldwide, from which more than two out of three were dismantled by the beaching practice –[1] i.e., on the tidal beaches in South Asia, including Chittagong in Bangladesh, Alang in India and Gadani in Pakistan (NSP, 2015a: 6). Almost all ships, however, reach their final destination under a new flag, such as Panama, St. Kitts and Nevis or Liberia. By means of this well-established procedure of 'flags of convenience', countries of origin and shipping companies resign from their responsibilities through prevention of a cost-intensive and sustainable disposal in the Global North (NSP, 2015a: 8). Ship owners and ship-breaking companies thus '*benefit*' from this arrangement and as a consequence endanger the physical health of thousands of labourers and the incur substantial environment risks. End-of-life vessels contain a considerable number of hazardous substances, including asbestos, oil-saturated materials and heavy metals, which are harmful for human health and the immediate environment.

The business of demolition is not only profitable on the level of sale and purchase but also for the participating South Asian economies. The high level of re-utilised materials of more than 90 percent of a ship's structure is sufficient to match the large domestic demand for steel and second-hand commodities (NSP, 2016: 4). Over the last few decades, the ship-breaking industry has become a crucial resource for a multitude of steel-related industrial branches. Hundreds of thousands of labourers are directly and indirectly involved in these economic structures (Gerostergiou, 2009).

This chapter focuses on 'waste mobilities' – i.e., on the mobilities of the 'waste-resource' ship and the associated socio-economic and ecological impacts within the Pakistani ship-breaking industry. It includes analyses of existing literature and reports of relevant organizations, results from a standardised survey of workers at Gadani Beach, as well as observations of several plots and interviews with stakeholders in Pakistan in 2013/2014.

The demolition market: movements, effects, dynamics and feedbacks

The demolition market plays a key role in the global shipping market cycle. In general, the life cycle of a vessel passes through four main markets (see Stopford, 2003): (1) the shipbuilding market, (2) the freight market, (3) the sale and purchase market, including the second-hand market and (4) the demolition market. These markets are connected, mutually dependent and closely linked by the supply and demand side (see Figure 9.1).

The dynamic of the demolition market, including the ship-breaking activities, depends on various economic factors at several levels. Changes on the world market have effects on the global shipping markets whereby the demolition markets act as a collecting basin, absorbing and reducing effects and serve to keep the market cycle in balance. In addition, the demolition market provides the opportunity to reduce the oversupply of tonnage, to boost the modernisation of the world fleet

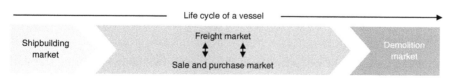

Figure 9.1 Interactions between the four main markets of the global shipping market cycle

both technically and ecologically primarily due to the demolition process of end-of-life vessels, which are characterised by less fuel efficiency and more hazardous materials (UNCTAD, 2015: 44).

Dynamics on the freight market, type and age of vessels and legislative frameworks, such as the implementation of stricter regulations in the field of waste disposal, are significant drivers, which move into the demolition market. In addition, the market demand depends on steel price and ship-breaking costs (Knapp et al., 2008).

The liberalisation of the global trade in the 1990s led to new altered circumstances: Increasing trade activities and the related rising demand for diverse types of vessels, such as bulk carriers, tankers, container and cargo ships to manage the volume of goods/freights has ended in a boom of the shipping sector with impacts on the markets of shipbuilding and second-hand (Kumar and Hoffmann, 2002). New shipbuilding nations – almost all of them located on the Asian continent (such as China, India and Vietnam) – penetrated the market. Prices for second-hand vessels ran up to two or three times the amount before and the price for new vessels went up, for example, by 17 percent in 2006. In addition, the increase in steel prices and the decline of the US dollar intensified the dynamics in the maritime sector. As a consequence, shipping companies cut back their demolition plans and kept their vessels longer in operation (Knapp et al., 2008).

On the other hand, a low rate of shipbuilding and an increasing demand for maritime transport services, caused by a flourishing world economy, did increase the price for maritime trade. Again, these tendencies have affected the related markets, including the second-hand market and the demolition market. Based on the low dynamics on the shipbuilding market, prices for second-hand vessels increased and smaller numbers of vessels were scrapped. All in all the demolition market – the last period of end-of-life vessels – acts as a buffer, balances and regulates the global shipping market cycle (EC, 2004).

Global economic crises, such as the financial crisis in 2008, have direct and indirect influence on the ship-breaking industry, short-term and medium-term. Confronted with lower freight rates, shipping companies attempt to adapt to challenging market conditions by renewing the fleet, selling obsolete vessels or older vessels, which are subsequently sent to ship-breaking yards (NSP, 2016: 6).

Ship owner versus ship breaker

Dynamics on the macro-level – the world economy – serve as an external actor for the demolition market and influence decisions on the micro-level between ship owner (sale) and ship breaker (purchase). At the level of individual decision-maker several indicators affect the decisions made (see Figure 9.2).

Shipowner

Running costs are the key attention of ship owners, including bunkering and staff costs. Confronted with increasing costs, caused by high bunkering, fuel costs or port taxes, can affect the economic efficiency and competitive capacity. Advancing

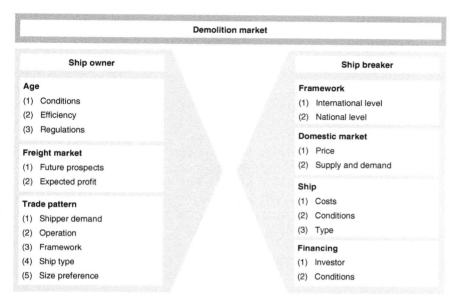

Figure 9.2 Indicators in the decision-making procedure

ship's age in combination with increasing repairing charges and maintenance costs can drop the economic value of a vessel (Gerostergiou, 2009: 7). All these variables can influence the ship owners' decision-making process to demolish a vessel. However, mobility costs for the '*transport*' of end-of-life vessels to the final destination, the ship-breaking yard, are secondary (MoEF, 2010).

An even more crucial factor is the realisable net value and regulatory framework. For example, age restrictions can mean ship owners are required to retail the shipping fleet ahead of the potential elapsed time. Both positive market conditions and an expectable positive capacity tend to the result that shipping companies stall the sale of vessels for demolition. Hence, vessels stay longer in operation or ship owners charge prices above the natural market level for end-of-life vessels.

In contrast, a low and/or stagnating freight market symbolises that shipping companies have a tendency to dispose of vessels on the demolition market (MoEF, 2010). The situation is similar in case of an over-capacity of vessels on the freight market. An over-supply leads to an increased appearance of vessels on the demolition market with the result that shipping companies have to sell less than the actual economic value. Moreover, there are several political frameworks on the global scale, which have impact, positive or negative, on the dynamics and mobilities on the ship-breaking level.

Ship-owner decisions are based on economic efficiency; they are motivated by the fact that freight rates defray the costs of running expenses. Global fluctuations in steel (scrap) prices are not the decisive factor in the process of decision making. End-of-life vessels are sent to regions, where ship breakers are ready to pay the highest purchase price (EC, 2004: 42ff).

Ship breaker

The decisions of ship breakers depend on the interaction of four principal values: (1) regulatory frameworks on different levels; (2) the domestic steel market; (3) ship-related issues, such as conditions, price and type; (4) and financing. Over the last few decades, the increasing steel demand on the Indian subcontinent has enabled both the competition of the demolition market and the capability of ship breakers to pay more for end-of-life vessels. In comparison, operating costs for plots, labour, transportation and machines have increased steadily from year to year, yet labour costs account for the major part of total costs.

Operating costs, accumulated by labour costs and regulations (including environmental and labour certificates), as well as import duties and taxes, have a critical impact on the scope of action during the buyout of obsolete vessels. Ship breakers have to calculate the anticipated costs for the purchase compared to the current traded price for steel scrap on the domestic market. Changing parameters, such as import duties or national taxes imposed by government are limiting the scope and profitability of ship-breaking companies. The results are low levels of activity on the demolition market (Gerostergiou, 2009: 9; EC, 2004: 45).

A further crucial variable is financing. In the regional context of South Asia, the ship-breaking industry is considered as capital intensive. Whereas shipping companies accumulate capital by the sale of ships, the purchase of end-of-life vessels requires financial resources of the ship breakers. Even though vessels diminish in value across their life cycle, the purchase price is beyond the financial resources of ship-breaking operators (Baloch, 2003; Helfre, 2013). Many ship-breaking companies are not able to realise a purchase without external funds. In Pakistan, for example, a complex and sophisticated financial concept has become firmly established: large domestic banking institutions (including Bank Al-Habib, Soneri Bank, Askari Bank, MCB Bank and Meezan Bank) act as financial backers and advance money to operators or acquire financial interests and receive in return the 'resource' ship (called 'Letter of Credit'). The financial circumstances vary from case to case depending on the ship breaker's financial resources (Ahmed and Siddiqui, 2013). In general rule, operators pay around 10 percent of the total sale price and get a credit of 90 percent by banks. This financial model, however, involves the risk of dependence and unequal power relations between banks and ship breakers.

New flag, other regulations, no responsibility

Before they are sent to the ship-breaking yards, end-of-life vessels are often re-staffed, renamed and re-flagged for the process of demolition. This seemingly trivial modification has extensive implications in terms of legitimate principles aboard a ship: "Where beneficial ownership and control of a vessel is found to lie elsewhere than in the country of the flag the vessel flying, the vessel is considered as sailing under a flag of convenience" (ITF, 2006).

The term of 'Flag of Convenience' describes the status of registration of a ship under a sovereign state. The ship operates under the conditions and regulations of the flag state. This common practice is closely linked to the ship-breaking cycle. Rarely, the country of the ship owner corresponds with the flag of the shipping fleet. The reflagging of end-of-life vessels, broken in substandard ship-breaking yards, becomes popular. Ship owners practice this in order to reduce the operating costs, to avoid registration fees and the legal framework of the original state (Galley, 2013). Grey or blacklisted flags by the Paris Memorandum of Understanding[2] are often used for the last trip to the ship-breaking regions at the Indian subcontinent. In 2014, the NGO Shipbreaking Platform (NSP) stated that 40 percent of all end-of-life vessels were sent under a grey- or blacklisted flag – such as St. Kitts and Nevis (64 vessels), Comoros (39) or Tuvalu (24) – to South Asia (NSP, 2015b). In 2015, the most popular end-of-life flags amongst all vessels that were scrapped on the beaches at the Indian subcontinent were Panama (74 vessels), Liberia (47 vessels) and Marshall Islands (42 vessels) (NSP, 2016). Many countries of typical end-of-life flags, including St. Kitts and Nevis, Comoros and Tuvalu, are offering 'last journey' packages to ship owners (NSP, 2015b).

Going once, going twice, going three times, sold!

The sale price is the subject of fluctuations and dependent on several factors, including price, age and type of vessel. Currently, the estimated demolition price for a tanker with 10,000 Light Displacement Tonnage (LDT) is approximately 3.5 million US dollar at the Indian subcontinent (Compass Maritime, 2017a). In March 2017, for example, the ship brokerage Compass Maritime Services reported a transaction of a 28-year-old bulk carrier with an empty weight of 18,812 LDT for 400 US dollar/LDT to Gadani, Pakistan (Compass Maritime, 2017b). In general, the average sale prices at the South Asian yards (with 300 US dollar/LDT) are considerably higher than direct competitors, such as China with 195 US dollar/LDT and Turkey with 175 US dollar/LDT (Hellenic Shipping News, 2016).

The disposal of obsolete vessels on the demolition market is an intransparent process due to the structural complexity of types of ships and the multi-scalar political and legislative interactions. Hence, processes of sale and purchase on the demolition market often take place in a legally grey area (Hossain and Islam, 2006). From a shipping company perspective, three principal avenues open up for the sale of an obsolete vessel: (1) direct sale, (2) brokering (3) and cash buyer (Figure 9.3).

In times of globalisation, the demolition market has adapted to fast-moving and highly competitive markets. While an end-of-life vessel is moving on the world's oceans from one place to another, prices for steel (scrap) are permanently in motion. Cash buyers estimate the potential market prices. They "work as a buffer between the end buyers and owners" (Gerostergiou, 2009: 5) and make renegotiations unnecessary. Finally, it is necessary and even more important for ship owners to pick qualified cash buyers carefully in terms of management, trade balance, market activities and stocks and core business (Gerostergiou, 2009: 16). Often, in the context of ship-breaking regions with beaching yards, they use the service of a middleman to distance oneself from the vessel and the dirty game of ship breaking, and its social and ecological impacts.

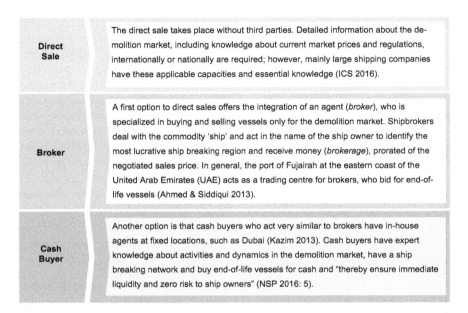

Direct Sale	The direct sale takes place without third parties. Detailed information about the demolition market, including knowledge about current market prices and regulations, internationally or nationally are required; however, mainly large shipping companies have these applicable capacities and essential knowledge (ICS 2016).
Broker	A first option to direct sales offers the integration of an agent (*broker*), who is specialized in buying and selling vessels only for the demolition market. Shipbrokers deal with the commodity 'ship' and act in the name of the ship owner to identify the most lucrative ship breaking region and receive money (*brokerage*), prorated of the negotiated sales price. In general, the port of Fujairah at the eastern coast of the United Arab Emirates (UAE) acts as a trading centre for brokers, who bid for end-of-life vessels (Ahmed & Siddiqui 2013).
Cash Buyer	Another option is that cash buyers who act very similar to brokers have in-house agents at fixed locations, such as Dubai (Kazim 2013). Cash buyers have expert knowledge about activities and dynamics in the demolition market, have a ship breaking network and buy end-of-life vessels for cash and "thereby ensure immediate liquidity and zero risk to ship owners" (NSP 2016: 5).

Figure 9.3 Three avenues for the sale of an obsolete vessel

The domination of the Indian subcontinent

Historically, the global ship-breaking industry has undergone two radical geographical shifts: from Western countries to East Asia and from East Asia to South Asia. Currently, ship-breaking zones are located in only a few countries: India, Bangladesh and Pakistan, as well as China and Turkey.

Until the 1960s, the industry of ship breaking was characterised by high standards, both technically and ecologically, and was located in some European countries (such as Germany, Italy and Great Britain) and in some coastal regions of the United States (Hossain and Islam, 2006: 2). In the 1960s and 1970s, the first geographical shift took place. Driven by changing economic conditions in East Asia, caused by an industrial boom plus an existing domestic market for re-rolled steel and low labour costs on the one hand and on rising labour costs and stricter regulations in countries of the Global North on the other, geographical shift to South Korea and Taiwan occurred (Kumar, 2009: 5). After two decades of East Asian dominance, the ship-breaking industry subsequently moved to the Indian subcontinent. This second shift was based on strict labour standards, environmental guidelines and advanced globalisation processes (Faez, 2011). Since the 1980s, the South Asian countries have become the centre of the ship-breaking industry.

The reasons for this dominance can be summarised as follows: The central governments of Bangladesh, India and Pakistan have, for example, ratified the Basel Convention.[3] However, the (un)conscious toleration and low enforcement of environmental, safety and working standards, low labour costs, corruption at various levels in combination with times of political instability enabled the establishment and the rapid expansion of the South Asian ship-breaking region on a global level (Gerostergiou, 2009). In comparison to ship-breaking zones in the Global North, the labour-intensive branch has benefitted from lower operating costs, primarily due to cheap labour costs. The strategic and geographical location close to several highly frequented maritime trade routes and non-seasonal conditions in terms of ship-breaking activities are crucial locational advantages of the Indian subcontinent (Hossain and Islam, 2006: 2).

In recent years, Chinese ship-breaking zones have been integrated into the global market driven by the economic recovery and extensive governmental subsidies (UNCTAD, 2015: 44). Around 90 percent of all end-of-life vessels are scrapped on the Indian subcontinent and China. In 2014, India was on top with 7.0 million GT, followed by Bangladesh with 4.9 million GT and China with 4.3 million GT and Pakistan with 4.1 million GT.

Ship-breaking regions show a specialisation in terms of type and size of vessels: Container ships are primarily demolished in India, bulk carriers in Bangladesh and oil tankers at Gadani Beach, Pakistan (UNCTAD, 2015: 44). In 2015, with a focus on the size of ships, the largest vessels moved to Gadani Beach, followed by Chittagong (Bangladesh), while yards at Alang (India) scrapped more medium-sized vessels (NSP, 2016: 6).

Pakistan: a ship-breaking nation

Located at Gadani Beach – in the economically weak province of Balochistan – the Pakistani ship-breaking industry can look back on a long history. In 1947, the year of independence from Britain, first informal demolition activities took place near the Gadani Beach (Kumar, 2009: 4). Already in the 1950s, ship breakers started efforts to establish a permanently and regular ship-breaking industry (see Figure 9.4). In the following decades, the activities constantly increased (Dawn, 2001). In 1971, the secession of the eastern part of the country (today Bangladesh) and the associated loss of market and trade links served as a catalyst for the ship-breaking industry to become a new domestic raw material supplier (Dawn, 2001). In addition, pushed by governmental measures, Pakistan's ship-breaking industry became the global market leader in the 1980s, with more than 30,000 workers directly employed (Kumar, 2009: 6; Dawn, 2009c, 2011; Masood, 2013). Changing parameters primarily caused by financial burdens in the form of high taxes and import duties on the part of the central government and a very competitive situation due to economic competition with other South Asian ship-breaking regions brought Gadani Beach into a deep economic crisis (SAJ, 2015). In the 1990s, activities nearly stopped and the Pakistani ship-breaking industry disappeared into the shadow of competition on the Indian subcontinent (Dawn, 2009a; Rana, 2010). In the early 2000s, ship breakers put pressure on the central government and Gadani Beach slowly recovered due to a tax break and reduced duties (Masood, 2001, 2013; Dawn, 2003; Khan 2013b).

Figure 9.4 Scrapped vessel at Gadani Beach
Source: Author

The sleeping giant: Gadani Beach

The ship-breaking area next to the small fishing village Gadani stretches over 18 kilometres along a sandy beachfront with a relatively small tidal range characteristic of the Arabian Sea. As a 'naval-restricted' area (Iqbal and Heidegger, 2013), it is connected to the National Highway and with the port city of Karachi, 50 kilometre south-east.

The ship-breaking zone at Gadani Beach comprises 132 demolition plots with different property statuses: the majority of the plots are under the private ownership of 'waderas' (landlords) and one in four belong to the Balochistan Development Authority (BDA, 2014). Many of the plots are inactive and are reminders of the former dominance of the area as market leader in the 1980s. In 2014, demolition activities were take place only on a third of all plots. Plots are often leased for an annually fixed volume of ship breaking to external ship-breaking companies.

Due to the limited availability of heavy machines, the demolition process is realised almost exclusively manually by a large number of workers. Compared to Bangladesh, however, Gadani Beach has marginally more heavy machines, such as cranes, excavators and steel winches driven by diesel generators. This means that an end-of-life vessel with 5,000 LDT can be demolished in 30 to 45 days, whereas at ship-breaking yards at Alang or Chittagong it takes around six months for breaking a ship of this size (Rana, 2010).

At the yards, the workers can be classified in five principal working groups: (1) foreman, (2) cutter group, (3) plate group, (4) wire group and (5) hammer group and other secondary activities, such as crane and truck drivers, and a wide range of unskilled helpers (see Figure 9.5). At present, roughly between 12,000 and 15,000 workers (almost all of them Pakistani citizens and half of them under 30 years of age) are employed in the physically demanding, male-dominated and labour-intensive industry (Dawn, 2009b). Around 850,000 persons, including labourers and their families, are directly or indirectly involved in the branch (Iqbal and Heidegger, 2013).

Many workers are hired by self-contained agents (as a kind of recruiting system), mainly from the marginal rural areas of the northern Pakistani provinces, such as Khyber Pakhtunkhwa and the semi-autonomous Federally Administered Tribal Areas region. Based on the physically and energy-sapping working environment at Gadani Beach, the primary target group of agents are unemployed, uneducated and unskilled young men. A poor education system, a high illiteracy rate, low alternative employment opportunities in combination with empty promises on the part of the agents are key drivers for the controlled internal labour migration in a north-south direction. Today, around two-thirds of all workers have male family members who also work in the ship-breaking industry. Officially, the industry does not employ children. Observations by the one of the authors, however, challenge this statement.

Employees mainly work on the basis of daily wages and without any formal labour contracts. Labour standards and human rights are severely limited because of inadequate regulations and legislations, corruption and lax governmental

Figure 9.5 Group of workers
Source: Author

enforcement on different levels. At Gadani Beach, two labour unions are present: the Gadani Ship Breaking Labour Union and the Ship Breaking Democratic Workers Union, under the umbrella of the National Trade Unions Federation (NTUF). Historically, the first labour union under the name of Ship Breaking Labour Union Gadani (short: Labour Union) had an unsavoury flavour. Formed in 1980 by operators, the key goal was to keep down the power, claims and rights of thousands of workers. Little has changed since then: labour unions are still influenced by contractors and operators. Key objectives are, for instance, salaries and regular working hours. Assertiveness by labour unions is often rare due to the low (official) 'membership' of workers – intensified by the uninterrupted powerful position of operators and policymakers. Daily wages are marginally above the average of branch-related industries, however, and due to socio-cultural structures, labourers are primarily responsible for the total income of families.

Despite the dangers inherent to the demolition process, workers at Gadani Beach are not trained and inadequately protected. Workers are exposed to hazardous materials and substances, released during the demolition at the unprotected beach zones. End-of-life vessels, in particular if vessels were built before the 1980s, contain a wide range of hazardous substances in their structures, such as asbestos or heavy metals. Almost throughout the entire demolition process, labourers are permanently directly or indirectly confronted with harmful substances, released as toxic fumes or solids (see Figure 9.6). The European Commission (EC, 2007) estimated that up to 130,000 tonnes of hazardous materials and other harmful substances are sent to the unprotected beaches of the Indian subcontinent

Figure 9.6 Welder at work

Source: Author

as components of ships originating from Europe every year. Improper dealing and incorrect temporary storage of hazardous substances during the demolition process indicate far-reaching negative impacts for the health of thousands of labourers and the immediate environment (Ilyas, 2014). The beach zone is covered by oil spills. Other pollutants are released into the sea.

The industry is frequently hit by accidents. Health problems or occupational accidents caused by the limited availability of protective equipment, inadequate safety measures, lax instructions, lack of knowledge and permanent exposure to hazardous waste are a daily routine (see Dawn, 2009c; Samaa, 2012; The News International, 2013; AFP, 2016; Hasan, 2016a). Many workers suffer under the hard physical activities and the permanent work in a dangerous environment as well. Health issues are closely linked with the dangerous work environment and working conditions. Common examples include back pain caused by carrying and lifting heavy ship elements, eye pain up to loss of vision caused by welding work undertaken without safety glasses and operating in a dark environment onboard, and respiratory problems due to breathing in toxic gases and hazardous fumes. Every fifth worker has had previous accidents at Gadani Beach. Typical injuries are bone fractures on joints, ankles and knees and cuts at the hands. In 2012, the NTUF recorded 12 fatal accidents (Iqbal and Heidegger, 2013). Gadani Beach is not prepared in case of life-threatening injuries. Neither medical facilities nor ambulance services are located there. The next available hospital – located in Karachi – is too far away to treat severe injuries.

Steel scrap: motor of an entire nation

The continuous growth of the ship-breaking industry in South Asia has played a major role in regional and national economic expansion since the 1980s (World Bank, 2010: 2). The high level of re-utilisation[4] – i.e., up to 95 percent of all ship elements – provides a key opportunity to supply the ever-expanding domestic demand for steel and re-utilised products (see Figure 9.7). The industry is an economic basis for thousands of labourers and their families on the one hand; on the other, the embedding of the 'waste' product ship in the form of regained steel and other usable materials is economically beneficial at various levels (Dawn, 2009a, 2009b). Notwithstanding economic fluctuations, this specific branch of 'waste' has become an essential motor for the domestic economy. In 2011 alone, the ship-breaking zone has provided around 70 percent of the country's total demand for steel and iron and manifested a unilateral dependence (The Express Tribune, 2011). The integration of steel scrap into the domestic economic cycle over decades indicates a certain degree of unilateral dependence.

Illegal imports of substandard raw material, such as steel pipes and other steel-related goods from Russia, the Ukraine and other former states of the Soviet Union, through the porous border of the neighbouring countries Iran and Afghanistan, however, impact the profitability of the Pakistani ship-breaking industry (Dawn, 2007; PakTribune, 2008).

Figure 9.7 Ship elements at the ship-breaking yard
Source: Author

A wide range of companies and branches depend on ship demolition as a source of '*raw*' material (supplier), primarily the construction sector, powered by the steady urbanisation process across the entire country (The News International, 2015). Scrap-melting plants (80) and re-rolling mills (334) are located in the provinces of Punjab and Sindh and in particular in the metropolitan areas of Karachi, Lahore, Islamabad and Gujranwala (World Bank, 2010; Khan, 2013a; Karimijee, 2013). Every day, around 100 to 150 truckloads of steel scrap are sent from Gadani Beach to Karachi, the largest urban metropolitan area (with roughly 25 million people) and national economic and financial hub of Pakistan. Here main customers are Amreli Steels, Steels Dewan, Nawab Steel and Razaque Steels (Khan, 2013a). The high-quality steel scrap enters the domestic market in two principal ways, as re-rollable scrap (around 70 percent of the total ship weight) or melting scrap.

Apart from the steel scrap, a broad spectrum of other re-utilised materials, including engines and pumps, cables and lines and other on-board items enter the domestic second-hand market, in the first instance via the large-scale Sher Shah Market in Karachi.

The recovered ship-breaking industry releases additional capital for the central government in the form of taxes. In comparison to the tax system in the competing countries Bangladesh and India, where a statutory fixed amount of taxes per annum on the import of end-of-life vessels is defined, the Pakistani ship-breaking landscape is based on another concept: In addition to an import tax of one percent of the vessel (purchase) price operators have to pay a fixed amount of 50 US dollar per ship tonnage. In recent years, the increasing activities at Gadani Beach are also visible in fiscal revenues from the ship-breaking industry. Within four years (2009 to 2012), the fiscal revenues increased by 600 percent, from 7 million US dollar to 42 million US dollar (Jamal, 2013). Therefore, "the argument is not that Pakistan as a developing country must break ship. The argument is rather that Pakistan breaks ships because it is [a] profitable business model."

But this apparent 'gold mine' is a play with fire. The Pakistani ship-breaking industry is directly exposed to the regional intense competition. History has proven that governmental pressure of high taxes and duties can cause the collapse of the ship-breaking industry with far-reaching socio-economic consequence for the entire country (Ali, 2013).

Mobility flows: waste, value and materials

When Sheller and Urry proclaimed a 'new mobilities' paradigm (2006), they argued for a stronger link between transport research and social theory and focused on the movement of human bodies and materials, but also of images and information. However, in applying what Cresswell (2014) has defined as "critical mobilities", adopting the term from Söderström et al. (2013), that disrupt taken-for-granted movements and encompass, for example, practices of 'off-shoring' waste, mobilities are central in approaching waste and waste material that does not simply disappear. In our attention to the mobilities of end-of-life vessels, though not in a strict sense of off-shoring waste, but rather the ships' dismantling and the (re-)use or recycling of materials, we argue that the movements and transformations of end-of-life cargo ships can be approached as 'critical mobilities' since these movements are neither one-dimensional and linear, nor from production to consumption or from south to north. Moreover, ship breaking encompasses processes of relocation and re-materialisation, both in terms of the waste materials' activities and performativities *and* the movement of value.[5]

Davies has considered waste's mobilities and 'waste' as the beginning of relocation and re-materialisation processes:

> These things called waste are moved (. . .) from place to place (and sometimes back again) and their constituent parts deconstructed, reconstructed and transformed, intentionally or otherwise, altering physical states and levels of toxicity; essentially waste has multiple mobilities.
>
> (Davies, 2012: 191)

Because waste mobilities obviously go beyond issues of transportation, Davies distinguishes four (related) sub-themes: among them (1) 'mapping flows' that are concerned with combining physical and political trajectories of end-of-life matter and bring together trade, regulations and environmental issues; thus focusing on legal as well as on ethical and moral aspects of moving and dumping waste, including hazardous substances. Yet to broaden this one-dimensional account of waste movement, the (2) 'following things' theme brings end-of-life objects, such as obsolete vessels, into commodity chain analysis by examining the complex constituencies of waste materials (see, e.g., Crang, 2010; Gregson et al., 2010).

In tracing global flows of commodities, most studies focus on commodity chains from production to consumption, and thus from the Global South to the Global North. Regarding end-of-life vessels and their demolition on the Indian subcontinent therefore requires at least two turns, for their mobility is usually directed from Global North to Global South and production and consumption are replaced by destruction, sometimes accompanied by reconstruction. Ships are then not only means of transportation for commodities and part of commodity chains but also commodities in themselves.

Transformation and movement of value in ship breaking

When cargo or container ships are not competitive any longer as means of transportation (e.g. due to a lack of capacity) and the scrap value of their materials is higher than their maintenance, they are sent to demolition markets on South Asian beaches to be destructed ('rubbish value ships', 'ship breaking as a global waste flow', see Crang, 2010; see also the aforementioned). This means that an ocean liner that has lost its competitiveness before it has balanced out its investment ('fixed capital'), but is then being scrapped in South Asia, the original fixed capital as a means of transport is devalued, but its single materials are (re-)used and thus 're-valued'. Referring to Marx's distinction between fixed capital (means of production and transportation and thus necessary for the entire process of production and capital accumulation, but not decisive for the profit-rate, e.g. vessels) and variable capital (labour force) and the finding that surplus value is primarily generated from variable capital (Harvey, 2010a), the 'ongoingness' of end-of-life vessels sheds different light on ship breaking: Whereas approaches to global production chains understand ships that are prematurely withdrawn from their transportation application as waste, the approach of "global destruction chains" helps to follow the "displacement" of value (see Herod et al., 2013: 378f), for example, re-utilisation as ship steel so that re-valuation results from devaluation. This, however, requires global spatial inequalities and an international division of labour regarding waste disposal – i.e., Harvey's conception of a 'spatial fix' is at work: The attempts to 'fix' a capitalist crisis spatially – by strategic productions of spaces and spatial relations – and by relocating production and in this case, destruction. Spatial mobility then presents a "spatial solution" (Harvey, 2010b) for capitalist problems and this mobility includes not only the relocation of production (due to reduced labour costs, and lower social and environmental standards abroad) but also the relocation of destruction and waste disposal.

Proposing waste as value (not as endpoint) and placing e-waste in global value chains and production networks of a 'rubbish recovery economy', Lepawsky and Billah (2011) furthermore argue for a sense of 'post-disposal value production' (see also Lepawsky and Mather, 2011; Gregson et al., 2010), including the activity of materials and the performativity of waste, but also the 'ongoingness' of economic life when ship components are transformed into new materials and commodities.

Taking this up, yet in a more Marxist sense of the capitalist character of waste recycling, Herod et al. (2013) rather stress this ongoingness as movement of value and differentiate between devalorisation and devaluation: At the end of the 'normal' working life of a cargo ship all of its value has been transferred to the freight it has transported (= devalorisation, the fixed capital has been transferred to the commodities and their value), but if it is destructed because of un-competitiveness, part of its original value is lost (= devaluation – i.e., destruction of value).

Conclusion

The ship-breaking industry at Gadani Beach illustrates that the mobility of waste (including value, capital and materials) is first of all not a typical (physical) movement within the global maritime transport system. Rather, in the context of the ship-breaking industry, mobility is present in form of (1) the mobility of value and capital, (2) the mobility of waste (3) and the mobility of materials, since the vessels classified as 'waste' undergo by the process of demolition a re-valuation, re-integration and release of (new) materials. Secondly, the South Asian ship-breaking regions depend on and manifest global inequalities – i.e., the demolition process depends not only on the unequal interaction between Global North and Global South but also on the unequal distribution of costs and benefits. At the local level, the workers and the environment are exploited for the profits of central governments and international operating ship companies.

The Pakistani ship-breaking industry discloses the unequal spatial relationships between Global North and Global South, and the mobility of capital, value, waste and materials by the ship-breaking industry: "Ships as waste bring the restless movement of globalization, the temporalities of objects, and the politics and aesthetics of waste into conjunction" (Crang, 2010: 1086).

The general market trends towards larger cargo and freight capacities of vessels and thus increasing tonnage of the world fleet on the one hand indicate an enormous potential of steel (scrap) supply for the ship-breaking zones over a medium-term period. Pakistan – preferring large vessels – can benefit from current trends. The inactive plots provide an enormous economic potential. On the other hand, the demolition process at Gadani Beach does not correspond with international guidelines in terms of labour and safety conditions and the dealing with hazardous materials. Recently, five workers died after a fire broke out inside a scrapped tanker at the ship-breaking yards at Gadani Beach in January 2017 (Schuler, 2017). Already in November 2016, a blast killed at least 26 workers (AFP, 2016). The demolition activities were stopped temporary (Hasan, 2016b).

A changed system at the level of the global ship-breaking industry is needed; however, it is only realizable if all relevant actors and stakeholders at the various levels are willing to assume responsibility in the fields of environmental and social standards. In the last few years, the pressure on the governments in shipowning countries to stop sending end-of-life vessels to regions of lax standards has been constantly growing.[6] In the same way, the receiving countries are called upon to refrain from disputed ship-breaking methods and to determine, implement and enforce measures of international, safety and social standards. An even greater challenge is the development and implementation of strategies for a sustainable future based on 'green ship-recycling', including the banishment of the beaching practice at coastlines at the Indian subcontinent.

Notes

1 Beaching is the most common ship breaking practice worldwide due to the low costs and marginal conditions regarding location and technical facilities. Other demolition approaches are 'alongside', 'slipway' and the most sustainable method, called 'dry-dock' (ILPI, 2016: 7f).
2 See the latest list of white, grey and black flags (2015): www.parismou.org/2015-performance-lists-paris-mou
3 The 'Basel Convention on the Control of Transboundary Movements of Hazardous Wastes and Their Disposal' (1992) is an international environmental regulation, which controls transports of hazardous materials across borders. All members of the European Union as well as Bangladesh, India and Pakistan have ratified the convention in the early 1990s.
4 From the authors' point of view, the term 'recycling' is avoided primary due to the fact that the term unifies positive, sustainable and environment-friendly associations, which, however, are not given within the demolition processes on the Indian subcontinent.
5 The former, however, referring to Actor-Network Theory, Science and Technology Studies and to the so-called new materialism, are left out here in favour of Marxist theory.
6 In the recent years, the demolition market showed a positive trend towards environmental standards. In 2014, the German company Hapag-Lloyd – one of the largest companies in the field of maritime transportation and logistics – turned away from sending obsolete vessels to the South Asian ship breaking regions.

References

AFP (2016). Death toll rises to 26 in Gadani shipbreaking blast. *Dawn*, 6 November 2016. Available at: www.dawn.com/news/1294669 Accessed 10 October 2017.

Ahmed, R., Siddiqui, K. (2013). Ship breaking industry in Pakistan – problems and prospects. *International Journal of Management, IT and Engineering*. 3 (9): 140–155.

Ali, S. (2013). Gadani ship breaking: A glimpse into the abyss. *The Express Tribune*, 29 July 2013. Available at: https://tribune.com.pk/story/583114/gadani-ship-breaking-a-glimpse-into-the-abyss/ Accessed 17 July 2014.

Baloch, L. (2003). Karachi. Shipbreaking trade set to achieve landmark: World's famous ship at Gadani. *Dawn*, 8 September 2003. Available at: www.dawn.com/news/114291 Accessed 16 June 2014.

BDA (Balochistan Development Authority) (2014). Gadani ship breaking projects. Available at: www.balochistan.gov.pk/index.php?option=com_content&view=article&id=713:gaddani-ship-breaking-projects&catid=57&Itemid=1058 Accessed 20 May 2016.

Compass Maritime (2017a). Compass maritime weekly report: Week 11. Available at: www.compassmar.com/reports/Compass%20Maritime%20Weekly%20Market%20Report.pdf Accessed 16 March 2017.

Compass Maritime (2017b). Compass maritime weekly report: Week 12. Available at: www.compassmar.com/reports/Compass%20Maritime%20Weekly%20Market%20Report.pdf. Accessed 26 March 2017.

Crang, M. (2010). The death of great ships: Photography, politics, and waste in the global imaginary. *Environment and Planning A*. 42 (5): 1084–1102.

Cresswell, T. (2014). Mobilities III: Moving on. *Progress in Human Geography*. 38 (5): 712–721.

Davies, A. R. (2012). Geography and the matter of waste mobilities. *Transactions of the Institute of British Geographers*. 37: 191–196.

Dawn (2001). Ship-breaking attracting entrepreneurs. *Dawn*, 24 December 2001. Available at: www.dawn.com/2001/12/24/ebr20.htm Accessed 14 May 2014.

Dawn (2003). Karachi. World's second-largest ship at Gadani. *Dawn*, 6 September 2003. Available at: www.dawn.com/news/113992 Accessed 18 May 2014.

Dawn (2007). Steel makers suggest imports to lower prices. *Dawn*, 27 February 2007. Available at: www.dawn.com/news/234820/steel-makers-suggest-imports-to-lower-prices Accessed 24 May 2014.

Dawn (2009a). 65 ships reach Gadani for scrapping. *Dawn*, 9 May 2009. Available at: www.dawn.com/news/463135 Accessed 4 June 2014.

Dawn (2009b). Ship-breaking picks up pace at Gadani. *Dawn*, 19 May 2009. Available at: www.dawn.com/news/830686 Accessed 19 April 2014.

Dawn (2009c). Karachi. Ship-breaking activities: Workers face health hazards. *Dawn*, 21 December 2009. Available at: www.dawn.com/news/509969 Accessed 10 April 2014.

Dawn (2011). Ship breaking at Gadani. *Dawn*, 23 October 2011. Available at: www.dawn.com/news/668410 Accessed 19 June 2014.

European Commission (2004). Oil tanker phase out and the ship scrapping industry: A study on the implication of the accelerated phase out scheme of single hull tankers proposed by the EU for the world ship scrapping and recycling industry. Available at: http://ec.europa.eu/transport/modes/maritime/studies/doc/2004_06_scrapping_study.pdf Accessed 10 May 2016.

European Commission (2007). Green paper: On better ship dismantling. Available at: http://ec.europa.eu/environment/waste/ships/pdf/com_2007_269_en.pdf Accessed 20 May 2016.

The Express Tribune (2011). Iron and steel: Ship breaking industry meeting 70 percent requirements. *The Express Tribune*, 28 July 2011. Available at: https://tribune.com.pk/story/218691/iron-and-steel-ship-breaking-industry-meeting-70-requirements/ Accessed 20 May 2016.

Faez, S. (2011). Ship breaking industry: A closer look. *Pakistan Today*, 26 August 2011. Available at: www.pakistantoday.com.pk/2011/08/26/ship-breaking-industry-a-closer-look/ Accessed 21 May 2016.

Galley, M. (2013). Flagging interest: Ship registration, owner anonymity, and sub-standard shipping. *Mountbatten Journal of Legal Studies*. 14 (1–2): 87–109.

Gerostergiou, E. (2009). Ship breaking: A study of the demolition market. Available at: http://digilib.lib.unipi.gr/dspace/bitstream/unipi/4633/1/Gerostergiou.pdf Accessed 12 November 2013.

Gregson, N., Crang, M., Ahamed, F., Akhtar, N., Ferdous, R. (2010). Following things of rubbish value: End-of-life ships, 'chock-chocky' furniture and the Bangladeshi middle class consumer. *Geoforum*. 41 (6): 846–854.

Harvey, D. (2010a). *A Companion to Marx's Capital*. London: Verso.

Harvey, D. (2010b). *The Enigma of Capital and the Crisis of Capitalism*. London: Profile Books.

Hasan, S. (2016a). 11 dead in oil tanker blast at Gadani ship-breaking yard. *Dawn*, 2 November 2016. Available at: www.dawn.com/news/1293729 Accessed 10 October 2017.

Hasan, S. (2016b). Call of resumption of ship-breaking activities in Gadani. *Dawn*, 2 December 2016. Available at: www.dawn.com/news/1299906 Accessed 10 October 2017.

Helfre, J.-F. (2013). Controversial shipbreaking dismantles stakeholder trust. Available at: www.shipbreakingplatform.org/shipbrea_wp2011/wp-content/uploads/2013/06/Sustainalytics-Shipbreaking-Report-April-2013.pdf Accessed 26 August 2016.

Hellenic Shipping News (2013). Too many ships in the world merchant fleet. Available at: www.hellenicshippingnews.com/984ef639-7f94-4d62-88a9-f80b3ecc6fb9/ Accessed 14 August 2016.

Hellenic Shipping News (2016). Weekly shipping market report week 43. Available at: www.hellenic shippingnews.com/wp-content/uploads/2016/10/ADVANCED-MARKET-REPORT-WEEK-43.pdf Accessed 16 March 2017.

Herod, A., Pikren, G., Rainnie, A. I., Mgrath-Champ, S. (2013). Waste, commodity fetishism and the ongoingness of economic life. *Area*. 45 (3): 376–382.

Hossain, M. M., Islam, M. M. (2006). *Ship Breaking Activities and Its Impact on the Coastal Zone of Chittagong, Bangladesh: Towards Sustainable Management*. Chittagong, Bangladesh: YPSA, Young Power in Social Action.

Ilyas, F. (2014). Toxic ship paints affect female snails at Gadani. *Dawn*, 4 September 2014. Available at: www.dawn.com/news/1129680 Accessed 20 May 2016.

International Chamber of Shipping (2015). Shipping and world trade. Available at: www.ics-shipping.org/shipping-facts/shipping-and-world-trade Accessed 22 April 2016.

International Law and Policy Institute (2016). Shipbreaking practices in Bangladesh, India and Pakistan: An investor perspective on the human rights and environmental impacts of beaching. Available at: www.klp.no/polopoly_fs/1.34213.1467019894!/menu/standard/file/Shipbreaking%20report%20mai%202016.pdf Accessed 20 September 2016.

International Transport Workers' Federation (2006). *Handbook*. 2nd ed. Washington, DC.

Iqbal, K.M.J., Heidegger, P. (2013). *Pakistani Shipbreaking Outlook: The Way Forward for a Green Ship Recycling Industry – Environmental, Health and Safety Conditions*. Brussels, Islamabad: Sustainable Development Policy Institute and NGO Shipbreaking Platform.

Jamal, A. (2013). Pakistan's ship breaking industry revives. *Central Asia Online*, 26 March 2013.

Karimijee, M. (2013). Shipbreaking: World's most dangerous job? *Global Post*, 21 March 2013. Available at: www.salon.com/2013/03/21/shipbreaking_worlds_most_dangerous_job_partner/ Accessed 28 April 2014.

Khan, A. S. (2013a). On the roll. *Dawn*, 6 January 2013. Available at: www.dawn.com/news/776752 Accessed 10 August 2014.

Khan, M. Z. (2013b). Gadani shipbreaking yard under threat. *Dawn*, 4 November 2013. Available at: www.dawn.com/news/1053903 Accessed 14 August 2014.Knapp, S., Kumar, S. N., Remjin, A. B. (2008). Econometric analysis of the ship demolition market. *Marine Policy*. 32 (6): 1023–1036.

Kumar, R. (2009). Ship dismantling. A status report on South Asia. Available at: www.shipbreakingplatform.org/shipbrea_wp2011/wp-content/uploads/2013/07/ship_dismantling_en.pdf Accessed 10 August 2016.

Kumar, S., Hoffmann, J. (2002). Globalization: The Maritime Nexus. In: C. T. Grammenos (ed.), *Handbook of Maritime Economics and Business*. London. pp. 35–62.

Lepawsky, J., Billah, M. (2011). Making chains that (un)make things: Waste-value relations and the Bangladeshi rubbish electronics industry. *Geografiska Annaler B*. 93 (2): 121–139.

Lepawsky, J., Mather, C. (2011). From beginnings and endings to boundaries and edges: Rethinking circulation and exchange through electronic waste. *Area*. 43 (3): 242–249.

Masood, A. (2001). Ship breaking attracting entrepreneurs. *Dawn*, 24 December 2001. Available at: www.dawn.com/2001/12/24/ebr20.htm Accessed 14 February 2014.

Masood, A. (2013). Gaddani ship-breaking industry waking up. *Dawn*, 5 August 2013.

Ministry of Environment and Forests (2010). Technical EIA guidance manual for ship breaking yards. Available at: http://environmentclearance.nic.in/writereaddata/Form-1A/HomeLinks/TGM_Ship%20Breaking%20Yards_010910_NK.pdf Accessed 20 August 2016.

The News International (2013). Two labourers die at Gadani ship breaking yard. *The News International*, 13 July2013. Available at: www.thenews.com.pk/archive/print/442334-two-labourers-die-at-gadani-ship-breaking-yard Accessed 24 April 2014.

The News International (2015). Ship breakers call for cut in sales, income taxes. *The News International*, 20 May 2015. Available at: www.thenews.com.pk/print/41330-ship-breakers-call-for-cut-in-sales-income-taxes Accessed 22 May 2016.

NGO Shipbreaking Platform (2015a). Annual Report 2014. Available at: www.shipbreakingplatform.org/shipbrea_wp2011/wp-content/uploads/2015/06/NGO-Shipbreaking-Platform-Annual-Report-2014.pdf Accessed 18 April 2016.

NGO Shipbreaking Platform (2015b). What a difference a flag makes: Why ship owners' responsibility to ensure sustainable ship recycling needs to go beyond flag state jurisdiction. Available at: www.shipbreakingplatform.org/shipbrea_wp2011/wp-content/uploads/2015/04/FoCBriefing_NGO-Shipbreaking-Platform_-April-2015.pdf Accessed 16 March 2017.

NGO Shipbreaking Platform (2016). Annual Report 2015. Available at: www.shipbreakingplatform.org/shipbrea_wp2011/wp-content/uploads/2016/05/NGO-Shipbreaking-Platform-Annual-Report-2015.pdf Accessed 28 January 2016.

PakTribune (2008). Ship breakers seek end to scrap pipes' smuggling. *PakTribune*, 6 April 2008. Available at: http://paktribune.com/news/Ship-breakers-seek-end-to-scrap-pipes%92-smuggling-199195.html Accessed 19 June 2014.

Rana, P. I. (2010). Record 107 ship dismantled at Gaddani. *Dawn*, 29 June 2010. Available at: www.dawn.com/news/961977/record-107-ships-dismantled-at-gaddani Accessed 19 June 2014.

Samaa (2012). Karachi: Three labourers die at Gadani ship-breaking yard. *Samaa*, 19 October 2012. Available at: www.samaa.tv/pakistan/2012/10/karachi-three-labourers-die-at-gadani-ship-breaking-yard/ Accessed 4 April 2014.

Schuler, M. (2017). Another deadly blast at gadani shipbreaking yard. Available at: http://gcaptain.com/another-deadly-blast-gadani-shipbreaking-yard/ Accessed 9 January 2017.

Sheller, M., Urry, J. (2006). The new mobilities paradigm. *Environment and Planning A*. 38 (2): 207–226.

Shipbuilders' Association of Japan (2015). Shipbuilding statistics, March 2015. Available at: www.sajn.or.jp/e/statistics/Shipbuilding_Statistics_Mar2015e.pdf Accessed 26 August 2016.

Söderström, O., Randeria, S., Ruedin, D., D'Amato, G., Panese, F. (2013). *Critical Mobilities*. Lausanne: EPFL.

Stopford, M. (2003). *Maritime Economics*. Padstow, TJ: International Ltd.

United Nations Conference on Trade and Development (2015). Review of maritime transport, 2015. Available at: http://unctad.org/en/PublicationsLibrary/rmt2015_en.pdf Accessed 26 April 2016.

World Bank (2010). Ship breaking and recycling industry in Bangladesh and Pakistan. Available at: http://siteresources.worldbank.org/SOUTHASIAEXT/Resources/223546-1296680097256/Shipbreaking.pdf Accessed 24 August 2016.

Part 4

Induced and unproductive mobilities

10 Unproductive mobilities and maritime system capacity

Jason Monios and Gordon Wilmsmeier

Introduction

This chapter explores the concept of unproductive mobilities. These exist in several forms in maritime transport, from transporting empty containers or fuel wastage to service and ship overcapacity. Two specific and related forms are analysed in detail: overcapacity of vessels due to the rush to order ultra-large container ships, which leads to a cascading down of vessels to medium routes that do not need them, and infrastructure undercapacity of ports facing the prospect of vessels cascading all the way down to the lowest tier, which may not possess the physical infrastructure to handle them. The chapter establishes the outlines of the concept of unproductive mobility as a result of capacity mismatch and then draws on previous work by the authors to demonstrate empirical applications of the concept.

Unproductive mobilities

As discussed in the introductory chapter of this volume, the mobilities literature highlights the challenges "of too little movement or too much, or of the wrong sort or at the wrong time" (Sheller and Urry, 2006: 208). Hannam et al. (2006: 3) note that, "Mobilities cannot be described without attention to the necessary spatial, infrastructural and institutional moorings that configure and enable mobilities." In this chapter, two interrelated examples of unproductive mobilities will be examined that link these moorings with the wrong sort of movement.

Monios and Wilmsmeier (2015) identified unproductive and induced mobilities in the global maritime transport system. As discussed elsewhere in this volume, unproductive and induced mobility can be observed in the movement of empty containers and the handling of containers at transhipment ports, as the search for greater economies of scale and density through hub-and-spoke strategies results in unproductive and induced mobility. This chapter will explore the relationship between capacity and utilisation as another kind of unproductive mobility. Mobility analysis requires knowledge of capacity and utilisation, where utilisation, or the degree to which equipment is currently being used, is commonly expressed as a percentage. Measurements of cargo moved do not paint an accurate picture as they do not include the share of unproductive or induced mobility, and few studies exist on capacity utilisation, either of vessels or of ports.

Not long after 16,000 TEU and 18,000 TEU ships became the accepted maximum, the new limit reached 20,000+ TEU. Designs for at least 22,500 TEU ships are actively being considered as small profit margins force operators to pursue ever-greater technological scale economies. Wilmsmeier and Sánchez (2017) ask, "How big is beautiful?" and evaluate the impact of the effective decoupling of supply and demand. They describe the rather cataleptic state of the maritime industry – a condition through which the traditional shipping cycle seems to be broken due to the diminished responsiveness or a rather trancelike state of the industry.

After the onset of the global recession in 2008, demand shrank just as large amounts of vessel capacity entered the market, leading to overcapacity and the resulting plunge in freight rates and charter rates. This was due to the cyclical nature of shipping and the time-lagged nature of large investments, meaning that vessels ordered at the peak of the market when rates were high and capacity was stretched came online as the market turned downwards. Similarly, vessel orders slowed, older vessels were scrapped early for a fraction of their value, slow steaming was employed to absorb excess tonnage where possible and many vessels were laid up. However, these measures taken by actors in the shipping market did not solve the challenges of overcapacity.

More slowly but just as noticeable was the arrival of additional port capacity. In regions where under capacity had led to a loss of traffic to competitor ports (e.g. UK ports losing traffic to continental European ports), major terminal expansions came online at a time of overcapacity, and some expansion plans were delayed or cancelled. Ports invest large sums upgrading their facilities and competing to receive vessel calls, but handling such demand spikes is difficult. Large container drops can result in inefficient crane utilisation, as the numerous large cranes required to service large ships are not all required between calls; furthermore, such numbers of containers cannot always be moved in and out of the port in a smooth manner. It has been estimated that a 19,000 TEU vessel dropping 8,800 TEU in a single call will necessitate 14,000 container moves, 6 feeders of 800 TEU, 53 trains (carrying 90 containers each), 3 barges of 96 TEU and 2,640 trucks (Grey, 2015). Yet large ports continue to invest in upgrades, fearful of losing their calls from the leading carriers.

Hall et al. (2006) noted that cheap energy (especially oil) and the success of transport modes such as container vessels in the latter decades of the 20th century led perhaps to an assumption of mobility and a tendency to overlook components of the reality on which that mobility rests. This tendency can be observed in the increasing ordering of larger vessels and port expansions in the years before the economic crisis hit in 2008. Indeed, many port expansions came on stream in the years following when such handling capacity was no longer needed. Likewise with vessels. In recent years we have observed in the over ordering of vessel capacity the results of these assumptions about never-ending mobility expansion with little attention paid to the actual influences, causes and drivers of this mobility. Transport demand has frequently been accepted as given rather than seeking to understand the forces behind it and how drivers for efficiency in some quarters may produce unintended inefficiencies in other ways. How these actions then impact in the future and on the actions of decision makers from both the ports and shipping lines, and by extension, the users of these services, and ultimately the customers, will be the focus of this chapter.

Overcapacity of vessels

Wilmsmeier and Sánchez (2017) question the "traditional and still prevalent argument . . . that the development of ever larger ships is driven by the search of economies of scale by shipping companies." This thirst for size has undoubtedly provoked overcapacities at sea and exerted significant pressure for port infrastructure development. But, as in any industry, a mismatch between supply and demand creates inefficiencies; in the case of transport, an industry that trades the bridging of space for time and money, it results in unproductive mobilities.

The average output rate and the capacity must be measured in the same terms (time, customers, units or dollars). The utilisation rate indicates the need for adding extra capacity or eliminating unneeded capacity. The challenge here is that, in a global industry like the liner shipping industry, the unneeded capacity on primary trade routes is shifted geographically to secondary and tertiary routes via the cascading of vessels. The cascading effect thus effectively widens the scale of unproductive mobility as it is decoupled from demand growth.

The traditional argument has been that supply of shipping capacity is a function of the overall volume of trade. Consequently, only if the volume of trade is sufficiently large can technological economies of scale be reached and make the use of bigger ships economically sensible. However, more recent developments of capacity supply and trade development have led to questioning the assumption that supply follows demand.

Figure 10.1 shows that between 2000 and 2004 demand growth exceeded fleet capacity expansion and since 2005 supply continuously outgrew demand, except for 2010. The continued trend is particularly noteworthy in the post-crisis period (after 2010); while fleet growth rates slowed down, growth rates in container throughput evolved at even lower rates. Post-crisis, annual fleet capacity growth oscillates between 5 percent and 9 percent. However, the global demand growth slowed from 7.9 percent in 2011 to 1.1 percent in 2015. It is important to point out that this hard slowdown is triggered mainly by economic and political changes in China (Drewry, 2016) and knock-on effects in other countries.

The disconnection between supply and demand, particularly the strategies of shipping lines to handle overcapacity while operating the vessels, becomes evident in the cascading of vessels from main to secondary and from secondary to tertiary routes. Figure 10.2 depicts the period with the strongest effect of cascading on South American routes (shaded area) between 2009 and 2013. During this period, one of the main strategies of shipping lines to cope with oversupply on main routes was to shift vessels to secondary markets. This shift was disconnected from demand growth on these secondary routes.

A further indicator of the disconnection of supply and demand is the ratio between nominal deployed capacity and weekly capacity. The lower the ratio of

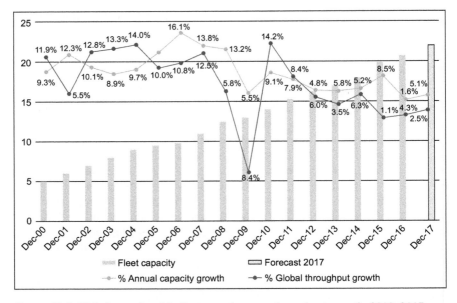

Figure 10.1 Global containership fleet growth versus throughput growth: 2000–2017
Source: Authors, based on data from Alphaliner

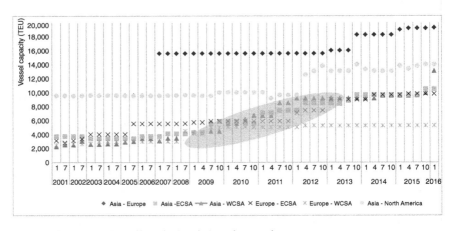

Figure 10.2 Cascading effects in South American main routes
Source: Authors, based on *American Shipper* various years

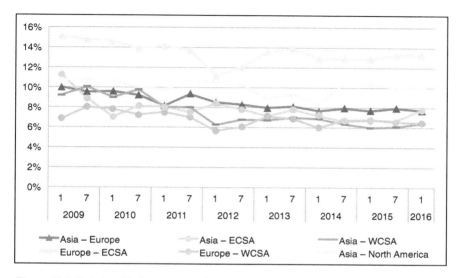

Figure 10.3 Relationship between nominal and weekly deployed capacity, main and secondary global routes to ECSA and WCSA, 2009–2016

Source: Authors, based on *American Shipper* various years

weekly capacity, the greater the disconnect between supply and demand, as low ratios can only be sustained with the support of other operational measures such as slowsteaming. Figure 10.3 depicts the evolution of this ratio in South America between 2009 and 2016. The results show that a particular deterioration can be observed on the east coast and west coast routes, which occurs in effect with the cascading of larger vessels into these routes.

Another approach to the same issue may be observed through the relationship between ship nominal capacity and call size. Glave and Saxon (2015) studied the movements per call of vessels serving large European terminals in 2014–2015. The research showed a high variability and thus only moderate correlation between the number of movements per call and vessel size.

In summary, the indicators and empirical evidence shown in this section underline an increasing disconnect and mismatch between supply and demand. The question that emerges is to what extent (from a temporal perspective) the industry can sustain the luxury of unproductive mobility and in how far this situation not only influences the economic sustainability but also the environmental and social sustainability of the sector.

Wilmsmeier and Sánchez (2017) show that container shipping lines are much less dependent on the "believed" economies of scale, but actually widely benefit and reap economies of scope. The consequence is that in the current scenario the estimated "benefits" of scale drive obsolescence of existing terminal capacity in two ways: a) through the push of larger vessels into secondary and tertiary markets where existing terminal infrastructure becomes incapable of handling and responding to the vessel requirements and b) where large terminal capacity created to cater for peak demands produces a temporal obsolescence due to the extended idle times at terminals, either one leading to a deterioration and inefficiencies in the container transport system (Wilmsmeier and Sánchez, 2017).

Mismatching of port and vessel capacity

Monios (2017) explored the impact on small ports dealing with the increasing size of feeder vessels as a result of cascading down from larger trades. Frequently overlooked, small ports provide the origin or destination of traffic for regions that do not have local access to a large port with direct international connections. Such locations already face the penalty of peripherality due to this additional transhipment of their trade at container hubs from large mainline vessel to small feeder vessel. Yet while much of the literature focuses on the fierce competition between large ports as they expand to be able to handle the calls of ever-larger mainline vessels, the effect on smaller ports who must expand to handle larger feeder vessels has received little attention.

From the perspective of small ports, cascading of vessels as discussed earlier presents a much more serious problem. If even medium traffic routes can expect to be served by vessels too large for their traffic, the case is even more acute for the trades below them, currently served by vessels around 4,000 TEU. Below that level are 2,000–4,000 TEU routes and, finally, small feeder routes currently served by sub-1,000 TEU vessels. Busy ports handling large vessels may not occupy valuable berth space with small feeder vessels below 1,000 TEU. Thus feeder routes linking small container ports with transhipment hubs may in the future be served by "super feeders" in the range of 2,000–4,000 TEU, which would mean some small ports have insufficient handling capacity to accommodate them. Such a situation would support the growth of regional second-tier hubs linked to main hubs, which can then serve the smaller ports either by smaller feeders or even land transport (thus raising issues relating to the quality and capacity of hinterland infrastructure links). The likely reality is a combination of the aforementioned strategies at different ports across the globe.

Monios (2017) found that there are 436 ports being served by sub-1,000 TEU container vessels. Of these 436 ports, 90 (or 21 percent of 420 confirmed data points) have berth depth less than 9.1m. Interestingly, the majority of these are in Europe and Asia, reflecting the extensive coastal and island geography of these continents compared to North and South America, which have fewer, larger ports (see Figure 10.4). Specifically, there are more river ports in Europe and more estuary ports in Asia, reflecting the geography of larger navigable rivers in Europe and the common occurrence of deltas and estuarial locations in Asia but rivers becoming less navigable upstream.

Berth depth of 8.7m is the average cut-off for vessels of 1,000 TEU, and that is using the design draft rather than the full depth required for a heavily laden vessel.

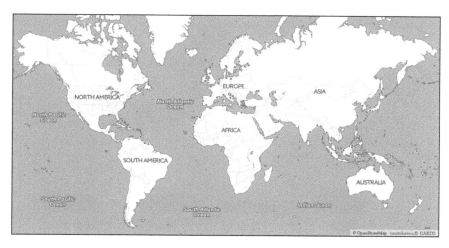

Figure 10.4 World map of small container ports with depth restrictions
Source: Monios (2017)

The existing sub-1,000 TEU vessel supply is under threat, with 15 percent already laid up, many operating vessels approaching the scrapyard (average age 15 years) and very few new vessels on order. This suggests that, as already inferred from the cascading on larger routes, sub-1,000 TEU vessels are likely to be replaced, at least to some degree, by larger vessels. Ports with poor landside accessibility cannot be served overland from a competing port in the same range, but even though they should then continue to be served, they may incur an additional cost for an operator to utilise less profitable smaller vessels or transship at a secondary hub from large to small feeder. Some opportunities for such concentration can be identified from the world map in Figure 10.4, which reveals that a cluster of such small ports may be identified in several locations, notably Southeast Asia, Japan, the Irish Sea and the (East and West) Baltic Sea.

An additional point of interest was that, while there exist vessels above 1,000 TEU capacity with suitably shallow design drafts, every one of the 1,000+ TEU vessels in the dataset has a full laden depth requirement beyond what any of these ports should be able to accommodate, which reveals that they were far from fully loaded (Figure 10.5). Thus the appearance of such vessels in the dataset does not mean that they offloaded any more containers than the smaller vessels, which is not an efficient use of vessels in the long term. In fact, it suggests that such vessels are already being cascaded even when they are underutilised, and if they are going to be utilised towards their capacity potential, then ports will need to deepen their berths. Furthermore, even if a port does upgrade to accommodate larger vessels, it will mean fewer calls, which puts other strains on the system.

The findings from Monios (2017) suggest that a greater rationalisation of smaller ports can be expected, with some expanding to handle larger vessels and

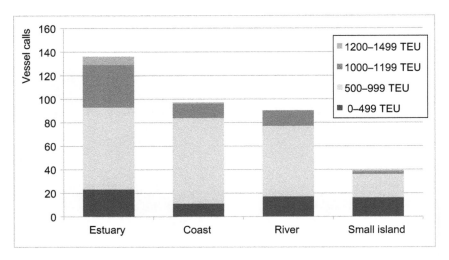

Figure 10.5 Vessel capacity calling at world container ports with sub-9.1m depth

Source: Monios (2017)

some disappearing from feeder schedules. Whether shippers currently utilising such ports will then be served overland or by smaller feeders or not at all will be the next question. Policymakers and planners supporting such shippers will need to consider how they can best serve them, by upgrading ports, upgrading connecting infrastructure to neighbouring ports, being prepared to subsidise their increasing transport costs or lose competitiveness to other shippers. The penalty of peripherality, already suffered by many producers and consumers not located on the main trade lanes, may soon grow worse. Many of these ports (although by no means all) are from countries with less effective governance regimes in place to develop the ports, especially as they will in most cases be publicly owned and therefore may find it difficult to justify large expenses for port expansion. Large international operators may take them on (or may already run them) if the price of expansion work is factored into their concession arrangement. But they could just as easily operate a different port where such constraints do not exist.

Conclusion

The discussion in this chapter reveals not only the existence of unproductive mobilities in a market where supply and demand have become disconnected, but it further illuminates the interconnections of unproductive mobility. From a system perspective, the unproductive mobility of mobile entities (vessels) entails, provokes and triggers unproductive mobility across different geographical scales and drives them into the spatially fixed port sector. As port infrastructure in many cases remains a public sector responsibility (even if the responsibility has been temporarily transferred to the private sector via concessions) the cenotaph of scale of a global private industry ultimately pushes its unproductivity back to society.

These strategies also derive in part from an oligopolistic market structure that regulators have done little to address. Thus, it could be argued that large vessels are not ordered as a response to market signals of customer demand, but rather as a sign of large carriers exerting their market power, as the large investments required cannot be matched by smaller competitors. The other aspect of the market power of carriers is not only in competition with other carriers but also in their relation with ports. Larger vessels enable carriers to make additional small savings on the cost per container shipped, but they cause much higher costs for the rest of the transport chain, from large spikes at terminals to larger inventory costs for shippers. Vessels are cascaded too soon in order to soak up excess tonnage, spreading unproductive mobilities throughout the system. From a system perspective, therefore, this strategy does not make economic sense, thus it can be concluded that the shipping market is not functioning correctly and market power of large carriers is distorting the market.

The question then becomes how to restore balance to the market. How to incentivise a healthy market, with busy ports that don't suffer demand spikes, vessels fully loaded and not causing customers to have infrequent large deliveries and large inventories? One could argue that the market should decide. If the carriers want to introduce large vessels and go bankrupt then that is their choice and customers will benefit from fierce competition. Yet the reality is not so simple. With large backers (e.g. public sector state backers for China Shipping or private sector conglomerates such as Maersk), carriers can sustain losses for several quarters or years in a row. That is not a healthy market and does not produce optimal results from a system perspective. This behaviour sends false signals that ultra-large container vessels are healthy; therefore, ports must compete to upgrade to handle those vessels, but it is society that ends up paying the dredging costs or expansion costs, especially when the ports end up sitting empty much of the time. So how can society respond? Is it time to consider new approaches to regulation? Such a solution is often politically unpopular but needs to be considered. Individual ports cannot individually decide not to upgrade because of the imperatives of competition. Could it be feasible for a country or region (e.g. the European Union) to introduce a regulation prohibiting vessels above a certain limit (e.g. 15,000 TEU)? Would that curb market power and reduce unnecessary expense by ports, or would it distort the market in another direction? It seems certain that shipping regulation is one of the big questions to be addressed by scholars in the next decade.

References

Drewry (2016). Diminishing returns? Are we entering a new period where the money to be made from ports and terminals is markedly less than it was? Spotlight Briefing, February 2016. Available at: www.drewry.co.uk/AcuCustom/Sitename/DAM/004/Diminishing_ Returns_Spotlight_Briefing_Feb2016.pdf Accessed 25 July 2017.

Glave, T., Saxon, S. (2015). How to rethink pricing at container terminals. McKinsey and Company. Available at: www.mckinsey.com/industries/travel-transport-and-logistics/ our-insights/how-to-rethink-pricing-at-container-terminals. Accessed 26 January 2016.

Grey, M. (2015). Age of the giants. Lloyd's List, 2 February 2015. Available at: www. lloydslist.com/ll/sector/containers/article456093.ece Accessed 16 March 2015.

Hall, P., Hesse, M., Rodrigue, J.-P. (2006). Reexploring the interface between economic and transport geography. *Environment and Planning A*. 38: 1401–1408.

Hannam, K., Sheller, M., Urry, J. (2006). Editorial: Mobilities, immobilities and moorings. *Mobilities*. 1 (1): 1–22.

Monios, J. (2017). Cascading feeder vessels and the rationalisation of small container ports. *Journal of Transport Geography*. 59: 88–99.

Monios, J., Wilmsmeier, G. (2015). Identifying Material, Geographical and Institutional Mobilities in the Global Maritime Trade System. In: T. Birtchnell, S. Savitzky and J. Urry (eds.), *Cargomobilities: Moving Materials in a Global Age*. Abingdon: Routledge. pp. 125–148.

Sheller, M., Urry, J. (2006). The new mobilities paradigm. *Environment & Planning A*. 38 (2): 207–226.

Wilmsmeier, G., Sánchez, R. J. (2017). Economies of scale in the liner container shipping industry: Challenging the beliefs – port management implications in decoupled supply and demand market conditions. Forthcoming.

11 Before the "hangover"?

Gordon Wilmsmeier, Marta Gonzalez-Aregall and Ricardo J. Sánchez

Introduction

This chapter analyzes the potential future consequences of the concentration processes and the problem of potential dominance position abuse in the liner shipping industry, which might reach far beyond creating barriers for new entrants and privileges for setting prices.

Only a few decades ago globalization was seen as an unstoppable force, the bringer of development and prosperity. "Rejecting globalization, was like rejecting the sunrise" (Packer, 2016). The liner shipping industry (based on the container, the "humble hero" – The Economist, 2013) was a, if not the, key element to make trading across borders cheaper. Within this process, the liner shipping industry was itself part driver and tool of liberalization and deregulation efforts. And in the 1990s, the growth doctrine resulted in an era of "hyperglobalization", where growth rates, privatization and liberalization were the ingredients to the global capitalist system. The liner shipping industry during these years engaged in expansivist strategies which found their symbol in the ever-increasing vessel sizes and geographical reach of companies' activities.

In the wake of the financial crisis, shipping lines' behaviour seemed to be indifferent to the changed environment and their expansionist strategy continued, ordering more and larger vessels. However, as the crisis prevailed cracks and limitations began to show in this endeavour. Thus the shipping lines are now facing a defiant situation.

On the one hand, they had ridden on the exponential growth of cargo mobilities and continued economic growth that had been fed and sustained by an also continuously growing capacity. On the other hand, the recent economic crisis and its aftermath in global trade has created a deceleration and on certain trades even decline of activity, which is now outmatched by the available capacity (Figure 11.1).

In previous times, "the industry found a solution to the problem of excess capacity in conferences and cartels, which work to control competitive relations between existing lines." (Marx, 1953). Now the industry initiated a strong restructuring of its market. Carriers started, more than ever, to share capacity on assets to manage overcapacity in various trade routes through alliances, mergers and different

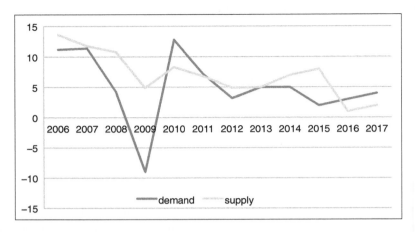

Figure 11.1 Evolution of demand and supply in container shipping, 2006–2016 (annual percentage change)

Source: Authors, based on data from Clarkson Research Container Intelligence Monthly, various issues

Notes: Supply data refer to total capacity of the container-carrying fleet, including multipurpose and other vessels with some container-carrying capacity. Demand growth is based on million TEU lifts. The data for 2017 are projected figures.

forms of acquisitions and collaboration.[1] While this "solution" makes sense from a shipping sector and shareholder perspective, the pace and level of these different arrangements might lead to a situation of abuse of a dominance position.

Based on the industrial organization theory, the shipping line market is a stable market with competition on quantities (capacity) but, in contrast to the theoretical framework, when concentration increases a reduction of prices can be observed. This situation seems to suggest competition on setting lower prices (limit pricing) through a dominant position (predatory prices) or setting prices close to costs (efficiency pricing). Although it is difficult to identify if prices are based on costs, it is important to monitor alliance behaviour through leniency programs and antitrust authorities in order to control a potential "explosive cocktail".

If the industry is converging towards a monopoly, economic theory establishes the need for regulation; however, the capacity of international action is limited, and institutions dealing with the shipping market currently have not established rules to solve this specific problem. In this regard, it is difficult to predict when the current "party" will end, but undoubtedly, the current changes will have consequences for the future of maritime transport and the sector.

Thus, in front of an unquestionable concentration process since 2013 (Sys, 2009; Gonzalez-Aregall et al., 2017), this chapter provides a look into a potential future in which the current "party" of low freight rates, decoupled supply and demand, as well as the silently accepted global concentration might create a "hangover" that will have to be paid by society at last as a consequence of market power[2] and the absence of a specific global regulatory framework. "Hangover" is defined as "a custom, habit, feeling, etc. that survives from the past" (Oxford Dictionary, 2017).

The rest of this chapter is organized as follows. Section 2 describes the main ingredients of the liner shipping industry. Section 3 outlines the basics of economic theory of industrial organization and the current state. Section 4 addresses the results and consequences. Finally, the last section is devoted to summarizing the main findings.

The cocktail – basic ingredients of the liner shipping industry

This section analyzes the main characteristics of the liner shipping industry to understand the current situation and relevant significance. The combination of external factors, such as economic growth and other elements produce a cocktail of dominance abuse.

The liner shipping business is a capital-intensive industry,[3] with high income risk due to the freight rate instability, subject to seasonality (Shashikumar, 1995) and imbalance constraints (Sánchez et al., 2003; Wilmsmeier, 2014). Besides, this industry is subject to perishable conditions of its services supply (Brooks, 2000; Sánchez, 2005; Sánchez and Wilmsmeier, 2011) as well as cyclical condition and inflexible capacity adjustment in the short run (Sánchez, 2005; Notteboom, 2012).

In the same direction, the liner shipping industry presents an intensity of capital use with high income risk due to the price instability and the perishable condition of services supply and where the differences in product structure generates diversity in the market (Brooks, 2000; Sánchez and Duesi, 2002; Wilmsmeier, 2014) with different production costs and competitive conditions (Gonzalez-Laxe and Sánchez, 2007). In this regard, there has been an inter-relation of three main factors: concentration, cyclical effects and economies of scale, scope and density.

First ingredient: concentration

Even on main shipping routes where a large number of shipping lines operate the market is not necessarily a competitive one. Indeed, alliances and cooperation of different type allow the firms to potentially agree on prices and market shares. In this regard, the authors question if this tendency of market concentration already implies a situation of market power, which is still potential and not yet exercised, but a possible scenario.

The liner shipping market concept is defined as "frequently called an economic or trading market, is the area in which prices tend towards uniformity allowing for transport costs" Sjöstrom (2002: 310), where issues like size of liner market and agreements between market agents are crucial. Also, existing studies fail to include the evolution of liner shipping networks from a network of direct services to a hierarchical hub-and-spoke network (Wilmsmeier and Notteboom, 2011).

Market competition and concentration has been studied for a long time through-out the expansion and crisis period (cf. Sys, 2009; Sánchez and Wilmsmeier, 2010; Gonzalez-Aregall et al., 2017) in different temporal and spatial configura-tions, allowing for close documentation of the processes and situation over the last two decades. However, fewer works discuss the theoretical approaches used for measuring market concentration and the threat of suffering from collusive behaviour and oligopolistic market structures in emerging markets (Sys, 2009; Sánchez and Wilmsmeier, 2011; Gonzalez-Aregall et al., 2017). Hirata (2017: 31), in his analysis until 2011, argues, "The economic implication of contestable market explains why alliance formation prevail," and he further states, "Technology advances make it possible to achieve market efficiency in absence of real entry/exit barriers and without actual competition, which is a highly significant implication for policy makers."

In general, competition authorities have tried and still aim to regulate and enforce competition laws. According to UNCTAD (2016) and based on the White Paper of European Shippers' Council, there are three main competition regulators in the world: the Ministry of Commerce from China, the Federal Maritime Commission from the United States and the Directorate-General for Competition from the European Union. Although they act autonomously, since 2014, they engaged in a cross-institutional manner on respective legal regimes and policies for the international maritime sector.

A regulatory approval of alliances is required in some jurisdictions such as China and the United States. The European Commission requires consortia members to conduct a self-assessment to ensure that there is no abuse of dominant position where market share exceeds 30 percent. (UNCTAD, 2016).

From a theoretical point of view, market power is defined as the possibility of a firm to fix prices above marginal costs. It enables a firm to apply behavioural strategies to maximize its surplus without running the risk of competition. Some authors affirm that the causality can be reversed and that a firm's conduct can shape the market structure. Thus the market structure would be endogenously determined. Therefore, behaviour can be used to create entrance barriers (Cable, 1972; Schmalensee, 1981). Thus, in the case of individual markets, such as shipping lines, entrance barriers can enable firms to hold market power against new competitors or allow only new entrants that form part of the existing alliances.

According to the theory, the shipping market is defined as a contestable market where it is possible to reach equilibrium in competition in terms of prices, volume and consumption; however, the existence of a barrier to new competing entrants to the market, as mentioned before, suppose an impediment due to their use of market power by the incumbents. Bogo (2000) observed in a contestable market the same results as a market in perfect competition. In the paradigm of contestable markets, the threat of new entrants effectively exists and the capacity of incumbents to use their market power should be limited.[4] However, according to Sánchez and Wilmsmeier (2010), it seems that the evidence indicates that there is a lack of contestability in the South American container markets, for example.

However, empirical evidence on market power differs. Clyde and Reitzes (1995) found a statistically relevant relation between prices and market share of conferences on similar routes, Fink et al. (2000) assures that prices are higher in such cases whereby Wilmsmeier and Hoffmann (2008) confirm this result, showing that in the Caribbean freight rates in trades with few service providers (one to four) are higher than in trades with more market players. Moreover, according to the industrial organisation literature, a small number of companies in one market do not necessarily lead to market power, because new potential entrants could challenge them by offering an attractive price level, whereas the pure existence of alliances by itself does not mean consistently price fixing agreements. In this line, Davies (1986: 311) argues that the "concept of contestability, for the maritime economist at least, is an eminently relevant analytical tool and one which has some very important implications for the policy maker."

During the last decades, maritime container transport has been concentrating in fewer larger carriers. Even if there are no market conditions allowing for the abusive management of prices, shippers have to face the fact of not being specialized in maritime transport and, many times, must negotiate freights through intermediaries (Brooks, 2000). Consequently, shippers thus have a low possibility of obtaining relevant information on the maritime transport market. These information asymmetries are also supported by discussion agreements (which provide the supply side with information access) which affect those members of the international maritime trade (demand side) with less access to information and less negotiation power. These are typically exporters and importers related to small and medium-sized industries. In addition, carriers are used to entering into long-term contracts with large shippers. This provides a clearer picture to those who can afford to negotiate this type of contract. The proliferation of alliances and mergers in the maritime sector, especially among carriers, has been the result of a widespread process intensified by a series of external factors that led to the creation of megacarriers and global strategic alliances in the industry. In turn, this enhances the attractiveness of the logistic business for large waterborne transport companies, increasing the concentration and control over markets. This is also supported by the typical short-term instability of the liner business, which may limit its rate of return in some segments of the economic cycle, and can be solved through the expansion to road and container logistics. Companies that are able to obtain cost profits by using a more intelligent logistics management will enjoy a very important cost advantage. The same logic is followed by liner expansion to port operation (Sánchez, 2005).[5]

Gonzalez-Aregall et al. (2017) not only identify the increase in concentration but also define "the black box" of concentration, which is defined by the difference in concentration level at the company in comparison with the alliance level. It can be referred as a "black box" since the actual level of collaboration within the alliances is generally unknown. Thus the authors stress significant differences and underline questions on the boundaries between the firm and alliance. In line with Sánchez and Wilmsmeier (2011), the authors show the variation of collaboration in different geographic contexts (routes) in terms of concentration levels and inequality. Since the economic crisis, the concentration process in the liner shipping industry has accelerated significantly in the global market, as 80 percent of global trade in terms of volume will be controlled by even fewer firms than today, leading to quasi-monopolistic and monopsonic market situations. A continuation of this trend might lead to competitive advantages for market leaders and a centralization of market power on few actors. A reduced number of competitors and close

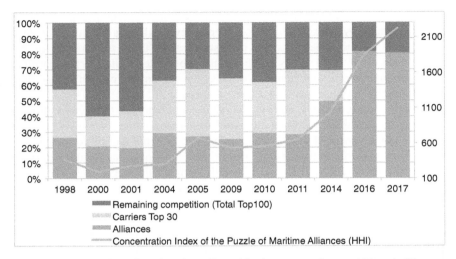

Figure 11.2 Evolution of market share liner shipping companies top 100 and alliances, 1998–2017

Source: Mouftier and Sánchez (2017)

cooperation also increase the interdependencies among actors and an increased reactivity of actions of the competitors.

Figure 11.2 shows preliminary evidence about concentration in the liner shipping industry through the estimation of the Herfindhal-Hirschmann Index (HHI) for the whole industry. As it is possible to observe, competition based on top-100 companies not included in alliances only takes 19 percent of total supply, meanwhile HHI has recently exceeded the threshold of 1,800 points.

Latest developments of falling demand caused further concentration in the shipping market (see Figure 11.1). Falling demand freed shipping capacity and thus increased competition as shipping lines aim for maximizing capacity utilization. At least three scenarios might arise: a) intensification of collective action of suppliers and thus "artificial" pricing, which does not reflect the real market situation, but is a protectionist measure of the industry, b) withdrawal of shipping lines from peripheral markets and concentration on key market areas and c) overcapacity leads to ruinous competition among suppliers, leading to a continued drop in freight rates, but as a result leaves markets with higher level of concentration as of today because competitors are pushed out.

Second ingredient: cyclical effects

Cyclical conditions produce positive and negative mismatches between supply/demand ratios that force companies to look for new markets and exploit new routes outside their traditional geography, encouraging further spatial expansion of activity in the sector (Sánchez and Wilmsmeier, 2011).

Associated with the cyclical condition arises the cyclical risk, which lies in the behaviour of companies ordering ship capacity. Additionally, the decision of acquiring and expanding a fleet must take the increase in the price of vessels, because of the maritime cycle, into account. The change in vessel prices can reach from a minimum of 50 percent to over 300 percent.[6] Since the shipping cycle is defined as the interaction between supply and demand in the maritime transport sector, supply provision will lag, especially when facing extremely dynamic exogenous demand. Fluctuations in the shipping cycle are closely linked to those of the business cycle, where decreases or shrinkage in aggregate demand will mean lower demand for transport services, forcing shipping companies to build fewer ships and scrap some of those that are not in use. Conversely, when aggregate demand increases during a cycle of economic expansion, it cannot be met immediately because the shipping companies are already managing existing demand. Figure 11.3 provides a simplified ten-step diagrammatic representation of the shipping cycle.

These phenomena are reflected in the variation of freight prices.[7] An economy in crisis causes the production, consumption and, consequently, transport as a derived demand, to fall. In the beginning of the shipping cycle, freight rates, industry revenues and profits fall (step 1) and, consequently, there are no incentives to add tonnage to the fleet (step 2). In turn, the demand for ships falls, more ships

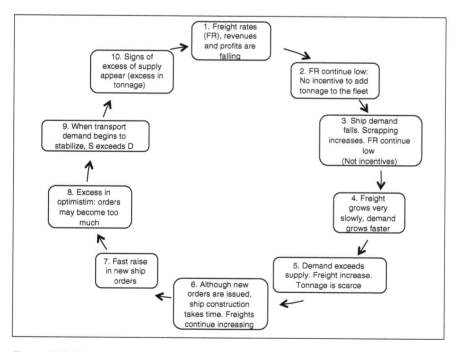

Figure 11.3 The "traditional" shipping cycle mechanism
Source: Sánchez (2005)

are scrapped or laid-up. Freight rates remain low (step 3). Steps 1 to 3 are the lower phase of the maritime cycle. In the moment, the economic growth starts to pick up (step 4), the fleet start to expand slowly in response, due to the time lag between ordering and receiving new tonnage, but transport demand grows more rapidly (because of the inelasticity). Steps 5 to 10 are the higher phase of the cycle: demand outstrips supply, capacity is scarce, freight rates rise while demand continues to exceed supply and orders for new shipbuilding increase rapidly. At a certain point, excess of optimism, and this positivist tendency, results in an excess of new vessel capacity orders. When transport demand begins to stabilize, supply exceeds demand, and signs of excess capacity appear. This mismatch triggers a "crisis" and the cycle returns to phase one.

The industry's first reaction in respect to the 2008 economic crisis was to reduce operating costs, restructure financial commitments and try to fit the decoupling between supply and demand (Sánchez, 2011). Recently, there was a change in the behaviour of new vessel deliveries, and a reduction of actual deliveries with respect to planned deliveries (Drewry, 2016). However, actual deliveries did not result in any reduction of capacity, which would be the expected behaviour within the traditional shipping cycle (Figure 11.4).

The side effects arising from processes linked to crises and peaks in the business cycle are tightly connected to the decisions made by economic agents, particularly in response to crisis periods. Stakeholders in the maritime sector are affected by economic recessions, since as aggregate demand weakens, so does

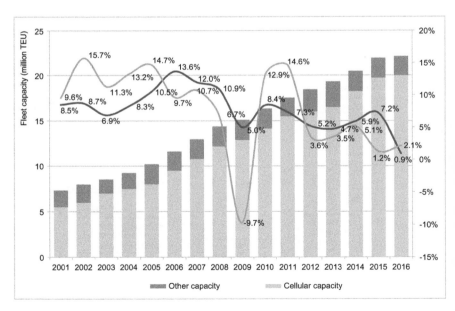

Figure 11.4 Global containership fleet growth versus throughput growth: 2000–2016

Source: Authors, based on Clarkson (several issues)

demand for goods transport, resulting in consequences for companies' profits. Along with this, the decisions made in the optimistic phase of the cycle can cause imbalances in companies' results. Hence shipping companies' operating margins declined throughout 2011 before rising again, with small fluctuations from one quarter to the next, although overall results have remained poor. Companies' fluctuating financial performance correlates exactly to changes in the global trade of goods and the wider economy, and specifically to the sustained overcapacity in the industry as well as this situation is clearly driven by low freight rates.

Following the traditional shipping cycle approach, after the crisis started in mid-2008, jointly with a drop in production, consumption and transport needs, freight rates, industry revenues and profits fell. In fact, initially the demand for shipbuilding fell and an increasing number of ships was scrapped or left idle. Freight rates remained low, confirming that the shipping cycle was in its lower phase. However, shipbuilding never stopped.

Under the "shipping cycle" traditional approach, trade and transport needs fall when a crisis occurs and supply exceeds demand. Consequently, freight rates, revenues and financial margins drop and shipbuilding are halted. This is considered as a natural reaction to low revenues because there are no incentives to add tonnage to commercial fleets.

However, after the 2010 "re-take-off", bigger liner shipping companies performed for the first time a "trilogy": increasing number of shipbuilding orders for new vessels, bigger ships and concentrated alliances. The trilogy is a clear detour from the traditional shipping cycle approach. In summary, there is sufficient reasoning to support the suspicion that the traditional mechanism of the maritime cycle has changed with bigger liner shipping companies (Sánchez, 2017).

Third ingredient: economies of scale

In a context of global competition, the role of shipping lines is challenging. The increase of ship size over the last two decades (Cullinane and Khanna, 1998) has undergone significant changes in the last years. According to Sánchez and Wilmsmeier (2017), economies of scale might be the most frequently used argument to explain developments in the liner shipping industry and challenges for port infrastructure.

Since 2008, many recurring arguments on bigger ships associated with concepts such as economies of scale, diseconomies, market equilibrium, "chronic" overcapacity, among others, are based on a set of important long-held beliefs that could eventually become myths. Among these are 1) only vessel size matters: big is beautiful, 2) all containers can be considered the same: the business of dry containers is usually mixed up with that of reefer containers, 3) supply follows demand and 4) individual vessel size generates economies of scale, independently from efficiency of networks or average operational speed, among others. Finally, this set also includes the continued assertion that, from a shipping line's point of view, economies of scale are the strategy to seek efficiencies. This is the perfect synopsis of those common beliefs.

The question is not, therefore, what we believe, but to critically reflect on the tendencies of the liner shipping industry to create an understanding of what shipping development principles and tendencies can tell us about port planning. The success of economies of scale cannot be questions, but they are only part of the "story" in the current success or failure of shipping lines. Further, a discontinuation of some traditional arguments and a diversification of the discussions seem indispensable not only to build research and strategies for the shipping market but also particularly to drive knowledge and research on future port development.

In connection to the previous "ingredients", facing the need to reduce costs through economies of scale and scope, and in order to take advantage of the know-how and have a fleet appropriate for the new requirements, many companies are now resorting towards strategic alliances not only with regional operators, as in the past (e.g. the Hamburg Süd takeover of Alianca), but also more specifically among the leading global companies.

Essentials of current events

According to Cabral (2000), industrial organization focuses on the study of markets and industries, specifically how firms compete with each other. Generally, economists analyze industries with reference to the structure-conduct-performance paradigm. In this regard, observable structural characteristics of a market determine the behaviour of firms within that market (Martin, 2000). More firms drive more competitive pricing and squeeze margins with firms earning no supra-normal profits.[8]

In some markets, the relevance of economies of scale in production induces that only one or few firms can efficiently produce in the market (Carlton and Perloff, 2005). Specifically, the shipping market is defined as a contestable market where it is possible to reach a competitive equilibrium with few firms being aggressive in their commercial offerings. However, the existence of entry barriers supposes an impediment to new competing entrants, and there is evidence that firms tend to collude and concentrate (Connor, 2006).[9]

In the case of shipping line business, it is an industry that may end up with few competitors as incumbents initially lower prices to drive rivals out of the market, and then the remaining firms merge and/or collude with their rivals using alliances and other coordinating arrangements.

Theoretical framework – the measurement

To reflect critically on the current situation, it is important to examine the strategies of the liner shipping industry from a theoretical point of view.

As mentioned earlier, there has been an increase of ship size over the last two decades (Cullinane and Khanna, 1998; OECD, 2015). Hence we suppose that the liner shipping industry is a stable market that competes on quantities (capacity) – i.e., the Cournot Model. This model assumes that the product is standardized and the two firms have identical and constant average costs with a common objective to maximize their profits (equation 1), where the price equilibrium depends on quantity (equation 2).

$$\pi_i = p(Q)q_i - TC_i(q_i)$$

$$\frac{d\pi_i}{dq_i} = p(Q) + \frac{dp(Q)}{dq_i}q_i - MC_i(q_i) = 0 \tag{1}$$

$$p^e(Q) = MC_i(q_i) + \left|\frac{dp(Q)}{dQ}\right|q_i \tag{2}$$

However, according to Martin (2010), if firms in Cournot duopoly have different unit costs, the firm with lower cost has a greater degree of market power. At the industry level, this is measured by the Lerner index of market power for the average firms (equation 3):

$$L_i = \frac{p^e - MC_i}{p^e} = \frac{MC_i(q_i) + \left|\frac{dp(Q)}{dQ}\right|q_i - MC_i}{p^e} = \frac{\left|\frac{dp(Q)}{dQ}\right|s_iQ}{p^e} = \frac{s_i}{\varepsilon}$$

$$s_i = \frac{q_i}{Q} \qquad \varepsilon = \left|\frac{dQ(p)}{dp}\right|\frac{p}{Q}, \tag{3}$$

$$L = \sum_i s_i L_i = \sum_i \frac{s^2_i}{\varepsilon} = \sum_i \frac{HHI}{\varepsilon}, \tag{4}$$

where $s_i = q_i/Q$ is firm i's market share and ε is the absolute value of the price elasticity of demand. Hence the Lerner index of market power is the ratio between Herfindahl index of seller concentration and the price elasticity of demand (equation 4). In sum, in a Cournot oligopoly with cost differences, there is a positive relation between concentration (Herfindahl index) and price – cost margin (Martin, 2010). However, in the case of the liner shipping industry, the current concentration process presents even lower prices than the ones we should expect from the previous model. Therefore, we brand the current state of the market as a "party", discussed in the following section.

Business parties

Price competition

Hence we observe competition on prices – i.e., Bertrand model. In this model, firms set prices rather than output. Assuming perfect information and identical products, the consumers buy the product with the lowest price. In the equilibrium, when each firm sets a price equal to marginal cost, each firm is maximizing its own profit. However, if the marginal cost is lower, there will be an incentive for firms to lower their prices. This situation, referred to as the Bertrand Paradox, yields the same result of fair perfect competition (Martin, 2010) and may reduce the number of sellers to the few ones that are more cost efficient and bigger.

Price war and collusion cycles

By the way, price competition suggests two situations. First, a price competition seems to suggest the existence of a fair price war between firms. This situation leads to a reduction of the number firms through alliances, mergers and acquisitions, and, consequently, the remaining firms collude with their rivals.

Second, since the last decade, the reduction of freight rates allows to reason that the liner shipping industry applies predatory prices. According to Carlton and Perloff (2005: 352), predatory prices are defined as a conduct of firms that

> first lowering its price to drive rivals out of business and scare off potential entrants, and then raising its price when its rivals exit the market. In general, the firm lowers price below some measure of cost; thus, the firm incurs short-run losses to obtain long-run gains.

In this case, an abuse of a dominant position can be observed. On the one hand, market concentration leads to exclusion for new entrants through alliances, mergers and acquisitions as well as entry of carriers in new markets. And on the other hand, although due to a lack of cost and price information, it is difficult to identify whether prices are above costs; however, the reduction of freight rates induce one to think that there exists either a situation of predatory prices or a fair price war between firms in the market.

Considering that shipping line firms are in a fair price war or predatory prices, a reduction of firms can be expected and when the party will be over to reach again the collusive phase. Figure 11.5 depicts these price war and predatory price phases and the collusive cycle idea.

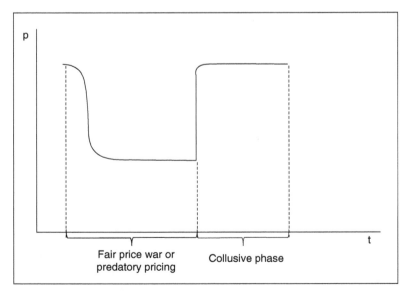

Figure 11.5 Price war, predatory prices and collusion cycle
Source: Own elaboration

Consequently, it is relevant to monitor alliance behaviour through leniency programs and national antitrust authorities and international cooperation. It seems necessary to monitor shipping line performance continuously over time to determine whether a potential risk of dominant position abuse exists. Such intervention to a potential risk has been applied ex-post in the past. Given the current situation the emergence of a collusive phase and rising prices, despite a continued mismatch of supply and demand seem a probable near future. However, due to the lack of substantial and differentiated of cost and price information, it is difficult to identify whether prices are above operating costs. Thus the following section discusses the potential risks and tries to identify signals towards an evolving hangover.

The aftermath

This section explores and discusses the first signs of potential future challenges.

First signs of "hangover"

The hangover might be interpreted with a double meaning here: a custom, habit, feeling, etc., that survives from the past, which is reflected in the continued belief in growth, and in its more common sense as "a severe headache or other after-effects caused by" partying in excess. While the first one rather applies to the liner-shipping sector, the second meaning illustrates the possible symptoms for the shippers and the economy.

One indicator to identify the potential first signs of the "hangover" are freight rates. As argued earlier, one reason why relatively little attention is being paid to the concentration process is that freight rates currently remain at all-time lows and thus the "party" mood of low transport costs distracts from the parallel developments in the sector. Despite small growth rates in economic development and the seeming recoupling of economic growth and trade activity, freight rates remain low in major trades (Figure 11.6), indicating that the mismatch of supply and demand has still not been solved.

In 2016, container spot freight rates remained low and volatile. In general, the level of freight rates on the selected routes is less than 50 percent of the rates in 2009 (Figure 11.7). Even further reduction of rates was stopped by shipping lines starting to effectively reduce capacity through network optimization, slow steaming, scrapping and more careful vessel deployment around the peak season. Figure 11.7 shows that average spot freight rates maintained their negative trend in most trade lanes in 2016. Particularly, some intra-Asian routes reached all-time lows. However, the development in some of the routes requires attention. By way of example, average freight rates in the Shanghai-South America (Santos/Brazil) trade increased over 250 percent between 2015 and 2016 (Figure 11.6). The *Journal of Commerce* (2016a) argues that this increase was a result of significant capacity reduction. This strategy was only possible because of the increasing concentration and alliances since this allows for sharing of capacity among lines and thus maintaining service levels.

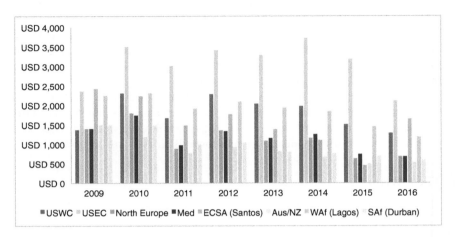

Figure 11.6 Selected container freight rates, Shanghai with different regions, 2009–2016, current USD per FEU

Source: Clarkson Research, Container Intelligence Monthly, various issues

Note: Data based on yearly averages. *Abbreviation, FEU, 40-foot equivalent unit.

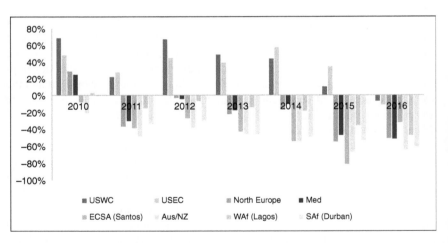

Figure 11.7 Evolution of container freight rates (FEU), Shanghai with different regions, 2009–2016, percentage change in comparison to 2009

Source: Authors based on Clarkson Research, Container Intelligence Monthly, various issues

Note: Data based on yearly averages. *Abbreviation, FEU, 40-foot equivalent.

The issue that emerges is, if these first increases in freight rates are a result of readjusting the match of supply and demand, similar developments can be expected in the other trade lanes over the next months and years. While the increase in general is positive for the industry, which was delivering services below operating costs, the question is, what will be the end of the line of this recovery? Or returning to the theme of the chapter, when will the recovery turn into pain (excessive freight increases) for the shippers? Once a level of pain is reached the question is, if there is still is a remedy to control the level of pain. Pain in this case should be translated in loss of competitiveness through high freight rates that causes distress and/or economic suffering.

The "hangover", but for whom – industry or society?

While the current hangover of the liner shipping industry is to a certain extent self-inflicted, the sector has found a response in mergers and alliances paired with other measures. Thus the current distress from low freight rates on company results can be expected be a temporary one and can be expected to also have clear strategic reasons, that are lifting the entry barriers for any new competitor and eliminating the weaker ones. This is reflected in the recent weddings among operators and some funerals (e.g. Hanjin).

As networks and collaboration do not evolve equally across regions and global industry concentration particularly affects more peripheral routes, and the current situation leads to a policy dilemma as in certain markets it might be difficult to interpret the boundaries between coordinative behaviour and tacit collusion. But just looking at concentration is too simple; the evolution of the maritime industry requires a systemic view reaching from the local to the global. "Powerful actors" are present in the market with relatively stable power relations across multiple spatial and temporal scales. This is creating a significant capacity to choose the timing of their strategic plays or to use stalling tactics to further their strategic interests.

Based on the arguments earlier, it can be expected that the "hangover" for society might be of greater relevance. It should also be noted that this "hangover" will emerge and spread in intensity in a spatially differentiated manner. Wilmsmeier and Hoffmann (2006) found that trade between poorer countries is burdened by higher freight rates than trade between richer countries. Global concentration will also have a stronger impact on secondary and tertiary routes as the number, given the volume of trade in general, have already been limited in the past. Thus the initially mentioned era of "hyperglobalization" that was expected to reduce poverty might be steering towards a phase in which the industry that mobilizes "the humble hero", despite all trade liberalization efforts, takes charge and might start to be the determining factor of competitiveness of a region or country. Potentially, playing a decisive role in the creation of adverse effects, to the point where the benefits of free trade might be consumed by individual companies' strategies. As this new power is found in relational positioning, expresses resource endowments, shapes intentions, defines strategic horizons and conditions the range of possible outcomes. Consequently, shifting power relations in the maritime industry require a spatialized understanding of power considering resources, capacities, positioning and strategies.

Conclusions and outlook for a cure

Is this the phase before the hangover? Does history repeat itself? If there is a "cure" to the appearing symptoms: it is difficult to identify. If prices are based on costs, it is important to monitor alliance behaviour through leniency programs and antitrust rules against market dominance, cartels and alliances. But the question is who is the respective entity to pursue and implement such regulation.

Considering the aforementioned characteristics and the discussion proposed, it is clear that there is no true possibility of repeating policies of state protected national merchant fleets, as the old-style protective policies. In fact, this would imply an effort allocation mistake. Instead, the design and execution of national maritime policies may set other important goals in terms of countries' development.

National, regional or global maritime policies should be consistent with regional and international policies, and contemplate to a certain extent the influence of interest groups. These policies should be included within the wider framework of transport, service and logistics policies. This is not only because vessels are integrated to transport chains but also because they interact directly with the different functions of a company using transport services, and because the modal choice decision affects production, financing and marketing strategies. In other words, transport may be a commodity, but all related services may be well differentiated and useful to relate companies in highly integrated and idiosyncratic distribution systems (Sánchez, 2005).

There are many examples of concrete possibilities for effective action in a new stage of national maritime policies, such as security, environmental and natural resource protection rules or antitrust laws and market transparency, to name just a few. To put this into a conceptualized framework, systemic characteristics should now orient national maritime policy design and application criteria, as well as push for their consistency with regional and international policies.

In addition, maritime policies may also include the participation of regional and national economic players in a broad field of action within the maritime business, made up of activities, regions and markets which, though being part of the global maritime business, do not have enough global dimension so as to encourage the involvement of global players, where specialization plays a key role and where all countries and trades, independent of size and economic development, have an important future and an active role to play within the large maritime world.

Notes

1 According to UNCTAD (2016), historically, liner shipping has been governed by different cooperative arrangements. Thus, originally in the form of conferences and later in the form of consortia, vessel sharing agreements, strategic alliances, capacity stabilization agreements and discussion agreements.
2 Defined as the possibility of a firm to fix prices above marginal costs.
3 Several articles consider that liner shipping industry presents intensity of capital (Chrzanowski, 1975; Graham and Hughes, 1985; Baird, 2000; Brooks, 2000; Harlaftis and Theotokas, 2002; Sánchez, 2005; Notteboom, 2012; Sheng and Yoshida, 2013: 20).
4 Generally, in order to analyze this concept, it is used two paradigms: First, the Structure Conduct Performance paradigm in which observable structural characteristics of a

market determine the behaviour of firms within that market (Martin, 2002). Second, the New Empirical Industrial Organization paradigm in which analysis of the "unobservable" price, marginal cost margin, from accounting data and focuses on the information of these margins.

5 For a further analysis of the evolution of alliances, mergers and acquisitions in the liner shipping industry over the last 25 years, see Mouftier and Sánchez (2017).
6 See Stopford (2009) for the shipping cycle evolution 1973–2007.
7 For more information, see UN-ECLAC *Maritime Bulletin 51*, 2012.
8 Amount profits close to fair rate of return on assets adjusted to industry risk.
9 The author finds several examples on cartel overcharge rates on shipping industry. For further detail see Connor (2006).

References

Baird, A. (2000). Port privatisation: Objectives, extent, process, and the UK experience. *International Journal of Maritime Economics.* 2 (3): 177–194.

Bogo, J. (2000). La privatización de un campeón nacional: El caso de YPF en Argentina. *Boletín Latinoamericano de Competencia.* 10 (1): 34.

Brooks, M. R. (2000). *Sea Change in Liner Shipping: Regulation and Managerial Decision-Making in a Global Industry.* Oxford: Pergamon Press. (now Emerald Books).

Cable, J. (1972). Market Structure, Advertising Policy and Interindustry Differences in Advertising Intensity. In: Keith Cowling (ed.), *Market Structure and Corporate Behavior: Theory and Empirical Analysis of the Firm.* London: Grey-Mills. pp. 105–124.

Cabral, L.M.B. (2000). *Introduction to Industrial Organization.* Cambridge, MA: MIT Press.

Carlton, D. W., Perloff, J. M. (2005). *Modern Industrial Organization.* 4th ed. Boston: Pearson/Addison Wesley.

Chrzanowski, I. (1975). *Concentration and Centralisation of Capital in Shipping.* Lexington, MA: Lexington Books.

Clyde, P. S., Reitzes, J. D. (1995). The Effectiveness of Collusion under Antitrust Immunity: The Case of Liner Shipping Conferences, Bureau of Economics Staff Report, Washington, DC: Federal Trade Commission. pp. 1–56.

Connor, J. M. (2006). *Global Price Fixing.* 2nd ed. New York: Springer.

Cullinane, K., Khanna, M. (1998). Economies of scale in large container ships. *Journal of Transport Economics and Policy.* 33 (2): 185–208.

Davies, J. E. (1986). Competition, contestability and the liner shipping industry. *Journal of Transport Economics and Policy.* 20: 299–312.

Drewry (2016). Diminishing returns? Are we entering a new period where the money to be made from ports and terminals is markedly less than it was? Spotlight Briefing, February 2016. Available at: www.drewry.co.uk/AcuCustom/Sitename/DAM/004/Diminishing_Returns_Spotlight_Briefing_Feb2016.pdf Accessed 25 July 2017.

The Economist (2013). The humble hero. 18 May 2013. Available at: www.economist.com/news/finance-and-economics/21578041-containers-have-been-more-important-globalisation-freer-trade-humble Accessed 28 July 2017.

Fink, C., Mattoo, A., Neagu, C. (2000). *Trade in International Shaping Future Rules for Trade in Services 75 Maritime Services: How Much does Policy Matter?* Washington, DC: World Bank. Mimeograph.

Gonzalez-Aregall, M., Spengler, T., Wilmsmeier, G. (2017). The liner shipping industry: Looking beyond firms – markets structure, competition and concentration. Paper presented at the annual conference of the International Association of Maritime Economists (IAME), Kyoto, July 2017.

González Laxe, F., Sánchez, R. J. (2007). *Lecciones de Economia Maritima.* La Coruña, Spain: NetBiblo S.L.

Graham, M. G., Hughes, D. O. (1985). *Containerisation in the Eighties.* London: Lloyd's of London Press Ltd.

Harlaftis, G., Theotokas, J. (2002). Maritime Business during the 20th Century: Continuity and Change. In: C. Grammenos (ed.), *The Handbook of Maritime Economics and Business.* London: Lloyd's of London Press Ltd. pp. 9–34.

Hirata, E. (2017). Contestability of container liner shipping market in alliance era. *The Asian Journal of Shipping and Logistics.* 33 (1): 27–32.

Martin, S. (2000). The theory of contestable markets. Department of Economics: Purdue University. Available at: www.krannert.purdue.edu/faculty/smartin/aie2/contestbk.pdf Accessed 9 October 2017.

Martin, S. (2002). *Advanced Industrial Economics.* 2nd ed. Oxford: Blackwell.

Martin, S. (2010). *Industrial Organization in Context.* Oxford: Oxford University Press.

Marx, D. (1953). *International Shipping Cartels.* Princeton, NJ: Princeton University Press.

Mouftier, L., Sánchez, R. (2017). The puzzle of shipping alliances in April 2017. Port Economics, 2017. Available at: www.porteconomics.eu/2017/04/20/the-puzzle-of-shipping-alliances-in-july-2016/

Notteboom, T. (2012). Container Shipping. In: W. K. Talley (ed.), *The Blackwell Companion to Maritime Economics.* Oxford: Blackwell Publishing Ltd. pp. 230–262.

OECD (2015). *The Impact of Megaships.* Paris: OECD/ITF.

Packer, G. (2016). Hillary Clinton and the populist revolt – the democrats lost the white working class: The republicans exploited it: Can Clinton win it back? *The New Yorker,* 31 October 2016. Available at: www.newyorker.com/magazine/2016/10/31/hillary-clinton-and-the-populist-revolt Accessed 28 July 2017.

Sánchez, R. J. (2005). *The Shipping Cycle as Determinant of the National Marine Policies.* Paris: Publishing Université de Paris X Nanterre – Universidad Carlos III de Madrid.

Sánchez, R. J. (2011). *Short-Term Fluctuations in Maritime Transport: FAL Bulletin (296).* Santiago, Chile: UN-ECLAC.

Sánchez, R. J. (2017). The shipping cycle in the international container market: Which will be the actual shipping cycle in the future of shipping, the traditional or a new one? CEPAL Working Paper. Available at: www.cepal.org/es/node/41866 Accessed 25 July 2017.

Sánchez, R. J., Duesi, E. (2002). The limits of port devolution. Paper presented at the annual conference of the International Association of Maritime Economists (IAME), Panama, October 2002.

Sánchez, R. J., Hoffmann, J., Micco, A., Pizzolitto, G. V., Sgut, M., Wilmsmeier, G. (2003). Port efficiency and international trade: Port efficiency as a determinant of maritime transport costs. *Maritime Economics and Logistics.* 5 (2): 199–218.

Sánchez, R. J., Wilmsmeier, G. (2010). Liner Shipping Networks and Market Concentration. In: K. Cullinane (ed.), *International Handbook of Maritime Economics.* Cheltenham, UK: Edward Elgar Publishing Ltd. pp. 162–206.

Sánchez, R. J., Wilmsmeier, G. (2011). Liner Shipping Networks and Market Concentration. In: K.P.B. Cullinane (ed.), *International Handbook of Maritime Economics.* Cheltenham, UK: Edward Elgar. pp. 162–206.

Sánchez, R. J., Wilmsmeier, G. (2017). *Economies of Scale in the Liner Container Shipping Industry: Challenging the Beliefs.* London: Kogan. (forthcoming).

Schmalensee, R. (1981). Economies of scale and barriers to entry. *Journal of Political Economy*. 89 (6): 1228–1238.

Shashikumar, N. (1995). Competition and models of market structure in liner shipping. *Transport Reviews*. 15 (1): 3–26.

Sheng, T. H., Yoshida, S. (2013). Analysis of key factors for formation of strategic alliances in liner shipping company: Service quality perspective on Asia/Europe route after global economic crisis. *International Journal of Social, Behavioural, Educational, Economic, Business and Industrial Engineering*. 7: 6.

Sjostrom, W. (2002). Modelling Competition and Collusion. In: Costa Th. Grammenos (ed.), *The Handbook of Maritime Economics and Business*. London: Lloyds of London Press. pp. 307–326.

Stopford, M. (2009). *Maritime Economics*. 3rd ed. London: Routledge.

Sys, C. (2009). Is the container liner shipping industry an oligopoly? *Transport Policy*. 16 (5): 259–270.

UNCTAD (2016). Liner Shipping: Is there a way for more competition? Discussion Paper, 224; United Nations Conference on Trade and Development Publications, Geneva.

Wilmsmeier, G. (2014). *International Maritime Transport Costs – Market Structures and Network Configurations*. Farnham: Ashgate.

Wilmsmeier, G., Hoffman, J. (2008). Liner Shipping Connectivity and Port Infrastructure as Determinants of Freight Rates in the Caribbean. *Maritime Economics and Logistics*. 10 (1–2): 130–151.

Wilmsmeier, G., Notteboom, T. (2011). Determinants of liner shipping network configuration: a two-region comparison. *GeoJournal*. 76 (3): 213–228.

12 The economic development effect of a transhipment port

The case of Gioia Tauro

*Mario Genco, Emanuela Sirtori
and Silvia Vignetti*

Introduction

In the past two decades, a large share of public investment in the EU Member States has been for infrastructures, a large proportion being in the lagging behind countries and Central and Eastern European countries and in the transport sector. Investments in the transport sector have been at the core of regional development policies aimed at reducing regional disparities all over the EU (Button, 1998; Cappelen et al., 2003; Spiekermann and Wegener, 2006; Sirtori and Vignetti, 2011). The rationale underpinning EU policies in the transport sector points to a number of considerations related to the increase in productivity and competition, accessibility to a broader range of goods and services, the reduction of the distance (across Western Europe and South-Eastern Member States and, within an individual country, between its main cities and peripheral areas) and, ultimately, contributing to the promotion of economic, social and territorial cohesion in Europe. More than other transport modes, maritime transport is prone to fluctuations of global economic trends and international trade. Containerisation and intermodal transport were determinant of port changes in the latter years. Container terminals have been growing at a fast pace together with the global fragmentation of production and thanks to major public investments. The global financial crisis not only had a negative effect on global freight transport demand but also called for a reconsideration of long-term sustainability of development strategies related to maritime freight transport infrastructures.

This chapter investigates the conditions under which benefits of transhipment ports may flow to the region or country hosting them. It does so by analysing the story of the port of Gioia Tauro.[1] Since its origin, the port of Gioia Tauro has been conceived as a project with significant potential to trigger economic development in the province and the whole region of Calabria, in the south of Italy. The geographical position, as well as the expanding transhipment market, turned the venture into an immediate success. In 2007, before the global crisis, Gioia Tauro was the premier transhipment hub in the Mediterranean. However, economic effect on the local economy did not materialise as expected. In addition, following the global crisis, the shipping market private investments were diverted to other destinations.

The anecdotal story of the Gioia Tauro port is assessed against a more comprehensive literature regarding the conditions for ports competitiveness and their impact on local development. The chapter illustrates the start-up, consolidation and performance of the port, and discusses the reasons explaining such performance. By relying on a wide number of direct interviews and the results of an ex-post, cost-benefit analysis, the authors assess the private as well as the social benefits achieved and ascribable to the port's construction. The analysis shows an emblematic story of great business success and unexploited potential for local development. The overall assessment of the economic impact of the project is mixed and illustrates that transhipment can create local development through the generation of indirect, spillover, effects, only if it is integrated into the national and international logistical system. Lessons learned point out the importance of factors such as political will, good governance and strong managerial response as key determinants of the long-term effects. These lessons, although drawn from an individual story, can be considered valid also in other contexts.

Ports as drivers of territorial development

Port infrastructure investments are associated with a number of possible direct, indirect and induced effects. Goss (1990) stressed how ports drive the economic development as they increase competition through enlargement of the market areas of firms, thereby reducing prices for consumers. Rodrigue (2017) highlights among expected benefits direct jobs creation, expansion of market opportunities of firms, establishment of new firms, taxes and custom duties partly earned by the port region, income to industries supplying the port with goods and services and which creates indirect employment. According to Abbes (2007), the EU ports are becoming no different from any other multi-product industry offering a range of services and Europe's competitiveness in the global economy depends increasingly on an efficient and cost effective transport and port system.

A special form of port activity is transhipment, a scheme of transport consisting of disembarking cargo from a large ship (or mother vessel) in an intermediate destination port and then embarking it onto smaller ships (feeder vessels) for onward transport to its final destination. Transhipment boomed during the 1990s as a result of the increase in international trade and more complex maritime networks, following globalisation dynamics, freight containerisation and the need to cut global freight transport costs. Major transhipment hubs are usually located along the main shipping routes that go through Panama, the Strait of Malacca, Suez and Gibraltar.

In recent years, significant public investments have been addressed to Mediterranean ports to build transhipment hubs or to enlarge previously existing ports for transhipment use. One of the first examples of transhipment hubs built in the Mediterranean Sea is the port of Gioia Tauro, opened in 1995 in the south of Italy. Other more recent examples are Algeciras in Spain, Tangier in Morocco and Port Said in Egypt. Ports require substantial capital investments which are generally secured, to a large extent, by the public sector (through the port authority or general funds) willing to attract private operators and investors and to trigger economic activities benefitting regional and national population. Besides geographical considerations related to the location of maritime mobility corridors, the decision to build a transhipment hub in a less developed area may respond to a twofold aim: take advantage from lower local labour costs so as to increase competitiveness and create opportunities for new businesses in order to support regional economic development.

The existing literature about the impacts of port on regional development is relatively scarce and usually focused on employment creation. Rodrigue (2017) stresses that empirical evidence about job multiplier figures is limited and that growth in traffic volumes is not associated with significant direct gains in employment.

A number of factors may affect the port's potential to stimulate economic activity nearby the port and along the transport corridors, but the way these benefits occur is not straightforward. This is even less so for transhipment ports. In fact, while the total transhipment activity in a market region is overall stable over time, individual transhipment hubs could experience significant fluctuation in their market share as a consequence of commercial strategies of private operators.[2]

As a reflection of the increasing international fragmentation of global supply chains and the resulting trade movements, international container shipping has been one of the most dynamic economic sectors (although severely hit during the global economic recession years), but is also characterised by fierce competition and highly risky investment strategies. A few major companies called to cope with an extremely volatile transhipment demand dominate the shipping market, although it is fragmented. To what extent the benefit for private shipping companies can also be enjoyed by local economy at large remains an open question.

Competitiveness and long-term sustainability of container terminals

Container terminals are crucial elements for the competitiveness of the fast changing global logistic networks. The transhipment market is dominated by a few major companies[3] who change their strategies quite quickly to react to context and market developments.[4] Quickly adapting to the increasing need of cutting costs and improving the quality and quantity of services offered is the only possible success strategy.

A number of factors determine the competitiveness of a container terminal (Caldeirinha et al., 2015; Notteboom and Rodrigue, 2011; Estache et al., 2005). Some of them are related to the infrastructure and terminal physical and structural characteristics and can be referred to as 'hard' factors. Among them, the geographical location is a first important element. Organisational capacity and the quality of handling equipment both at the quay and parking areas are other key aspects.

Other relevant competitiveness factors are more 'soft' elements and are related to the capacity to design and manage high-quality and integrated services. In a very competitive context, more than the geophysical characteristics of the infrastructure, the quality and reliability of the service provided, not only by the private operators but also by all the actors providing ancillary services, are particularly important. A vital success factor is the capacity to maintain high productivity levels in order to cope with competition from other emerging ports and develop proactive commercial strategies aimed at medium to long-term agreements with shipping companies, in order to stabilise traffic flows in the medium run. As stressed by Dyck and Ismael (2015), some of those features may be policy related and have to do with governance systems and regulatory frameworks.

The globalisation of maritime traffic and the recent process of decentralisation of port functions and management have resulted in a complex system of the European port governance structures, presenting a multiplicity of models depending on the level of decentralisation, the role of private operators and the responsibility of management and administrative functions. The nature of the global logistic chain and the way the decision making works is such that there is the need for highly technical capacity and expertise to act with large global players and financial institutions.

As stressed by many scholars (see among others Juang and Roe, 2010; Notteboom and Winkelmans, 2004) the ability to combine handling with logistic services has become an important issue for the port survival and has transformed many shipping companies into logistics management organisations. Thus the capacity to provide a full-fledged menu of services along the entire logistic chains (including inland transport, storage and distribution) is a crucial element to guarantee long-term sustainability of a container terminal.

The capacity to integrate maritime transport services with ancillary services downstream the logistic chain not only helps in meeting the customer needs but also helps in creating value-added services on the territory, enabling spill over effects on local economy. Some logistic functions, such as pre-assemblies, preparation and customisation, labelling, packaging and distribution, if performed at terminals, can boost economic development in the region.

At the same time, industrial and logistical development requires quite a long timeline to plan, implement and operationalise the related infrastructures and services, since they involve railway connections, firm localisations, territorial marketing and transfer of know-how and technical skills. They require coordination between different service providers and transport operators, both maritime and inland. The nature of these initiatives is such that in order to generate some tangible results, a medium to long-term perspective is needed together with excellent strategic capacity and solid governance structures.

This is even more necessary for transhipment ports in a development perspective since per se they are not particularly appropriate for triggering larger development effects. Because of its specific characteristics (Figure 12.1), pure transhipment tends to generate very little or no value added and development in the area where the port is located, since income is generated only where containers arrive at their final destination, where they are cleared (customs duties and value-added tax), opened and processed. A study estimated that when the goods are cleared through customs, stocked, handled and distributed through adequate and efficient transport infrastructures, employment, turnover, profits and State revenues significantly

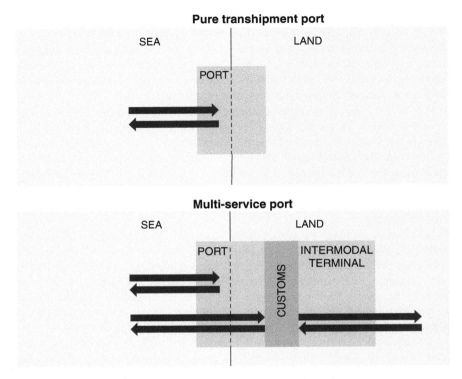

Figure 12.1 Container flows in pure transhipment and multi-service ports
Source: Authors

increase.[5] In other words, transhipment can create local development only if it is integrated into the national and international logistical system.

The port of Gioia Tauro: context and origin

The story of the port of Gioia Tauro takes place in the least developed region of Italy. Gioia Tauro is a municipality in the region of Calabria, on the Tyrrhenian coast. During the 1990s, at the time when the port was build, regional per capita GDP was more than 40 percent lower than the Italian and European average. Unemployment rate was among the highest of the EU.[6] A limited industrial activity and a wide and long-standing gap between Calabria and the national average in the level and quality of infrastructure endowment contributed at constraining the development prospects of the region. The ancient and deep-rooted presence of organised crime, which has always tried to profit from business activities in the area, especially those related to the use of public funds, represented an additional determinant of a poorly enabling context.

The story of the port dates back to the beginning of the 1970s. The port was built in a rural area where the Government committed to build a large steel plant, which was expected to generate about 7,500 jobs. Huge public investments (about 400 million Euro up to 1992) were undertaken to dig the seabed and build the artificial channel. However, due to the crisis of the steel industry, the project was eventually abandoned, and the port, for the most part already constructed, remained unused. For many years after its construction, many plans for possible alternative uses of the port were designed and later abandoned, with increasing frustration of the local population. In 1993, Angelo Ravano, founder of Contship Italia S.p.a., a global container carrier, asked the Italian Government for the use concession of the area, with the idea to convert the unused dock basin into a container terminal for transhipment traffic. The company obtained the concession of 2,450 metres of quay for transhipment purposes for a 50-year period. In a Programme Agreement signed by the Ministry for the Budget and Economic Planning, the Ministry of Transport, the Calabria Region and Contship Italia, the latter[7] committed itself to invest almost 150 million Euro by 2001 on civil works and equipment, and to provide one million TEU (20-foot equivalent units) of container traffic and 450 new jobs by 2001. The national and regional authorities invested 43 million Euro for civil works to adapt the existing infrastructure to the needs of the transhipment activity. Furthermore, an application for funding was submitted to the European Commission and a grant amounting to 40 million Euro[8] was approved for the project addressed, among others, to provide training activities for the labour force.

Strong arguments supporting the port project were related to the promise of development for the Calabria region and the reliability and good reputation of the private investor. According to Contship Italia Group (1994), the expected financial return for the private investor from the project was estimated to be equal to 19.60 percent. On the public side, specific objectives were not only to implement the transhipment terminal but also a power plant and additional port-related activities to be localised in the industrial zone overlooking the port area. In order to manage the port services it was planned to set up a consortium of private and public actors with a promotional mandate. The result of a socio-economic cost-benefit analysis indicated an expected socio-economic return on investment of almost 12 percent from these actions.

In September 1995, the first ship entered the port, three years before the completion of the construction works in the port area. The main infrastructure consists of an artificial channel running parallel to the coastline, with an entrance and an evolution basin, two long quays and a large land area behind the channel, designated for industrial usage. The total port area corresponds to about 3.5 million square metres, with a channel 220 metre wide and 3 km long.

The transhipment activity is carried out on an area of 1.5 million square metres (Figure 12.2), on the main quay by Medcenter Container Terminal (MCT), the operator belonging to the Contship Group. There is also a car carrier terminal, BLG Logistics,[9] which in 2007, before the economic crisis, handled 75,000 cars. Some maritime companies are working as suppliers for the terminal operator, providing additional maritime services such as custom operations, assistance for the loading and discharging of cargoes, warehousing and distribution.

Figure 12.2 Satellite image of the port of Gioia Tauro
Source: Google Earth

Hard factors at the basis of the success

Soon after the start of port operations, Contship plans proved to be realistic and underpinned by a thorough understanding of the shipping market context and development scenarios. In the 1990s, maritime freight traffic was undergoing a structural change at the international level brought about by freight containerisation. At the same time globalisation dynamics emphasised the importance of maritime traffic in the Mediterranean Sea for manufactured goods coming from the Far East to European markets: Since 1988, the Mediterranean container market has had an average annual growth rate of 10.5 percent[10] and Mediterranean traffic share of total European traffic rose from 25.8 percent in 1993 to 31.4 percent in 1995.[11]

Gioia Tauro soon became the premier commercial and industrial transhipment hub in the Mediterranean Sea. In Italy, container traffic increased from 2.31 million containers in 1993 to 4.82 million containers in 1997 (+108 percent) and Gioia Tauro reached a market share of 29 percent, quickly overtaking the port of Genoa, which remained at 24 percent during the 1993–1997 period.[12]

Newspapers began to spread this positive news story and economic development expectations of the regional population were high. Only ten months after opening, the level of traffic at Gioia Tauro rose above the ex-ante forecasts; traffic and employment targets were achieved earlier than foreseen (1997 rather than

2001). The transhipment and related activities created additional direct and indirect employment for MCT (reaching 1,200 people in 2007, the point of maximum expansion) and the shipping companies providing direct services to MCT. The list of all companies which were operational in the Gioia Tauro area counted about 2,200 employees in 2009.[13] Some new transport and logistics companies have been established thanks to the port activities, in addition to one manufacturing company which processes products (coffee) imported via Gioia Tauro.[14]

The great interest shown by the main shipping companies for the port of Gioia Tauro and the success experienced in the early stages by the terminal operations can be explained by four factors. First, its central position in the Mediterranean Sea and proximity to the Suez-Gibraltar sea-route made it an ideal transhipment location for companies wishing to make only one call in the Mediterranean. Secondly, thanks to the depth of the seabed (12.5–15.0 m), landside infrastructure and mechanical equipment, the port could accommodate the biggest container ships and support large-scale transhipment operations. Thirdly, the port was able to offer competitive prices because it took advantage of the previously built facility whose costs had already been written off. Fourthly, an experienced and highly skilled management team committed to providing a quality service was operating it. The strong commitment of Contship Italia was clear when the company decided to implement on its own (including investing extra money up-front in anticipation of funding) some of the investments expected to be carried out by the public sector[15] in order to avoid delays in the start-up of the project activities.

Soft factors as missed opportunities

The port operators and public authorities relied too much on the port's outstanding geophysical characteristics (depth of the seabed, length of the quay, strategic central position), disregarding other strategic aspects such as the competitiveness drivers of the global shipping market. The reduced working hour of some port service (for example related to the custom check), along with higher average hourly labour cost,[16] lower productivity[17] and higher taxes[18] compared to other competing ports, especially in North Africa, were and still represent the main competitiveness problems of Gioia Tauro.

Despite the promising start, Gioia Tauro failed to maintain and reinforce its leading position over the years. As early as 2004, it was already growing at a slower pace than its competitors in the Mediterranean Sea (Figure 12.3). The financial and economic crisis lead to a dramatic contraction in global traffic flows.[19] This exacerbated port competition and raised the need for high productivity levels in the Mediterranean ports, which translated into cost savings for shipping companies. Other ports (especially Algeciras in Spain, Tangier in Morocco and Port Said in Egypt) undertook important investments to build or strengthen their transhipment hubs, with the help of significant public investments.[20] On foot of this competition and the shrink of global maritime trade in the aftermath of the world economic crisis, Gioia Tauro lost market share and its leading position in Mediterranean transhipment. In 2010, Port Said and Algeciras ranked first and second as Mediterranean transhipment hubs.

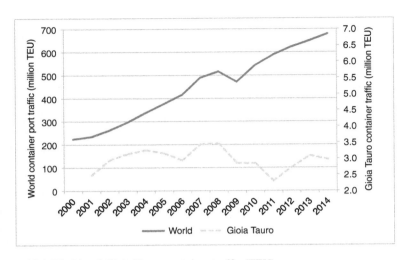

Figure 12.3 World and Gioia Tauro container traffic (TEU)

Source: Containerisation International, Containerisation International Yearbook; Gioia Tauro Port Authority

The loss of port competitiveness went hand by hand with the disappointing effects on local development. Since the 1990s, a number of other publicly funded interventions were put in place with the goal of creating the conditions for the development of 'the broad area of Gioia Tauro'. Interventions were aimed at diversifying business activities in the port of Gioia Tauro and, especially, developing the industrial zone behind it. Such an area, covering 3.6 million square meters, was supposed to be a driving force for local development. In 1997, a Master Plan was prepared, envisaging a railway link between the port and the Rosarno rail station; the improvement and upgrading of the road network; the creation of an intermodal transport system; a maritime link between Gioia Tauro and Milazzo in Sicily (Ro-Ro traffic); the implementation of a plan for industrial development; and additional infrastructure investments and the establishment of a free trade zone. In addition, in 1998 an application for a Global Grant was submitted by the local authorities to the European Commission, aimed at supporting the creation and development of small and medium enterprises (SMEs) in the area around Gioia Tauro mainly through a system of financial aids accompanied by guidance measures. The anticipated impact on employment was the creation or safeguarding of at least 450 permanent jobs through the launching of 35 new initiatives and the equipping of some 25 hectares with facilities for SMEs. National policy instruments for industrial promotion (in particular Law 488/92) were also used to facilitate the location of new enterprises linked to the port activity.

All the attempts aimed to the development of the broader area of Gioia Tauro and consolidation of port activities failed. The Master Plan was not implemented mainly due to lack of involvement of the provincial authorities and local munici-palities in its preparation, as well as conflicting interests on the actions to under-take. As to the Global Grant, strong initial enthusiasm and financial incentives encouraged entrepreneurial activity, however often lacking a precise strategy and expertise. Unlike other Italian historical ports, the Calabria entrepreneurial class generally lacked the necessary know-how for maritime-related activities. As a consequence, only few businesses survived.

Intermodal transport did not take off either. In the original plans, it was rec-ognised that Gioia Tauro had the opportunity to become an intermodal centre where containers could have been loaded and unloaded not only on ships but also on trains and trucks, to reach their destination markets in Italy and Europe. This opportunity, which other transhipment ports (such as Malta) do not have, was clear in the mind of Contship and Italian authorities when the project was approved in 1994, and contributed to raising expectations for the port. While road transport is the most affordable way to connect Gioia Tauro to the neigh-bouring Southern regions, railways is more convenient for longer distance.[21] In the early years of port activity, the volume of containers handled by land grew from 4 percent in 2003 to 5.5 percent in 2006.[22] Currently, it remains at 4 percent.

Technical studies[23] highlight that the main factor which prevented intermodal transport from growing is related to infrastructural limits in the Italian (especially Southern) railway system,[24] which are still unresolved. Besides infrastructural con-straints, the reduction in port business over the latest years contributed to decreas-ing the demand for intermodal transport.[25]

In 2010, the national government, regional and local authorities and the Euro-pean Commission signed a Framework Programme Agreement. The programme, which foresees almost 600 million Euro of public investments, is another attempt to trigger the development of the logistics district and the intermodal platform nearby the port. The overall goal is to transform the port from a pure transhipment hub into a multi-purpose port, more suitable to generate positive spillover effects on the local economy.

To date the implementation of the interventions finalised at improving the port's intermodality and bringing new economic activities in the port area has been severely delayed. According to the latest information available,[26] while the infrastructural works to connect the port to the railway network have been final-ised, the works to realise the new railway terminal are still ongoing. The full development of the intermodal transport is, however, subject to the completion of other investments to connect Gioia Tauro with the railway corridors towards North of Italy (Gioia Tauro – Salerno) and Apulia (Gioia Tauro – Taranto – Bari). As to initiatives to promote business creation, no major achievements have been recorded. The Region Calabria has submitted to the Parliament a proposal to establish a Special Economic Zone in Gioia Tauro, offering fiscal incentives for the implementation of new investments and for the operation of SMEs which decide to localise in Gioia Tauro, but the proposal is still pending approval.

Long-term performance

Despite the initial positive expectations and enthusiasm at local, regional and national level, today, a sense of frustration prevails among local people. While this partly reflects the unrealistic level of expectations raised during the initial phase of the port development it is undeniable that there is a significant unexploited potential related to the port despite many years (and much public resources) spent trying to trigger broader effects.

The results of the ex-post cost-benefit analysis support these findings. The long-term economic rate of return on the project over a 30-year time horizon (1994–2024) is positive (10.44 percent). The main economic benefit produced is via the employment created. However, economic benefits are not as significant as expected ex-ante because of the limited effects generated by the port on local development. The project's economic viability heavily relies on the pre-existence of the unused port infrastructure, originally built to serve the steelwork plant. If the port had had to be built specifically for the Contship operation, it would not have been worth doing at all. Therefore, the socio-economic benefits produced so far stem from the consideration that a past, expensive and unsuccessful public investment was turned at least to a fruitful business operation providing some employment effects.

The failure to realise a logistic pole and an industrial zone linked to the tranship-ment activity limited the port's capacity to trigger economic development in the Gioia Tauro area, as previously mentioned. Since the context was not suitable for such a development operation to spontaneously generate positive development effects through a bottom-up process, the role of public institutions and the gover-nance structure underpinning their actions were a key ingredient determining the observed performance. Broader development effects could be achieved only by an integrated and coordinated plan fostering business creation, transport connections and high-level services for port-related activities, combined with the long-term commitment of highly experienced and dedicated professional resources.

Surprisingly, the key constraints to economic development of the port were recognised from the beginning and the necessary actions were actually identified. However, a lack of coordinated, strategically oriented and focused implementation efforts determined the failure of all attempts made. This resulted from the existence of a large number of institutions and stakeholders involved in the decision-making process, with unclear and/or overlapping responsibilities,[27] and a general lack of motivation and coordination at different levels, which provides incentives for short-termism and opportunistic behaviour in the managing structures of key institutions.

Port governance is an issue not only in Gioia Tauro but also in the entire Italian context. As pointed by the ESPO (2010) survey on European Port Authorities, the Italian Port system is suffering from a delay in the reform process[28] aimed at addressing the current lack of integrated planning and management of the entire logistic supply chain at the national level. Differently from other EU countries (for example, Spain), Port Authorities in Italy have limited autonomy, especially at the financial level (for example, they cannot autonomously decide to decrease or can-cel the anchorage tax[29]), and this hampers their capacity to manage the conflicting interests of port operators, claiming for a tax reduction in order to increase competitiveness, and other stakeholders.

A fragmented sharing of responsibilities did not help with the attraction of new firms to the port. Judiciary evidence and press articles pointed to some complaints from local entrepreneurs of poor transparency and excessive bureaucracy in the allocation of locations in the industrial area. Organised crime also played a role. It has a strong interest in and influence on the port and port-related activities, and its pressure hampered the implementation of the business initiatives.[30]

In this fragmented national scenario, political support for the port system was more responsive to the pressures of local lobbies than to a transparent and consistent strategic vision. Although the high visibility of the project and the attention of public opinion would have been expected to play a positive role in enhancing political commitment to results-oriented behaviours, there are shared opinions that the political turnover at national and regional levels led to discontinuity of strategic direction,[31] slowing down the process and creating institutional impasse.

Conclusions and lessons learned

Defined as 'the metaphor of a modernisation process without development' or the 'largest industrial development project ever promoted in the Mezzogiorno', the port of Gioia Tauro is an emblematic story of great business success and unexploited potential for local development.

The Gioia Tauro project was initiated in an entrepreneurial spirit. The project design and its implementation involved a new business activity in the changing global market for maritime services. The underpinning rationale for public funding was related to the ambition to trigger growth at the regional level. The challenge from this perspective was how to take advantage of a smart but self-contained business operation, betting on the generation of positive side effects. In the end, however, the project was unable to reconcile the tensions between the ambitions of both the private business and the policymakers, and the difficult local context.

Since the beginning of the project it was clear to national and EU public decision makers that the transhipment terminal would not generate, per se, a significant impact on the area in terms of economic development, unless a number of institutional, socio-economic and political context specific conditions were in place. These conditions were related in particular to the strengthening of infrastructures and other softer interventions in order to capture a larger share of goods going through the port, by offering other services or attaching segments of the supply chain, which could generate value added within the territory.

However, developing a logistic pole and an industrial zone related to a transhipment activity of international significance, in the difficult context of Gioia Tauro, proved to be a too ambitious plan for the weak governance of the port system. Limited coordination of stakeholders with different responsibilities and interests, and the lack of a strong and long-term political support prevented from taking full advantage of the socio-economic opportunities that a promising business idea was expected to produce.

This interesting case history highlights two main lessons. The first one is that insufficient mobility of goods by land can significantly hamper the development potential of transhipment ports: transhipment hubs can have spillover effects on the territory only if accompanied by services that add value to the cargo instead of simply moving containers between vessels. Similarly to Gioia Tauro, the port of Valencia is facing the need to increase rail and port connectivity to the hinterlands, in addition to improve the port infrastructure endowment, so as to retain competitiveness (Sànchez Brox, 2014). The port authority has already announced an investment plan for remodelling road and rail connections.[32] On the other hand, the port of Tangier in Morocco and, outside the Mediterranean Sea, the Dubai hub port, show how the ports' integration with internal communication networks and ancillary infrastructures (such as free trade zones) can be instrumental to boost growth in traffic and economic activity around the ports (Ducruet et al., 2011; Akhavan, 2017).

The second lesson is how important is to have strong institutional capacity and governance structure for the success of a large port infrastructure. The integration of the Port of Tangier into a long-term public investment plan was key not only to make the Tangier Med port one of the most competitive transhipment hub in the Mediterranean Sea but also to spur local dynamics of economic growth and employment creation, which are expected to pave the way towards a better regional balance within the country as a whole. In addition to investments in the port complex, the Government has made concerted effort to open up business possibilities in a number of sectors, by improving inland transport infrastructure, creating industrial zones and attracting enterprises with a range of fiscal incentives (Oxford Business Group, 2014). The strategy also comprises the reconversion of the old port of Tangier into a marina with a view of favouring cruise tourism (Ducruet et al., 2011). The strategic combination of the interests and expectations of local public authorities, global private players, other national private and public operators and, ultimately, local population is a fundamental condition for positive regional development effects to be triggered by transhipment ports. Indeed, while technical expertise and private entrepreneurship are relatively easily available on the market, political commitment, entrepreneurial capacity in the public sector and coordination mechanisms are much rarer conditions.

Notes

1 This chapter draws from a study carried out by the authors on behalf of the European Commission, DG Regional and Urban Policies, on a sample of ten major infrastructure projects in the transport and environmental sector co-financed in the period 1993–1999 by the Structural and Cohesion Fund. The full reports of that study are available at the following link: http://ec.europa.eu/regional_policy/en/policy/evaluations/ec/1989-1999/#1 (visited on the 1 January 2017).

2 As stated by Rodrigue (2015), "The usage of transshipment hubs remains a decision made by maritime shipping companies that do so to organize their shipping networks. Such decisions can change if a company revises the allocation of its assets and its commercial strategy."

3 The continuous need for high and risky investments (for example, for the purchase of ever-larger ships) facilitates market concentration dynamics.

4 After the financial crisis in 2009, some shipping companies were considering to no longer cross the Mediterranean Sea but to circumnavigate Africa, as in the past, in order to save the cost of navigating the Suez Canal.

5 When moving from pure transhipment ports to multi-purpose ports "turnover goes from 300 to 2.300 euro, profits from 20 to 200 Euro, income for the State from 110 to 1,000 Euro and for every 1,000 handlings 42 jobs can be generated, instead of 5", from Gian Antonio Stella, Corriere della Sera, 5 July 2011, quoting the Ministry of Transport.

6 Eurostat data.

7 More precisely its subsidiary Medcenter Container Terminal, MCT henceforth, created specifically to operate the transhipment port.

8 This and the previous figures are in nominal terms at 1993 prices.

9 BLG Logistics was also owned by the Contship Group. Since 2016, it has been partly taken over by Automar Logistics (Grimaldi group).

10 Source: European Commission (1996).

11 Bruno Dardani (1996). Mediterraneo alla riscossa, in Il Sole-24 Ore, 23 May 1996.

12 Committee for the Coordination and Development of the Gioia Tauro Area (1997, p. 8).

13 Including MCT employees.

14 In 1999, the European Commission acknowledged the positive results achieved by the port, by stating, "The results and the international actors in the sector confirm the positive assessment and the confidence about the terminal, which is more and more considered as a strategic port at the global level. The constant growth of traffic volumes and number of ships requires, almost continuously, the purchase of additional equipment and the recruitment of additional employees. [. . .] The co-financed investment by the European Commission succeeded in promoting the take-off of an auto-propulsive development that produced, as an additional effect, acceleration of the growth rate of the port" (European Commission, 1999).

15 For example, it was MCT who bought fire protection equipment and trained the rescue emergency teams.

16 According to Eurispes (2010), the average hourly cost of a transhipment worker in 2009 is 22.1 Euro in Italy, 3.1 Euro in Morocco and 1.9 Euro in Egypt. Similar differences are experienced in case of white-collars costing 22.9 Euro in Italy, 10.1 Euro in Egypt and 7.9 Euro in Morocco

17 As a matter of example, productivity level of cranes (in terms of crane moves per hour) is 23 in Gioia Tauro as compared to an average of 30 in Mediterranean ports and a range between 27 and 32 in international container ports (Source: C-Log, 2008; UNCTAD, 2010).

18 In Gioia Tauro the total cost of calling on the port (including anchorage tax, piloting, towing and mooring) is 25 percent higher than in Port Said and 500 percent higher than in Malta (Source: Eurispes, 2010).

19 Using UNCTAD (2010) words, "The year 2009 witnessed [. . .] the sharpest decline in the volume of global merchandise trade. In tandem with the collapse in economic growth and trade, international seaborne trade volumes contracted by 4.5% in 2009. While no shipping segment was spared, minor dry bulks and containerized trade suffered the most severe contractions".

20 For example, the Spanish ports, in particular Valencia, Algeciras and Barcelona, grew thanks to their new quays directly linked to the railway system and to the attention paid to the quality of the service supply. On the other hand, the Egyptian Port Said established with success a free trade area that helped it achieve exceptional growth rates (63 percent in 2005–2007 and almost 32 percent in 2007–2009).

21 Transporting one container to Milan costs approximately 680 Euro by train and 1,250 Euro by truck. By contrast, railway transport costs to Naples are slightly higher than for truck, amounting respectively to 530 Euro and 450 Euro (C-Log, 2008).

22 Data provided by Calabria Region.

23 C-Log (2008).
24 Too small tunnels, lack of electrified rails or double tracks, especially in the Southern regions, are not suitable for long freight trains carrying almost 3m-high containers (the modern 'High Cube' containers).
25 It has been pointed out by interviewees that Grand Alliance was the shipping line that mostly used the railway gateway.
26 Press release: Bankitalia: continua la crisi del porto di Gioia Tauro, 16 June 2016, Il Giornale di Calabria. www.giornaledicalabria.it/?p=50240.
27 For example, a long-running dispute exists between ASI-REG and the Port Authority, regarding the ownership of a vast area of the industrial zone and, consequently, the allocation of competencies over the area. There is a shared opinion among the interviewees that this situation paralysed on many occasions the decision-making process, delaying and jeopardising the successful implementation of public actions.
28 The last port reform (Law 84/1994) took place in 1994. It shifted competence from the public to the private operators and introduces a new classification of ports and port labour activities.
29 This requires a decree from the central ministry.
30 Past trials mentioned criminal pressures on some political decision-making processes; for example, an 'influence' was said to be clear in the draft of the port Master Plan advocated during the Prodi government, however no politicians or public managers directly involved in the port activities were ever convicted in this regard.
31 In the period 1993–2010, ten different national governmental coalitions were in power, the longest-lived being the Berlusconi government in the period 11–06–2001/23–4–2005. Over the same period, five different coalitions followed one another at the regional level.
32 Port Strategies press release: www.portstrategy.com/news101/world/europe/valencia-plans-233m-investment. Accessed on 30 March 2017.

References

Abbes, S. (2007). Marginal social cost pricing in European seaports. *European Transport / Trasporti Europei*. 36: 4–26.

Akhavan, M. (2017). Development dynamics of port-cities interface in the Arab Middle Eastern world – the case of Dubai global hub port-city. *Cities*. 60: 343–352.

Button, K. (1998). Infrastructure investment, endogenous growth and economic convergence. *The Annals of the Regional Science*. 32 (1): 145–162.

Caldeirinha, V., Felício, J. A., Dionísio, A. (2015). The effect of port and container terminal characteristics on terminal performance. *Maritime Economics & Logistics*. 17 (4): 493–514.

Cappelen, A., Castellacci, F., Fagerberg, J., Verspagen, B. (2003). The impact of EU regional support on growth and convergence in the European Union. *Journal of Common Market Studies*. 41: 621–644.

C-Log (2008). Analisi delle opportunità logistiche dell'area retroportuale di Gioia Tauro (Analysis of the logistic opportunities of the area of Gioia Tauro). Technical report, Project OSMETE – Centro di Monitoraggio e Osservatorio Tecnologico, 29 January 2008.

Committee for the Coordination and Development of the Gioia Tauro Area (1997). Nota per il Signor Presidente On. Romano Prodi, Dossier Gioia Tauro: Attività in Corso e Primi Risultati; Nuove Iniziative di Sviluppo e Master Plan; 2° Fase della Programmazione Negoziata, Department of Economic Affairs – Council of Ministers, December 1997.

Contship Italia Group (1994). *Medcenter Container Terminal di Gioia Tauro*. Technical Document Attached to the Request of Co-Financing from the European Commission.

Ducruet, C., Mohamed-Chérif, F. Z., Cherfaoui, N. (2011). Maghreb port cities in transition: The case of Tangier. *Portus Plus.* 1 (1). Available at: www.reteonline.org

Dyck, G. K., Ismael, H. M. (2015). Multi-criteria evaluation of port competitiveness in West Africa using Analytic Hierarchy Process (AHP). *American Journal of Industrial and Business Management.* 5: 432–446.

ESPO European Sea Ports Organisation (2010). Fact findings survey 2010. Available at: www.espo.be/index.php?option=com_content&view=article&id=126&Itemid=86 Accessed 25 July 2017.

Estache, A., Perelman, S., Trujillo, L. (2005). Infrastructure performance and reform in developing and transition economies: Evidence from a survey of productivity measures. World Bank Policy Research Working Paper 3514. Available at: https://openknowledge.worldbank.org/handle/10986/8844

Eurispes (2010). Prevenzione e Sicurezza: tra crescita economica e qualità della vita. Available at: www.eurispes.it/index.php?option=com_content&view=article&id=1503:cagliari-gioia-tauro-e-taranto-60-milioni-di-euro-in-5-anni-per-salvare-piu-di-9000-posti-di-lavoro-a-rischio&catid=40:comunicati-stampa&Itemid=135 Accessed 25 July 2017.

European Commission (1996). Expertise sur le Grand Project "Porto di Gioia Tauro, DG XVI – Regional Policy and Cohesion Rome, February 1996.

European Commission (1999). Grande Progetto Gioia Tauro, Rapporto finale di esecuzione (Final Implementation Report), vol. I, 30 July 1999.

Goss, R. (1990). Economic Policies and seaports, part III: Are port authorities necessary? *Maritime Policy and Management.* 17 (4): 235–249.

Juang, Y., Roe, M. (2010). Study on success factors of development strategies for intermodal freight transport systems. *Journal of the Eastern Asia Society for Transportation Studies.* 8: 710–720.

Notteboom, T., Rodrigue, J. P. (2011). Global networks in the container terminal operating industry Part 2: The future direction of terminal networks. *Port Technology International.* PT50–03–2: 1–4. Available at: https://people.hofstra.edu/Jean-paul_Rodrigue/downloads/PT50-03_2.pdf

Notteboom, T., Winkelmans, W. (2004). Factual report – work package 1: Overall market dynamics and their influence on the port sector. ITMMA, Belgium: European Sea Ports Organisation (ESPO).

Oxford Business Group (2014). A rising tide: The northern region is a hub of industrial activity from The Report: Morocco. Available at: www.oxfordbusinessgroup.com/overview/rising-tide-northern-region-hub-industrial-activity Accessed 30 March 2017.

Rodrigue, J. P. (2015). Transhipment hubs: Connecting global and regional maritime shipping networks. Available at: www.porteconomics.eu/2015/09/17/transhipment-hubs-connecting-global-and-regional-maritime-shipping-networks/ Accessed 25 July 2017.

Rodrigue, J.-P. (ed) (2017). *The Geography of Transport Systems.* Fourth Edition, London:Routledge, 440 pages. ISBN 978-1138669574.

Sànchez Brox, M. (2014). Competitive global ports for regional economic development: The port of Valencia. Msc thesis. Radboud Universiteit Nijmegen. Available at: www.planet-europe.eu/fileadmin/files/Masters_theses_cohort_1/Mario_Sanchez_Brox_PE_MAThe_2014.pdf

Sirtori, E., Vignetti, S. (2011). Infrastructure Investment Opportunities in the EU New Member States: The Role of Regional Policies. In: M. Florio (ed.), *Public Investment, Growth and Fiscal Constraints: Challenges for the EU New Member States.* Cheltenham, UK and Northampton, MA: Edward Elgar Publishing Ltd. pp. 265–287.

Spiekermann, K., Wegener, M. (2006). The role of transport infrastructure for regional development in south-east Europe. *Journal for Labour and Social Affairs in Eastern Europe*. 9 (1): 51–61.

UNCTAD (2010). *Review of Maritime Transport*. UNCTAD/RMT/2010. New York and Geneva: United Nations Publication.

13 The unproductive and induced mobility of empty container repositioning in peripheral regions

Jason Monios and Yuhong Wang

Introduction

The movement of goods between locations of production and consumption relies on a complex global logistics system that is underpinned by immobile freight infrastructure and particularly transfer points such as ports, which are nevertheless constituted by an institutional mobility of governance, regulation and investment that has changed a great deal in the last few decades. Therefore, the freight system, when considered from a mobilities perspective, exhibits several of the characteristic features identified in the seminal early papers on the mobilities paradigm. The classic definition of mobilities by Sheller and Urry (2006: 208) as "too little movement or too much, or of the wrong sort or at the wrong time" could certainly apply to the movement of empty containers as discussed in this chapter. Similarly, Hannam et al. (2006: 3) recognise the "necessary spatial, infrastructural and institutional moorings that configure and enable mobilities", which in this case are observed in the decisions regarding container repositioning taken at a global level that have implications for local and regional actors.

The modernisation of port operations has resulted in huge changes to the freight system, notably through the advent of containerisation and the resulting overhaul of ships and ports to accommodate this new technology (see *The Box* [Levinson, 2006] for a historical account of the advent of containerisation). Now approximately 28m containers are in existence and well over 600m TEU of containers are handled at ports worldwide each year. While much research has been undertaken on globalised trade flows and mega ports, less attention has focused on the more human scale, leading to the need in recent years for the application of the mobilities paradigm to the freight sector, although in only limited approaches to specifically maritime issues (see introduction to this volume).

The mobility of freight containers themselves is an interesting topic that has received only scant attention thus far, yet Shaw and Sidaway (2010: 509) noted, "Viewing the rather mundane technology of shipping containers as an agent . . . and a means of production reveals it to be at the heart of momentous shifts." While containers are often viewed primarily in their maritime role, their role on land is increasingly being considered, whether that be their intentional role carrying goods overland or what happens when the system does not function as intended.

Creswell and Martin (2012) explored what happens in the case of accidents when damaged containers disgorge their previously private contents. Cidell (2012) considered the mobility of shipping container from an inland perspective, analysing the negative consequences of containers travelling far inland and pausing there. A certain degree of immobility or pausing is inevitable within a system of mobility, but what happens when that state obtains for longer than deemed acceptable? And who makes such a decision? Cidell's work considers the attempts to eliminate or redirect the immobility of containers when viewed as a negative consequence of their mobility. Inland stakeholders such as local government try to influence a situation on which they traditionally have little control, which is a similar focus to that adopted in this chapter. Whereas in Cidell's work, the focus is on local authorities attempting to remove empty containers, this chapter considers those same stakeholders attempting to attract them for the use of their exporters. Comparing these two approaches underlines the importance of perspective and imbalance in transport that the mobilities paradigm seeks to foreground: one region's surplus containers are another region's desirable resource. As noted by Cresswell (2010: 550), "mobility is a resource to which not everyone has an equal relationship." But how do such regions come to play these roles in the global trade system and what other factors influence their ability to secure an active agency?

Martin (2013: 1021) considered the container, and the wider system of containerisation, as an "attempt to create an integrated and continuous global surface devoid of differences between ocean and land." Standardisation was of course essential to the global adoption of the container and the elimination of difference discussed by Martin (drawing on Steinberg, 2001) sheds light on the core-periphery issue exemplified in the case in this chapter. The globalised containerised logistics surface promotes an assumption that all mobilities are equal and all have equal access to this universal system while in reality there are power differentials represented spatially, between those located at hubs with high degrees of centrality and intermediacy, compared to those located on feeder routes or spokes in the hub-and-spoke system. Martin highlights the huge amount of effort underpinning an apparently frictionless system, one aspect of which is the repositioning of empty containers as discussed in this chapter.

The technology of the container is obviously mobile, and, indeed, it is what facilitates the particular type of mobility obtained by modern freight systems. Of course, freight moved before containers were adopted but containerisation has allowed much more efficient movements and the erosion of local and regional specificity in trade profiles. Now cases exist of containerising previously bulk commodities, such as coffee and grain, sometimes for the efficiency savings and sometimes purely to utilise otherwise surplus containers that would have to be moved empty back to their origins. Yet containers are more mobile than the freight inside them. They begin life empty and are transported to the location of the freight where they are stuffed, then transported to their destination, which may include many periods of stasis, and then after the freight is discharged they are once again empty and must be moved or "repositioned" to another location for reuse. Maritime containers are thus examples of both unproductive and induced mobility as classified by Monios and Wilmsmeier (2015). Unproductive (as they often sit in depots necessitating a certain slack in the system) and induced (their movement, especially the extra movement on top of the freight move itself, is induced as a result of the freight demand, rather than being moved for its own sake).

Moreover, containers are not just repositioned locally between users, but, due to the imbalance of imports and exports in global trade, large numbers of containers must be shipped empty across the world. In some cases, the imbalance in global trade that leads to the repositioning problem has a disproportionate effect on peripheral regions located at a distance from the main trade lanes, producing global inequalities. East-south routes dominate world trade but the north-south axis suffers a relative lack of connectivity, not just at a global level (e.g. South America and Africa vs Asia-the West) but regionally (e.g. Southern Europe vs the Northern Range), which results in imbalances, unproductive mobility and waste of resources. Thus the global system of containerised trade is a form of mobility that facilitates growth for some but not for others. It could even be argued that, pre-containerisation, when ships took much longer to traverse the globe and the transport cost was a much higher proportion of the total cost, a short extra distance to divert from major trade lanes was less of an issue, whereas now with global east-west movements between large hub ports, the extra transhipment to feeder vessels to serve peripheral north-south ports puts them at a greater disadvantage. Thus greater drives towards efficiency in the maritime system deepen the divide between better-connected and less-connected ports and the regions they serve.

This chapter explores the acting capacity of regional stakeholders who seek to improve the situation for their local shippers. The methodology is based on a single in-depth case study of a peripheral exporting region within a country that is an overall net importer. The Scottish case was selected because it is an instructive case where the cost is unavoidable, but the proportion of the empty repositioning cost bundled into the full container movement price paid by shippers has the potential to be addressed through policy or lobbying solutions. As almost the entirety of previous discussions in the literature have been based on cost optimisation, this qualitative approach of exploring how regional stakeholders attempt to influence the situation has the potential to produce findings of relevance to other regions facing the same problem, and to shed light on the different types of mobilities and the power plays constraining them. The case study is used as an illustrative case, based on research conducted in 2012–13; the quantitative data has not been updated for this publication in order to remain accurate at the time the interviews were conducted, but there have been no significant changes since then that would affect the discussion.

Empty container repositioning

Global container movements are increasing in comparison to actual trade, due to increasingly complex liner networks and the need for transhipment. Global container flows are comprised not just of trade between countries but a large proportion of interchange movements as well as the movement or "repositioning" of empty containers, all of which increase both transport and management costs. These structures necessitate the repositioning of empty containers across the globe (e.g. from Western importers back to eastern exporters) as well as within regions or port ranges (e.g. from feeder ports back to hub ports). The number of empty container handlings has risen sharply as has total world container movements, but the percentage of total handlings represented by empty movements has changed little since 2000, reaming steady at around 20 percent.

In an ideal scenario, a loaded container would travel from origin to destination, where it would be stripped and then reloaded for export to a new destination. In practice, there is not always an export load waiting; therefore, once a container has been emptied the empty box will be taken back to the nearest port or nominated depot. It may then wait there for a period of time until a local exporter requires it, or it may be sent back or "repositioned" to the Far East, where there is a guaranteed shipment waiting to fill the container. Western countries generally are net importers, meaning there are not enough export loads to fill all the containers that arrive there with imported goods. Even if an export load is likely to be available, if the container must sit idle for more than one to two weeks then the loss of revenue means that the container owner would rather send the container to a location where a load will be found immediately.

Containers cost money to move, so the more empty or unproductive moves that take place, the higher the cost. The shipping line will therefore build a proportion of this repositioning cost into the total price charged for the full container movement. Exporters in peripheral regions face a disadvantage compared to better-located competitors who do not have to pay this additional cost. The problem is further complicated in the case of a peripheral exporting region within a country that is an overall net importer. Thus exporters in a peripheral country such as Scotland who require the provision of empty boxes have to pay this additional cost, which disadvantages shippers, penalising their trade costs compared to their competitors located near large ports with a greater supply of empty containers without an additional cost.

The majority of papers on this topic use cost optimisation models to find the lowest cost balance of allocation and distribution of containers across a complex system (see Braekers et al., 2011, for a good overview). Modelling approaches can provide support on which cases suit a particular route, which port choice will lower handling costs and which cases suggest repositioning back to the Far East for high demand and higher freight rates versus leaving them in a more distant port to await an export load. This is useful for a complex system with many nodes and links in which a user desires to find the optimum balance of allocation and distribution. However, such models provide less insight into the decision-making process. Such decisions are often made at the global level to manage containers on a macro scale with little consideration for a small exporting region requiring around 50,000 TEU of empty containers per year. Therefore, most papers on cost optimisation have also treated the decision on a global level. But the cost must still be paid. Some other innovative research has explored the possibilities for foldable containers (Moon et al., 2013). While it has been shown that the concept itself is feasible and could save money, widespread adoption of these containers by container lessors and shipping lines is required before the value can be exploited by Scottish shippers. Besides the optimisation of operational decisions to lower costs, it is rare for authors to consider managerial or policy solutions, or lobbying to influence global decisions on routing or cost recovery to reduce the burden on peripheral shippers who often do not feature in the thoughts of global decision makers. Lopez (2003) was a rare case of examining the decision-making process of shipping lines, but this was focused on the decision of inland transport of containers. This gap in the literature will be addressed by the current chapter.

The main cause of the need to reposition empty containers is due to a trade imbalance. In the case of an exporting region within an overall importing country or port range, the situation is more complex. This is because the empty container is already in the country after being emptied of its imported contents, but the shipping line has to decide if it will transport the empty container a few hundred miles on a feeder vessel to a specific region to serve the exporter, then return the loaded container to the hub port and onwards for global export. This is not always attractive to shipping line managers, as will be discussed more next. Also, for peripheral regions, demand is not high enough to have several empty depots and sources of containers needing to be optimised in a mathematical model. The problem is related to business strategy and influence rather than schedule optimisation.

Container ownership is another important factor. It has been estimated that there exist about three containers for every container slot in the world fleet, to account for overland movements as well as taking up the slack in the system (Rodrigue, 2013). In 2008, at the peak of world container shipping just before the recession, there were about 28 million TEU of containers in existence (UNCTAD, 2009). Most of these are controlled by shipping lines, either through ownership or by leasing them from container leasing companies, who provide flexibility for shipping lines who do not want to take the risk of purchasing too many containers. Shipping lines own approximately 62 percent and the remaining 38 percent is owned by leasing companies (Theofanis and Boile, 2009).

The problem with this system, as far as this study is concerned, is that a separate shipping line owns (or at least controls) each container. So if a Scottish exporter is a customer of carrier A, any boxes from carrier B that are sitting idle at a nearby port are not available to this exporter. Carrier A will need to bring an empty container, while the empty boxes belonging to carrier B may be unproductively repositioned elsewhere to serve carrier B's customers. This results in additional movements and costs. There have been some attempts in the industry to solve this problem, through the use of box pools (so-called grey boxes because containers are normally clearly branded for each shipping line), but the problem has not yet been resolved (Theofanis and Boile, 2009).

The choice of carrier or merchant haulage also plays a significant role. Under carrier haulage, the shipping line has control of the container and can manage repositioning more effectively, incorporating inland depots or direct transfer to a new customer. Under merchant haulage, the customer must return the empty container immediately to the port or nominated depot. Not only does the carrier have less visibility of the container under this scenario but also the container is more likely to travel unnecessarily long distances because the capacity for triangulation is reduced.

While the overall cause of the repositioning problem is an unresolved trade imbalance, perhaps the largest barrier to resolving the problem is that it has several causes which may not all be relevant in each case, or may be present in varying degrees. It is, first of all, necessary to distinguish between actually not having enough boxes when/where needed and a situation where they are being provided but at an additional cost.

The first reason for lack of empty containers is a case where there is no service linking the relevant supply and demand ports, or a lack of capacity or frequency on such links. If a line is not already serving this location on its main routings, it can position containers there by altering its feeder routings or by using slots on another feeder line, or, if need be, by leasing additional containers. An additional component of this problem is if services exist but the correct equipment types are not available in sufficient numbers and at suitable times. Second, there is the simple fact of the cost of transporting and handling the empty container, which must be recovered by the shipping line. Third, the opportunity cost of leaving empties waiting for a load or managing such small movements to small exporting regions when it is simpler just to move all boxes on east-west trade routes, empty them then send them back for guaranteed immediate reuse in Asia at a higher freight rate.

The Scottish case

In 2011, UK ports handled a total of 8.1m TEU, split into 4.1m inbound and 4m outbound or 5.9m loaded and 2.2m empty. The top-five ports were responsible for 86 percent of all container movements, displaying the high concentration in the container port sector. While the UK port system can be seen as mature, Wilms-meier and Monios (2013) showed that that a number of secondary ports have successfully taken on the "challenge of the periphery" and now seek a strategy that allows them to develop into new regional centres.

Figure 13.1 shows total inbound and outbound container flows at UK ports since 2000. The figure shows that inbound and outbound flows are relatively matched overall. Of total flows of 8.1m TEU in 2011, total inbound flows of 4.1m TEU matched total outbound flows of 4.0m TEU. However, the problem is that total loaded movements accounted for only 5.9m TEU, leaving 2.2m TEU of unproductive empty movements. The United Kingdom's 27 percent proportion of empty containers is the highest of any EU country handling more than 1m TEU annually (Figure 13.2).

Figure 13.1 shows that imports are almost exclusively laden (representing imported goods), while outbound flows are more balanced between full and empty containers (reflecting the large volume of empty containers being repositioned back to the Far East). Thus the United Kingdom is shown to be a net importer of containerised goods, in common with many European countries. A small proportion of the empty outbound containers will be double counted representing

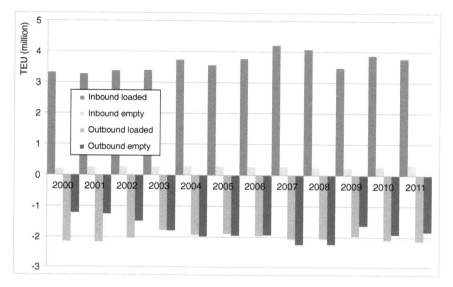

Figure 13.1 Full and empty movements at all UK ports by direction

Source: Authors, based on DfT (2012)

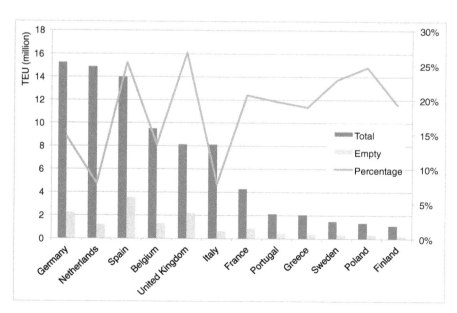

Figure 13.2 Total and empty container throughput at EU countries, 2011

Source: Authors, based on Eurostat (2012)

Note: The figure only shows countries handling more than one million TEU annually

repositioning around the United Kingdom – for example, from Felixstowe or Tee-sport to Grangemouth – but the majority of outbound empty movements will be going via deep-sea routes back to the Far East, as the United Kingdom does not produce sufficient exports to fill these containers.

Figure 13.3 shows empty movements by port and direction in 2011, with Felix-stowe and Southampton truncated for ease of presentation. The figure shows that the only ports that import more empties than they export are Forth Grangemouth, Greenock/Clyde, Goole, Aberdeen, Cardiff and Harwich. The Scottish ports have a significant imbalance, with Forth Grangemouth (east coast) and Greenock (west coast) showing serious imbalances. Scottish ports import a disproportionate num-ber of empty containers to fill with whisky exports. Scotland's problem is thus the reverse of the rest of the United Kingdom: it is a net exporter of containerised goods (by sea), thus it has a deficit of imported containers.

Looking specifically at Scotland's primary container port of Grangemouth, Fig-ure 13.4 shows that in 2006, only 12,557 TEU of empty containers were brought into Grangemouth, but as inbound loaded containers declined, the number of empty imports tripled. The result is similar, although less pronounced, at the pri-mary west coast container port of Greenock.

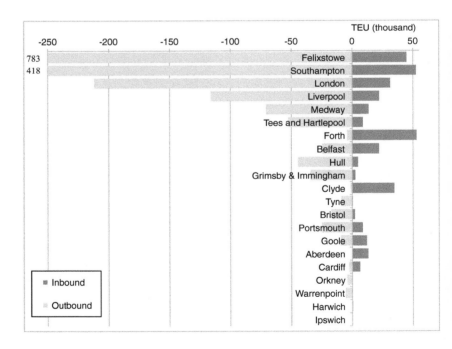

Figure 13.3 Empty movements 2011, by port and direction (with Felixstowe and South-ampton truncated)

Source: Authors, based on DfT (2012)

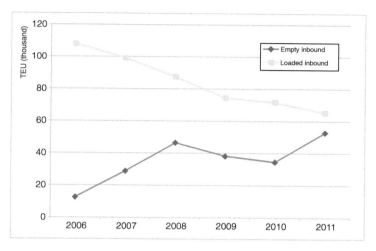

Figure 13.4 Inbound containers at Grangemouth 2006–2011
Source: Authors, based on DfT (2012)

This imbalance is due largely to the centralisation of distribution strategies in large UK hubs. So, for example, in the United Kingdom, large distribution centres in the middle of the country receive the majority of British containerised imports, which are then distributed around the country by road and to a degree by rail. This means that the exporting region of Scotland receives most of its imports overland by trailer, with the result that it does not then have the empty containers it needs for exporting. Northbound flows are predominately in 45ft pallet-wide road trailers (and swap bodies) and southbound flows are in 20ft and 40ft deep-sea boxes either through Scottish ports or by rail to English ports. Scottish exporters thus have to pay shipping lines to bring empty maritime boxes to Scotland, so this is a direct cost to Scottish shippers and by extension the Scottish economy. Thus both industry and government stakeholders have an interest in solving this problem. The map in Figure 13.5 shows UK container traffic at ports and the arrows indicate the domestic flow of containers. Full maritime containers move from Felixstowe (and other ports) into DCs in the Midlands and empty containers come back. These destuffed goods travel to Scotland overland in trucks, meaning that empty containers need to be moved north by ship.

Figure 13.6 shows that, while the majority of empty containers being repositioned to Grangemouth and Greenock are coming from UK ports (and are thus classed as domestic in Department for Transport [DfT] figures), some are coming from feeder vessels from European ports. The figure reveals that other European ports are sending empty containers to Scottish ports, particularly Belgium and the Netherlands to Grangemouth (the same is true for the west coast but in that case it is from Ireland to Greenock). These are not so surprising; what is of special interest

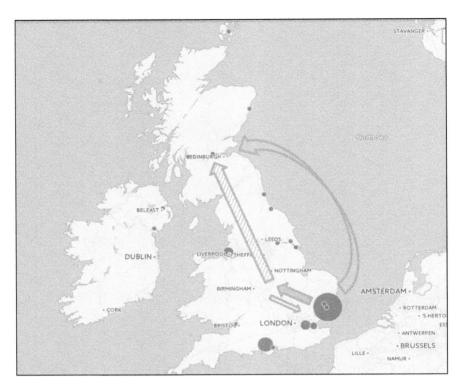

Figure 13.5 Map of the United Kingdom showing UK container traffic in 2012 and movement of full and empty containers to and from Scotland

Note: Solid/hollow arrows indicate full/empty containers moving between southeast ports and the Midlands, shaded arrow indicates trucked movements north to Scotland, hollow curved arrow indicates empty containers moving north to Scottish ports

Source: Authors

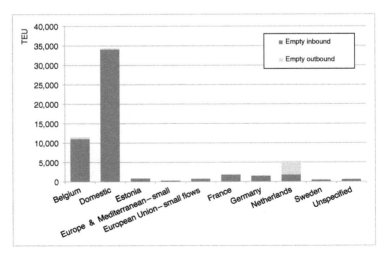

Figure 13.6 Empty inbound and outbound at Grangemouth 2011, by country of loading/unloading

Source: Authors, based on DfT (2012)

Table 13.1 Shipping lines calling at Grangemouth

Type	Shipping line	Main port	Calls	Vessel(s)
Short sea intra-Europe	Samskip	Rotterdam	Tilbury, Grangemouth, Hull	300/800 TEU
Feeder (open-user)	Unifeeder	Rotterdam/ Hamburg	Felixstowe, Immingham, Tees, South Shields, Grangemouth	700/970 TEU
Feeder (open-user)	BG Freight	Rotterdam/ Antwerp	Grangemouth, Tees	350/800 TEU
Feeder (dedicated)	MSC	Antwerp	Dunkirk, Grangemouth	900 TEU
Feeder (dedicated)	CMA CGM	Zeebrugge	Immingham, Tees, Grangemouth, Rotterdam	700 TEU

Source: Authors, based on port information and interviews

is that 3,508 TEU of empty containers left Grangemouth for Dutch ports in 2011. This outbound movement of empty containers is part of a shipping line strategy that will be explored in the interviews.

Table 13.1 lists current liner services calling at Grangemouth and reveals the connections on which these containers are moving. An interesting finding form this table is that one is shortsea intra-European (Samskip), two are open-user feeder services (Unifeeder, BG Freight) and two are dedicated feeder links of deepsea lines (MSC, CMA CGM). So a lot of feeder traffic on which empty equipment moves is on multi-user feeder services that carry containers from various shipping lines.

Figure 13.7 shows size and age of container vessels calling at Scottish ports in a representative one-month period in 2013. The figure reveals that vessel size ranged from 144 TEU to 974 TEU, with an average capacity of 697 TEU. The age distribution shows that most vessels are relatively young, but with a significant amount of capacity around 20 years old. This represents a problem because with the sulphur emission control area in the North Sea becoming more stringent in 2015 (Cullinane and Bergqvist, 2014), vessel owners are unlikely to invest in upgrading engines on such old vessels to meet the new sulphur requirements of 0.10 percent m/m. Newer vessels on these routes, in addition to the increased cost of fuel, will add to feeder costs.

Wilmsmeier and Monios (2013) showed how northern ports are pursuing ambitious development strategies to insert themselves as second-tier hubs, such as Liverpool on the west coast and Teesport on the east coast. These will challenge the role for Scottish ports without sufficient capacity for ever-increasing feeder vessel sizes. Scotland's current primary east coast container port at Grangemouth can handle vessels up to around 1,000 TEU and a proposed new container port at

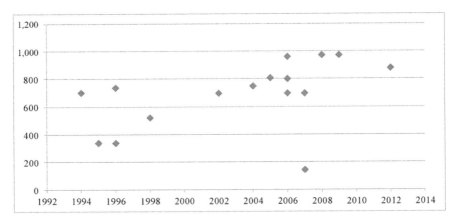

Figure 13.7 Size (TEU) and age of container vessels calling at Scottish ports 23 October–22 November 2013

Source: Authors, based on data from Marine Traffic

Rosyth is expected to accommodate vessels up to around 1,600 TEU. However, anything larger than that could not be handled and could have knock-on effects on the structure of Scottish supply chains.

The search for solutions

The only true solution to the lack of empty containers in Scotland is to increase containerised imports, thus providing the empty containers for exporters. However, until this happens, local and regional stakeholders meet regularly to discuss potential ideas that may provide partial solutions. This section presents the results of interviews conducted in 2012–13 with key stakeholders such as ports, shipping lines, shippers and public sector representatives, which explored possible strategies available to each group of actors, while remaining cognisant of the underlying trade imbalance.

According to the interview results, three scenarios where a shipping line could act are the alteration of service routing, influencing inland depot consolidation and better management of empties at ports. The Scottish case showed that, while sufficient services exist to Scottish ports, the routings are undesirable. Some services on the east coast move empties from UK ports (including Grangemouth itself) to hub ports on the continent (primarily Antwerp) and then back to Grangemouth. Likewise, on the west coast, the interviews revealed that CMA CGM used to move empties from Liverpool in the United Kingdom to Le Havre on the continent then all the way back up the west coast to the Scottish port of Greenock. The shipping line was encouraged through conversations with the port operator to modify their service routing. Now they run a local triangular service linking Liverpool (United Kingdom), Greenock (United Kingdom) and Dublin (Ireland) that then links with the service that joins the United Kingdom and the continent, thus removing the distance travelled by the empty containers and lowering costs. Another example was a feeder service at an Irish port not having sufficient turnaround time to drop its loaded containers and pick up empties so the empties were often left on the quay. Stakeholder discussions encouraged the line to alter the schedule so enough time was allowed. Speaking directly to the shipping lines can, therefore, achieve a change of schedule. While this sounds rather obvious, the fact that routing decisions are taken at a higher level means such local concerns are not always recognised without lobbying by local stakeholders.

Inland consolidation is another option where a shipping line can improve empty container availability. Shipping lines can move the inland empties under a variety of organisational models (e.g. outsource, contract with road or rail companies; Lopez, 2003), and they may own their own inland depots or more commonly rent space at an inland port or container facility to store their empty equipment. The selection of merchant or carrier haulage can play a significant role as the high incidence of carrier haulage in the United Kingdom means that the shipping line decides the inland haul. The location of the majority of empty equipment that travels inland is in the Midlands, and overland transport from there to Scotland is not any cheaper than moving a box port to port by coastal feeder. It could be possible to place containers on empty slots on northbound rail services on the Anglo-Scottish route, but these trains are generally well loaded in that direction. The occasional slot for a handful of containers would not be frequent or regular enough to be built into the management systems of shipping lines.

Better empty management at ports is, in theory, the simplest and easiest option. However, even if successful, this only accounts for a small proportion of required boxes. This has also been tried unsuccessfully before with "grey boxes". This will only partially resolve the problem, as the shortage in peak season will remain. Yet it only requires administration to be effective and may even provide good public relations for shipping lines through the green credentials of reducing empty movements.

One interviewee suggested that shipping lines could provide better information on box availability to their key customers through a website or email list. Obviously a shipping line would not make a public announcement of their empty movements, but if they set up a trusted organisation – for example, in the Scottish case just a collective of whisky exporters – they could send them daily updates about empty availability to make sure they were all used and none left the port.

The scenario of managing empty equipment at ports also involves port actors. Ports with a surplus of outbound empties have an interest in solving the problem, even if it is not directly their problem but that of the shipping lines. Ports charge shipping lines if they leave containers at a port longer than an agreed time. In regions with a surplus of empties, they increase charges to incentivise lines to take them away, but in a region such as Scotland with an excess of demand, supportive policies could lower such charges to encourage lines to leave empty equipment at the port until needed. Of course, the carriers may have their own reasons for not wanting to leave the empty at the port awaiting a customer if they can get a load elsewhere.

One interviewee gave an example of a port in Ireland lowering its port dues for carriers bringing empty containers (or leaving them there) in order to ensure they are brought to that port and thus there for their exporting customers. Such a solution can help a small port retain business from exporters. Before that solution, some shippers had been getting an empty truck from Dublin, and, since the truck was already there with the empty container for them, they would just fill the container and then send it back by truck to Dublin anyway so the port of Cork was losing this business. A regional British port like Teesport would consider such a reduced charge but only if it brought additional business. For example, they might give a discount if northbound empties moved from Teesport to Scottish port Grangemouth and the southbound loaded containers then were feedered from Grangemouth back to Teesport to link with a service there. If the southbound loaded containers from Grangemouth went to another port then there would be no benefit to the operator of Teesport.

It is possible for shippers with complementary equipment requirements to collaborate. In the United Kingdom, southbound shippers, particularly whisky exporters, use ISO containers, while northbound flows such as secondary retail distribution moves in road trailers and, to a lesser extent, 45 ft curtain-sided swap bodies on rail wagons (Monios, 2015). A potential solution that has been mooted by stakeholders is the possibility for one or the other to change their equipment usage so that both could use the same. Southbound whisky exporters could send their loads in trailers then transload into containers in the Midlands for onward transport to container ports, and the trailer will then pick up the northbound retail flows. Alternatively, northbound retail flows could move in the empty maritime containers available in the Midlands, and then once the load is deposited in Scotland, the empty container could be available for the southbound whisky flow.

This would be a neat solution for two large sectors to work together rather than many small shippers and such large shippers enjoy strong bargaining power with liner shipping companies. On the other hand, demand for different container types may vary, and it can be difficult to match freight flows. Moreover, whisky exporters retender their carrier contracts every year or two, and a change in carrier, thus a change in box ownership, could destabilise the northbound retail flows, which is undesirable for this sector. Another reason this solution has not yet been put into practice is that southbound whisky cargo is very valuable and opening trailers to reload into containers is not desirable. Competition among shippers within the same industry sector could also be a disincentive, as could be the commercial sensitivity of price negotiations.

The Scottish government already operates grant schemes for both infrastructure and operating costs involved in shifting freight flows from road to rail and water. It could be possible for such schemes to be extended to subsidise empty container movements, but they are in most instances already moving by water, so there is no modal shift. Such a scheme could, however, be justified if it were only available to SMEs in the sense that it is supporting local exporters. It would likely be politically and practically difficult to implement and would not be resolving the issue but merely moving the cost from shippers to the taxpayer.

What the public sector and other supporting actors can do, more profitably, is lobby shipping lines and ports with local knowledge and influence their decisions where possible. It was shown earlier that shipping lines can be encouraged to alter their service routings and schedule times, and ports can be incentivised to provide discounts where it is in their own interests. There is therefore a role to be played by such organisations in sharing information between stakeholders.

Conclusion

The aforementioned options can be reduced to four policy or intervention scenarios: establishing a new service or diverting a current service, inland consolidation of containers, empty management at Scottish ports, northbound/southbound shipper collaboration. The analysis has shown that none of them are currently feasible because the market is too small. Returning these findings to the mobilities perspective advocated earlier in the chapter, the limited agency of local and regional stakeholders identified in this study highlights the disproportionate negative effects suffered by those at the wrong end of the global imbalance, particularly peripheral regions. They do not enjoy unfettered access to the global trade system, despite it being promoted as an enabler of trade and a seamless logistics surface. In fact, previously well-connected and traditional maritime countries such as Scotland now find themselves at a trade disadvantage. The storage of containers, this statis, or pausing within the hyper-mobile system of containerised trade, represents the immobility that underpins mobility, but the spatial disparity of where these sites of immobility are located exerts a significant influence on access to trade mobility. Regions with empty container depots enjoy access while those with insufficient flows and insufficiently concentrated and connected mobility providers (in this case shipping lines) do not allow the agglomeration of such necessary resources in Scotland. This results in significant unproductive and induced mobility, leading to excessive costs not faced by better-connected regions. Yet ongoing attempts to resolve the issue through innovative management and cooperation strategies remain unfulfilled.

References

Braekers, K., Janssens, G. K., Caris, A. (2011). Challenges in managing empty container movements at multiple planning levels. *Transport Reviews*. 31 (6): 681–708.

Cidell, J. (2012). Flows and pauses in the urban logistics landscape: The municipal regulation of shipping container mobilities. *Mobilities*. 7 (2): 233–246.

Cresswell, T. (2010). Mobilities I: Catching up. *Progress in Human Geography*. 35 (4): 550–558.

Cresswell, T., Martin, C. (2012). On turbulence: Entanglements of disorder and order on a Devon beach. *Tijdschrift voor Sociale en Economische Geografie*. 103 (5): 516–529.

Cullinane, K., Bergqvist, R. (2014). Emission control areas and their impact on maritime transport. *Transportation Research Part D*. 28: 1–5.

DfT (2012). Port statistics. Available at: www.gov.uk/government/statistical-data-sets/port01-uk-ports-and-traffic Accessed 29 May 2013.

Eurostat (2012). Country level – volume (in TEUs) of containers handled in main ports, by loading status. Available at: http://epp.eurostat.ec.europa.eu/portal/page/portal/statistics/search_database Accessed 29 May 2013.

Hannam, K., Sheller, M., Urry, J. (2006). Editorial: Mobilities, immobilities and moorings. *Mobilities*. 1 (1): 1–22.

Levinson, M. (2006). *The Box: How the Shipping Container Made the World Smaller and the World Economy Bigger*. Princeton: Princeton University Press.

Lopez, E. (2003). How do ocean carriers organize the empty containers reposition activity in the USA? *Maritime Policy & Management*. 30 (4): 339–355.

Martin, C. (2013). Shipping container mobilities, seamless compatibility and the global surface of logistical integration. *Environment & Planning A*. 45 (5): 1021–1036.

Monios, J. (2015). Integrating intermodal transport with logistics: A case study of the UK retail sector. *Transportation Planning and Technology*. 38 (3): 1–28.

Monios, J., Wilmsmeier, G. (2015). Identifying Material, Geographical and Institutional Mobilities in the Global Maritime Trade System. In: T. Birtchnell, S. Savitzky and J. Urry (eds.), *Cargomobilities: Moving Materials in a Global Age*. Abingdon: Routledge. pp. 125–148.

Moon, I., Do Ngoc, A.-D., Konings, R. (2013). Foldable and standard containers in empty container repositioning. *Transportation Research Part E: Logistics and Transportation Review*. 49: 107–124.

Rodrigue, J.-P. (2013). The repositioning of empty containers. Available at: http://people.hofstra.edu/geotrans/eng/ch5en/appl5en/ch5a3en.html Accessed 29 May 2013.

Shaw, J., Sidaway, J. D. (2010). Making links: On (re)engaging with transport and transport geography. *Progress in Human Geography*. 35 (4): 502–520.

Sheller, M., Urry, J. (2006). The new mobilities paradigm. *Environment & Planning A*. 38 (2): 207–226.

Steinberg, P. (2001). *The Social Construction of the Ocean*. Cambridge: Cambridge University Press.

Theofanis, S., Boile, M. (2009). Empty marine container logistics: Facts, issues and management strategies. *Geojournal*. 74 (1): 51–65.

UNCTAD. (2009). *Review of Maritime Transport*. Geneva: UNCTAD.

Wilmsmeier, G., Monios, J. (2013). Counterbalancing peripherality and concentration: An analysis of the UK container port system. *Maritime Policy & Management*. 40 (2): 116–132.

Index